Finding the Way Home

A Compassionate Approach to Illness

Gayle Heiss

QED Press
Fort Bragg, California

Finding the Way Home: A Compassionate Approach to Illness

Copyright © 1997 by Gayle Heiss

QED Press
155 Cypress Street
Fort Bragg, CA 95437
1 (800) 773-7782
fax: (707) 964-7531
email: qedpress@mcn.org

Cataloging in Publication Data

Heiss, Gayle, 1947-
    Finding the way home : a compassionate approach to illness / Gayle Heiss. — 1st ed.
      p. cm.
    Includes biographical references and index.
    ISBN 0-936609-35-4
    1. Sick—Psychology.   2. Chronic diseases — Psychological aspects.
    3. Chronically ill—Family relationships.   4. Healing — Psychological aspects.   5. Helping behavior.   6. Love — Psychological aspects.
    7. Grief.   8. Death.   I. Title.
R726.5.H447 1997
155.9'16—dc20   96-24392
                                      CIP

For their support and expertise, *QED Press* would like to thank Sal Glynn, Michele Rubin, Meredith Phelan and Marla Greenway.

Cover design by Mark Gatter
Book production by Cypress House
Manufactured in the USA
First Edition

1 3 5 7 9 10 8 6 4 2

Dedication

to Larry
for providing safe passage
with his sheltering love

If fate throws a knife at you,
there are two ways of catching it —
by the blade and by the handle.

— Oriental Proverb

Contents

Part Three
In Good Company: Illness and Relationships

Acknowledgments

Sometimes actions we would not ordinarily take are called forth from us by extraordinary circumstances. This book is such an act. Illness is such a circumstance.

Grappling with my own illness stirred the writer in me but, by itself, summoned neither the vision nor the resolve to complete a full-length book. It was by walking shared ground with other people moving through illness that I gained some momentum. I was vitalized; if they could live those experiences, I could write them.

I extend my enduring gratitude to the members of the support groups I facilitate and to countless others who have entrusted me with their most intimate concerns about living with illness. I hope I have honored their trust and fully conveyed, as much as words can, a sense of what it is like to struggle on the physical level yet shape a life at the soul level.

These remarkable people have provided me with much more than material for a book. They taught me about the resilience of the human spirit under even the most difficult of circumstances. They gave me the opportunity to see how loving relationships can heal the deepest wounds. They lessened my own fears about pain, disability, and death by inviting me in to witness theirs. I credit my compatriots in illness not only with energizing me to write a book; they showed me how to script a personal life story that includes not only illness but many other chapters as well.

An illness invariably tests relationships; so does writing a book. My family and friends have been exemplary in their support and patience with me on both accounts. Without their willingness to accommodate to the erratic nature of my literary as well as my physical needs, I doubt that I could have undertaken such a demanding project. And their continual encouragement helped me see it through to completion.

Susan Larkin inspired me to form a support group for people living with illness. The Northern California chapter of the Arthritis Foundation, Mendocino Coast District Hospital in Fort Bragg, and Redwood Coast Medical Services in Gualala each sponsored the program at various points in its evolution. I am grateful for their support of the idea and their belief in me.

I imagine that few writers would characterize the relationship with their publishers as respectful and considerate, let alone warm or caring. I have had the good fortune, however, to work with the people at *QED Press,* where I have always felt there is an interest in my well-being as a person as well as an investment in my success as an author. Their faith kept me going, and their flexibility accommodated my pace.

A manuscript in progress is a fragile entity. Like anything else in its formative stages, it has strengths and weaknesses, active periods and dormant periods. My husband Larry has offered a steady, reassuring presence throughout each phase. He has accompanied me word by word, sharing my excitement during the growth spurts and providing me with needed perspective during the growing pains. I consistently felt from Larry that he was as committed to this book as I was, despite the intrusions it made into our daily life. His feedback has also been invaluable — as someone whose life has been touched by illness (mine), as a health care provider, as a sensitive reader, and as a skilled writer.

There are scores of others who, in less obvious ways, have helped make this book a reality. I wish I could enumerate the many people who have influenced and inspired me throughout my life; their cumulative guidance is reflected on every page. Two of those people are my parents, Lil and Sam Resnick. I offer my heartfelt appreciation to them for their constant love and devotion.

People often ask me, "How can you do the work you do without feeling burdened or defeated?" "Why would you write a book on such a depressing subject?" Ironically, I find this work the most rewarding I have ever done. I have learned that meeting *all* of life's experiences openheartedly engenders the richest human connections. It is an affirmation of life to be willing to encounter its full depth and dimension.

Neither my work nor my book is intended to fix people or their circumstances. I would indeed feel drained if I were trying to change things that are beyond my control. Rather, my aim is to accompany people through their experiences, to offer them understanding and perspective, to help them not feel so alone. I have been fortunate to be on the receiving end of such caring support and find it fulfilling rather than draining to pass it on to others.

Of course there is heartache in this work. It is work of the heart — but also of the spirit. Healing separation with love is a sacred process. That I have found a way to be part of this process, I am eternally grateful.

Introduction

When I developed an illness twelve years ago, it arrived somewhat like an eviction notice. I could no longer rest securely in the life I had arranged, in the place in the world I had known as my own.

I considered not moving. Perhaps an illness and all of its implications could be ignored, tossed away like a letter bearing bad news. I quickly found, however, that I was no longer in a comfortable fit with the old and familiar; somehow everything looked different and in need of rearrangement. When I reached for my usual props, I found they were just beyond my grasp. Staying put felt like losing ground.

For a while I stood in the doorway, a narrow, undefined space but one that allowed me to buy time. Illness stretches us; I found myself straddling two worlds, one outdated and one unknown. I needed time to establish my footing and sense of direction.

The geography of illness is sketchy, confusing. Suggested routes can begin to look like a maze, and we still get lost in strange, dark corners of fear and uncertainty, pain and loss. Although helpful to some extent, the maps others drew for me could never reflect the alternate routes, turning points, detours, and backtracks — the choices I needed, still need — to make my own way.

Intuitively I headed toward other people also experiencing illness. I suspected that they too might be testing out new territory, hoped that our paths might intersect or run parallel. I began facilitating illness support groups, a gathering of wounded healers, a lost-and-found for the human spirit in the process of transformation. From our collective experiences we recognized that "home" is ultimately a resting place we cultivate inside of us. It is an internal refuge we bring to whatever place we settle. Our point of arrival may not appear far from the home we left, but worlds have been traveled in the meantime.

The awareness we bring home remains with us, moves in like a Zen master, there to call things into question, to remind us that things are not always as they seem, to keep us awake, on track — and at home with ourselves. The support group members say we are chronically aware.

Our culture applauds a sense of adventure, honors those who willingly sacrifice personal security and put themselves at risk for the sake of a larger purpose. We call those people courageous, creative. They are.

What if we have no choice, as is the case with illness? Although not as dramatic or public, is the journey less heroic? Is internal distance less of a measure than actual miles or milestones? Is making peace with vulnerability a large enough purpose?

How we answer these questions often depends on how close to illness we stand and whether or not we are paying attention. A close-up view reveals the remarkable human ability to be tossed out of everyday existence and somehow land on one's feet. With an ongoing illness this can happen repeatedly.

For the most part our culture hasn't acknowledged this less tangible aspect of an encounter with illness, implying instead that a serious illness brings our adventures (other than medical) to a close. This attitude is slowly changing as holistic approaches to health care gain wider acceptance. Mental, emotional, and spiritual dimensions are beginning to be addressed along with the physical as important components of health and illness. Many people with illnesses are finding among health care providers, and among loved ones and friends, increasing recognition that an illness is a life-altering event, not just a collection of physical symptoms.

Yet in spite of this growing public awareness, those of us who live with illness experience something that remains largely hidden from view, even from those who are closely monitoring us for outward signs of improvement. This "something" is elusive because it happens beyond the linear world of cause and effect, more or less, better or worse; it reflects the difference between healing and curing. It is a hunch we have that perhaps we don't have to be broken or diminished by illness, that we can remain intact and live with integrity, even with physical limitations. And when we act on this hunch, we are honoring a natural, impelling force that moves each of us in unique ways to reach the fullest expression of ourselves.

My reason for writing this book is to validate this search for wholeness, healing, that wends its way through the other, more obvious, steps toward physical cure. My purpose is not to cover comprehensively the experience of living with an illness, but to clarify an aspect of it that receives less attention than medical treatments and outcomes. From my own experience and from talking with others in support groups, the healing process that unfolds can be so subtle that it is barely conscious. It is difficult to tease apart from everything else that is happening and, like intuition, more likely to be questioned than trusted. Putting words to an experience can make it more real, both to ourselves and to others, but the unraveling and reweaving we do in a life with illness is difficult to describe. And because redefining one's place in the world is carried out on such personal terms, we hesitate to reveal this inner world to others who might find it incomprehensible.

During the eight years I have been facilitating support groups, and talking and corresponding with others who are ill, some of the most rewarding moments have come during the interchanges that begin, "I've never really told anyone this before..." or, "This might sound crazy, but...." These revelations are usually not about some skeleton in the closet, some hidden shame. The words are often an early attempt to define a shift in the way of seeing and experiencing the world that feels strong and authentic, yet still too new — or in some cases, hidden too long.

Another comment I hear over and over again is "I don't feel so alone now; I thought I was the only one." Each of us knows, of course, that we are not the sole individual with a particular disease or symptom; we feel alone with our *experience* of illness. My hope is that this book will link the reader to others with illness, each also feeling alone, each with an evolving story inside and a hunch about how to live it. I also hope to help close the gap between people who are ill and their family members, friends, caregivers, and health care providers by clarifying that what sustains us through life generally is what sustains us through illness. In each of us resides an energy, a spirit, that seeks out meaning in the world and connections with others. My wish is that increased identification with our common needs and aspirations will bring increased understanding and communication.

This book is neither an attempt to draw broad conclusions based on individual experiences nor an attempt to present those individual experiences as success stories to emulate. Rather it is intended to acknowledge, to underscore, indeed to proclaim sacred, the individual human life as a unique unfolding of events and responses to those events. I offer the examples as a testimony to the infinite ways people move through the difficult role of unhealthy patient while trying to retain or retrieve an enduring sense of healthy person. I hope to draw attention to all that is *right* with people who are ill, to encourage more respect, patience, and support for the ways one needs to *be* with an illness to feel healed, aside from what one has to *do* to treat the body.

This book is more about being than doing, or perhaps about trusting that being will organically evolve into doing where healing is concerned. I realize this slow make-it-up-as-you-go approach differs from many of the popular self-help, step-by-step, streamlined approaches to healing. I know many people who are helped by the structure and the hope that such programs offer, especially in the midst of the fears and uncertainties surrounding illness. Others, however, find a "one size fits all" approach constraining; they feel pressure about getting on the program or feel guilty about not meeting with success. Whether we piece together our own program of healing or find an existing one that suits us well, we are exercising the right to choose. This freedom, all the more precious in the context of the losses and limitations of illness, invites us to appreciate the opportunities to shape our life and live it well.

Several years ago, my ten-year-old nephew asked me a question that was a prelude to telling me that he could say the names of all the states in alphabetical order in less than seventeen seconds. The question he asked was this: "Do you think you hold the world's record for anything, I mean, just anything?" I responded, "I suppose

I do, but not for anything anybody else would ever notice. Well, I guess we all could be in the *Guinness Book of Records* for something." My nephew's question and subsequent seventeen-second performance revealed to me a boundless faith in the human ability to find something unique to express and a way to express it. Illness challenges us to hold on to that faith and to see in ourselves and each other continual possibilities.

Part One

Living the Questions:
Illness and Uncertainty

...be patient toward all that is unsolved in your heart and...try to love the *questions themselves* like locked rooms and like books that are written in a very foreign tongue. Do not seek the answers, which cannot be given you because you would not be able to live them. And the point is, to live everything. *Live* the questions now. Perhaps you will then gradually, without noticing it, live along some distant day into the answer.

— Rainer Maria Rilke
Letters to a Young Poet[1]

Part of being alive is accepting that things are changing all the time. Being *fully* alive requires a flexible and creative response to change; life's struggles often arise from a rigid attempt to keep things exactly the same.

Yet we naively expect that our physical bodies will stay the same, year after year, decade after decade. We are surprised to find that we are neither immune from inevitable change or unforseen illness, nor protected from sudden accident or permanent injury. When these occur, we are faced with one of the greatest challenges to our ability to accept change. The threat of physical vulnerability dramatically presents the ultimate issue we all must confront sometime in life: facing who we are when it is no longer possible to continue in our familiar roles. That challenge is intensified by another issue that surfaces with an illness — our own mortality. So we are hit with the question, "Is your ever-shortening life meaningful to you or anyone else?"

Facing illness means finding a way to live one's life so that the answer to that question is an unqualified "yes." Because every person is a unique individual surrounded by unique circumstances, each person lives that question in his or her own way.

John Muir, the California naturalist, once said, "When we try to pick out anything by itself, we find it hitched to everything else in the universe."[2] The questions triggered by an illness are like that; each seems to pull in others that go still deeper, reach out further, and uncover long-held, often unexamined assumptions and expectations. Illness disrupts not only the usual ways of functioning in the world but of understanding the world — and especially trusting it. Spiritual concerns often arise for the first time or intensify in importance. Perspectives shift along with priorities, and self-esteem and self-awareness are severely tested. These profound changes and disturbing questions translate, of course, into emotions: fear, anxiety, confusion, helplessness, hopelessness, alienation, disappointment, grief. But emotions change along with everything else. In the words of Rachel Naomi Remen, M.D., a cofounder and the medical director of the Commonweal Cancer Help Program, "Human beings have the capacity to grow bigger than their challenges."[3] Understanding the painful issues and emotions embedded in illness is the first step toward transforming them.

Chapter One

To Know We Are Vulnerable

When you have come to the edge
of all the light you know
and are about to step off
into the darkness of the unknown,
faith is knowing
one of two things will happen:
There will be something solid
to stand on,
or you will be taught how to fly.

— *Face to Face Quarterly Bulletin*
Sonoma County AIDS Network[1]

Personal Limitations

About a year after I became ill, I was talking on the telephone with a longtime friend who lives in another city. I told her about the changes in my life over the past year, and she asked, "What has been the biggest change?"

"Finding that sheer will no longer works," I responded without hesitation.

We agreed that sheer will had been a constant in both of our lives, not merely handy but essential. "That's something I just take for granted," my friend said. So had I.

Illness is humbling. When daily life consists of canceled plans, postponed projects, and jobs left undone, we are constantly reminded of our limitations. Depending on the nature of the illness, the usual modes of planning and doing may be affected dramatically or subtly, progressively or episodically. But affected they are, along with our pride. As our accomplishments become reduced in number and proportion, we can feel reduced in personal status as well. If we have become accustomed to reasonable success in meeting our goals and commitments, we can feel inadequate when unable to goad a weary body toward the tasks created by the mind. Competence and integrity, roles and relationships, independence and security are called into serious question. People often describe feeling overwhelmed, out of control, trapped. Somewhere I heard the comment, "Humility is making friends with the facts." Such facts make demanding friends.

At the very least, the ability to be efficient and adhere to busy schedules is compromised; we can't move as quickly or sustain energy as long. The familiar "second wind" may be replaced by a less dependable "second breeze." Once-reassuring comments like "Relax; it will all get done somehow" or "Don't worry, it's not that important" provide little comfort when the very fabric of life feels threadbare. Seemingly minor endeavors assume major importance in terms of energy required and implications for self-esteem.

In her book, *Plaintext: Deciphering a Woman's Life*, Nancy Mairs describes the impact of multiple sclerosis on her daily existence:

> Each morning that I wake up, that I get out of bed, is a fresh event, something that I might not have had. Each gesture that I make carries a weight of uncertainty, demands significant attention: buttoning my shirt, changing a light bulb, walking down stairs. I might not be able to do it this time. Inevitably the minutiae of my life have had to assume dramatic proportions. If I could not love them, delight in them, they would likely drown me in a rage and in self-pity, that tempting, obliterating sea.[2]

Illness indeed demands attention to detail. I had always considered myself a patient person, on friendly terms with the small and particular, but monitoring my body as a way of life tests that patience to its limits.

A good friend, Kate, is a poet and therefore someone who shares my love of detail. She also knows me well. Shortly after I became

6

ill, she wisely gave me a haiku by Issa that I tacked up near my desk
for daily sustenance.

> snail,
> climb Mt. Fuji —
> oh slowly[3]

My illness is Sjogren's syndrome, an autoimmune, connective
tissue disease that causes inflammation of muscles and joints. It
also affects the exocrine glands (which produce secretions
throughout the body) and can potentially damage other organ systems as well. Although some of the symptoms are peculiar to
Sjogren's syndrome, the unpredictable pattern of pain, discomfort,
and overwhelming fatigue is characteristic of many chronic systemic illnesses. Because the people who attend the support groups
have a variety of physical problems, we talk less about the details of
specific symptoms and more about the challenges of living with
and transcending them. But a major frustration for most of us is
the profound exhaustion that rolls in like the tide. "Moving
through molasses" is how one person describes it. Another says,
"It feels like someone pulled out the plug." And another experiences "gravity itself as a major force with which to contend."

Last winter a series of severe rainstorms pounded the Northern
California coast, resulting in intermittent power outages, some
stretching into several days. Scheduled plans and normal activities
came to an abrupt halt without electricity, telephone, running
water, or heat other than a woodstove. The basic tasks of survival
and self-care (chopping wood, carrying water) consumed all my
time and energy. I could only guess when the power would be restored, and for how long — before another storm hit.

"This all feels oddly familiar," I thought. A chronic illness is
much like an ongoing series of personal power failures, and just as
unpredictable in terms of onset, duration, and frequency. And no
matter how many times you flick on the light switch in hopeful
desperation, when the power is off, there's no juice in the system.

When an illness is characterized by fluctuations, "good days" are
interspersed with the others. Long-awaited and unpredictable,
these cherished days are often greeted with packed agendas and

high expectations. They offer a chance to make up for lost time — and to check again about sheer will. On many occasions people arrive at the support groups looking strained and in pain to report they are recovering from a good day — of overdoing it. The wife of a man with congestive heart failure came to the group for help in understanding why certain days she could not coax her husband out of bed, and other days she could not coax him down from the roof where he was cleaning the gutters.

People vary in terms of life circumstances — family support/responsibilities, employment options/commitments, financial resources/obligations, and personal/interpersonal goals — as much as they vary in terms of illnesses, symptoms, and any treatment or health-related routines. For many people, mountains of paperwork and stressful appointments connected with medical or disability insurance are additional factors with which to contend. Consequently, people have unique ways of trying to piece together a workable fit between personal standards and responsibilities on the one hand, and the ebb and flow of symptoms on the other hand.

For those with a demanding level of responsibility or limited financial or emotional support, the bare essentials of living occupy center stage — and the show must go on. These people do not have much latitude to pursue a mutual accommodation between bodily needs and outside demands. A woman with asthma describes negotiating some days with the uneasy awareness that "one more thing will throw me over the edge." Asking for or accepting help are reasonable options but also are emotionally charged ones. (See Chapter Nine for more discussion.)

Others have fewer outside obligations or expectations impinging on them, but self-generated standards and goals, even old habits, can compete with compelling intensity against recurrent physical needs. For these people, and I frequently stand among them, stirring the body from needed slumber to keep pace with an aroused spirit has both its rewards and its price.

An incident that illustrates the consequences of overplanning happened a few years ago, during a beautiful spring and period of wishful thinking. I tried to fit too much into my life and was exhausted, scattered, and distracted. Filling my car with diesel fuel at a self-service pump was the most expensive example of my lack of mindfulness. A few days later, I was sorting through the paper trash to separate it for recycling. Somehow a little red sticker landed on my shirt and appropriately labeled me "40% off." The percentage struck me as fairly accurate.

Even for those of us who do eventually, or at least periodically, reconcile the differences between illness and the rest of life, the partnership is usually not one marked by a high degree of spontaneity or casualness about making commitments. It's a fragile relationship, easily thrown off balance by a change in condition or a change in plans.

If we could forecast our personal storms, it would also simplify our relationships with others. With or without an illness, we all like to feel in control of our lives and secure about our plans. It is frustrating for people on either end of rearranged schedules or last-minute disruptions. For the ill person, there is the superimposed discomfort of knowing we are the source of disappointment, whether we decline in the first place or have to back out later.

Often people who enjoy good physical health overestimate the capabilities of people who are ill, as well as underestimate our motivation and sincere desire that things proceed as planned. Sometimes truly caring family members and friends accept the fact of limited reserves, but still feel that available energy should be reserved for *them*. Many people in the support groups I facilitate talk about the ongoing tug-of-war between establishing health-dictated personal priorities and being available for the needs or wishes of others. We would like to do both; a tentative response often reflects this ambivalence.

As one person frequently reminds her friends, "This is not the flu...." Out of necessity, most of us tend to develop some personal strategies for the long haul. The ways people describe these strategies reflect the substantial challenge involved in just meeting a "typical day": energy rationing, redefining "go," redefining "blowing it," picking one small task to accomplish each day, having a hierarchy of possibilities requiring different levels of energy, and remembering "the first rule of holes" — when you're in one, stop digging.

Several years ago, a family with two children spent the weekend at our home. Toward evening on one of the days of their visit, the eight-year-old, who had been continually busy and active, collapsed in a heap in the middle of the living room. His parents and older brother sang out almost in unison, "Oh, oh, Benjamin's gone floppy again," as they headed over to scoop him up. I watched this young child's unedited response to his body's demands, and his family's warm and supportive response, with more than casual interest or mere adult amusement. I decided to rename my own low points "going floppy"; it is an accurate description of the experience, and the picture of Benjamin that it conjures up somehow helps. "Going floppy" has become a household term.

Illness, of course, encompasses larger issues than going floppy and the strategic problems of time and energy for daily tasks. Severe symptoms, unrelenting pain, progressive disability, or a terminal diagnosis can dislodge a person from life altogether. Two women who attend the support groups are gifted musicians who each search for a way to improvise a new life, develop variations on lifelong themes, and create harmony from the discord.

Judy had been singing most of her life, since childhood. She says that singing is largely what got her through her life, much of which had been difficult. Extremely versatile, she sang and composed a wide range of music, but was especially loved by her fans for the way she sang the blues. In her mid-forties, Judy developed Meniere's disease, a disorder of the inner ear that causes hearing loss and hypersensitivity to sound, as well as frequent and severe attacks of vertigo. Judy now can neither sing herself nor listen to live music without precipitating an attack. Well-meaning suggestions that encourage her to compose music instead, and to remember all that Beethoven accomplished in spite of his deafness, offer little comfort to someone who had always sung out her life on stage.

During the meetings Judy has often described her experience of performing, how she transported herself to some magical place where boundaries of time and space disappeared, and how she could feel the audience come with her. She explained, "I was never really acquainted with the person offstage, wasn't sure I wanted to be. When I became ill, I realized I didn't even know the woman who doesn't sing."

> I always thought I'd be singing until the day I died, that I'd be croaking out the blues in some dive like Alberta Hunter. Never mind making money or selling records.

At one of the meetings, I was describing a day of heartbreak and pain in my own life. Judy was sitting next to me; she reached over, gently touched my arm, and said, "Baby, it sounds like you had the blues." Judy's vehicle had been song, but her enduring gift is communication, an ability to hear, feel, and express, and to move others with that expression. Although those close to Judy cherish her lyrical observations about people and life, Judy still longs to put music to the words.

Renée Roatcap is a conductor. Her career was well on its way with the San Francisco Opera when lupus, undiagnosed at the time, caused her to give up the work she loved. The pain, fatigue, frequent infections, and intolerance to fluorescent lights that are symptomatic of lupus made the demands of her job impossible to meet. She began coaching other musicians at her home, a bittersweet experience for an accomplished musician and performer. Tempted back into performing, recording, and composing by her irrepressible creative drive, Renée formed a string band called Gypsy Gulch. As her lupus progressed, causing cognitive and behavioral impairments, she became unable to continue with the band. Since that time, Renée has been struggling to keep her creative spark flaring more intensely than her lupus. She expresses this determination in the following poem, which she calls "Motionless Transcendence":

> In those moments of darkest despair
> when every sinew aches and every limb feels like lead
> When your loneliness is greatest
> because your experience cannot in fact be shared:
> Being "human" is not a better or superior choice
> but a yoke of cognizance with endlessly looping memories
> and worse, the imagination of frighteningly real possibilities.
> In those moments of darkest despair

Finding the Way Home

it may take all your strength
to seek out and kindle a tiny spark of Life-Spirit:
to form a thought contrary to your physical experience.
But if you can fill yourself with Love
and find your Pool of Worthiness
You will discover your Personal Truth
And with this knowledge
you are set free
— through Motionless Transcendence —
to let your doubts and fears be washed away.

One the many projects Renée keeps afloat in her pool of possibilities is an ingenious system for teaching harmony by using simple geometric shapes and their combinations to represent musical intervals. The "pictographs," however, are not orchestral scores, and like Judy, Renée misses the active role she enjoyed in the musical world.

Philosopher Sam Keen encourages people to develop their gifts, to listen for their calling. He goes on to say, "Incidentally, the thing calling you never says, 'To whom it may concern....' If you have a calling, it means that what you have to give is correlated with something that the world needs."[4] For people like Judy and Renée, who have found their calling and then are robbed of the opportunity to follow it because of illness, it is a leap of faith to assume a voice will beckon again.

Unable to imagine what call would come to a person with Sjogren's syndrome, I continued, for as long as I could, my work as the owner and teacher of a small preschool attached to my home. Shortly before I finally made the decision to close the school because of my health problems, I was dressing for an evening Halloween party to be held at the home of one of the children. In spite of flaring symptoms and exhaustion, I covered myself with my costume, reflecting on my habit of covering my symptoms as well. I thought, "My true disguise for the evening? I'm coming as a healthy, well-adjusted preschool teacher." No one guessed the truth that night, but the disguise was wearing thin.

I had always loved my work and continued to love the *idea* of

12

doing that work, but refused to acknowledge that it was no longer a positive experience because physical limitations were getting in the way. I simply didn't feel well enough, enough of the time, to do it with ease or to meet my own standards. It left me feeling defeated and too drained to do anything else I enjoy.

When I could no longer continue, I closed the school, after nine years in operation, to take care of my health and to_____. I tried to fill the gap by pushing the pieces of my life neatly into place: I had experience working with children, I had a chronic illness, therefore I should work with children with chronic illnesses. I had a finger in the dial, ready to telephone all the local pediatricians so I could locate those children — and relocate myself.

But, as editor and satirist H.L. Mencken pointed out, "For every problem there is one solution which is simple, neat, and wrong."[5] Luckily I sensed on some level that I needed to wait and see rather than hurry and do. It was the first time that I truly acknowledged, since becoming ill three years earlier, that things would have to change.

The Human Condition

In the process of adapting to the personal limitations specific to a particular disease, the larger issue of human vulnerability enters our awareness — and takes up permanent residence. The susceptibilities of the human body, and ultimately our mortality, are part of the human condition.

When first presented with a diagnosis, many find the news startling: "How ironic that *I* should have physical problems; I've always been so healthy." But by definition, *every* person is physically healthy until he or she develops symptoms or an illness, just as we all are alive until we die. Although each of our personal struggles may be intense, we have not been singled out for the task. Everyone who has been blessed with a life will have to face, in their own unique circumstances, physical vulnerability. Were this common vulnerability recognized and acknowledged more openly in our society, people who live with illness might not feel so separate from those who do not. I recently saw a bumper sticker that read, "I am woman, I am invincible, I am tired." I consider this admission of vulnerability a promising sign.

The following Sufi tale, "The Man Who Was Aware of Death," offers a graphic example of the precarious nature of human existence — and of the human tendency to deny it:

> There was once a dervish who embarked upon a sea journey. As the other passengers in the ship came aboard one by one, they saw him and — as is the custom — asked him for a piece of advice. All the dervish would do was to say the same thing to each of them; he seemed merely to be repeating one of those formula which each dervish makes the object of his attention from time to time.
>
> The formula was: "Try to be aware of death, until you know what death is." Few of the travelers felt particularly attracted to this admonition.
>
> Presently a terrible storm blew up. The crew and the passengers alike fell upon their knees, imploring God to save the ship. They alternately screamed in terror, gave themselves up for lost, hoped wildly for succor. All this time the dervish sat quietly, reflective, reacting not at all to the movement and the scenes which surrounded him.
>
> Eventually the buffeting stopped, the sea and sky were calm, and the passengers became aware how serene the dervish had been throughout the episode.
>
> One of them asked him: "Did you not realize that during this frightful tempest there was nothing more solid than a plank between us all and death?"
>
> "Oh, yes, indeed," answered the dervish. "I know that at sea it is always thus. I also realized, however, that I had often reflected when I was on land that, in the normal course of events, there is *even less* between us and death."[6]

Although illness steals a certain innocence, it leaves something valuable in its place. In exchange for illusions about the secure and predictable, we acquire a wisdom about some deeper truths: Things don't always happen to someone else, but they don't happen exclusively to us either. With the knowledge of our vulnerable position in the world both personally and as a member of our species, we are doubly humbled.

But humility and wisdom go hand in hand. Only when we are humble are we truly open, and only when we are open do we truly learn. Preconceived notions of who we are and how the world operates can cloud our vision and prevent us from perceiving things as they are. We can depend on the illusion of our invulnerability if it's never been significantly tested; we can feel certain about our authority and competence as long as our actions, by and large, have the predicted outcome. And if we've managed, so far, to escape serious loss or disappointment, we might assume that we can continue to approach life on an a la carte basis.

An illness often awakens a more accurate and profound understanding of the world. It highlights the paradoxes of the human condition, and the futility of a life driven by attachment to transitory pleasures and aversion to unavoidable pain. "Illness has made me look at the way sweet things and hard things come and go — like beads strung across life, some dull, some shiny," says a woman with liver disease. Recognizing that everything in life is subject to change and impermanence better prepares us to live in accord with the inevitable uncertainty and ambiguity. Similarly, recognizing that we are each unique and vulnerable draws us together as one of a kind who share a common fate.

Karren, a woman who has lived with chronic pain most of her life, likes to engage with life's ironies through art. Although the level of her pain remains intense, over the years the site has shifted from severe abdominal and chest pain due to familial Mediterranean fever — now in remission — to head and neck pain, the result of a serious injury. Her artistic mode of expression has also shifted from the traditional canvas to what she calls "art with a pulse."

Karren is a tattoo artist (who goes by the name of Chinchilla in the tattoo world), and she approaches her work with reverence. She sees it as a way to transform the human body from a vehicle for pain into a symbol of transcendence: "Pain happens to us; tattoos we choose."

Karren explains that choosing a tattoo is a statement of freedom: I can do anything I want, I have total control, and my body can express it. It's a powerful antidote to the experience of illness, which can lead one to opposite conclusions. Since tattoos are forever, Karren also finds in the "indelible commitment" a way to grapple with the unsettling notion of impermanence: "Every night they will go to sleep with you and be with you when you wake up. They will even accompany you to the grave."[7] Karren wears along her own spine a tattoo of a woman embracing a skeleton:

> Above their heads is the yin-yang symbol, which represents the balance of life and death.... I chose this tattoo to accompany me throughout my life because of the profound statement it makes to me about my own mortality. I will eventually surround it with colorful exotic flowers to soften the still-disturbing feelings I have about my own mortality.[8]

We commonly armor ourselves to hide our vulnerability rather than embellish it. Yet, when we do exhibit our human limitations, we invariably display a growing self-awareness and resourcefulness as well. A member of the support group put it this way in a letter to a friend, written after the first meeting she attended:

> In listening to the people in the group, I realized that illness really just accelerates the process of growth in life, on some levels, because almost everyone who has experienced long-term chronic illness bumps up against the hard issues in life all at once. Compressing dealing with those issues in a tight time frame while under stress, physical and otherwise, can really bring out some amazing things in people. I was overwhelmed with the courage, hope, strength, and compassion of those people. I really wish you could have been there to hear some of their experiences. Although my asthma and your migraines may not be such terrible curses in the scope of things, it was heartening to realize that in dealing with those illnesses, we've probably dealt with a great deal of life's difficulties and are better people for it.

The qualities ill people applaud in one another are not necessarily recognized by "civilians," a term used by a man with heart disease. Those of us with compromised health are considered the exception to the norm; we tend to be relegated to a lower status rather than elevated for our compensating strength.

Kay is a woman whose active life was dramatically altered by a succession of four heart attacks within a brief period of time. She expressed at one of the support group meetings an understandable but troubling reaction that many of us have toward those who live unencumbered by health concerns: "I've never considered myself an envious person, but now I find that I am jealous of other people, yes, especially of their good health and the freedom that gives them. I don't like feeling that way about others."

We talked at length about the different connotations of the words "jealousy" and "envy." Jealousy implies the desire to keep something away from others and guard it as our own. Envy signifies an awareness of the advantage enjoyed by another, accompanied by the desire to possess the same advantage. We agreed we don't begrudge anyone else good health; we just want it too. What *can* cause us to feel alienated from people who are well is a casualness about health concerns, an assuredness that takes a sound body for granted, and sometimes a certain arrogance that assumes "that will never happen to me."

Living with the knowledge that anything can happen to anybody keeps us grounded in what Buddhists call the non-dualistic nature of reality, the fluidity between the good news and the bad news. If we are aware of the complete range of possibilities on the continuum, we can feel distressed about our limitations or fearful about the future and, at the same time, grateful for the *relatively* agreeable nature of our current circumstances, given what could have happened or hasn't happened yet. This Zen tale imparts the unpredictable nature of change and its consequences.

> There was once an old Chinese farmer who had a mare. One day the mare broke through a fence and ran away. "Now you have no horse to pull your plow at planting time," the neighbors said. "What bad luck this is."
>
> "Good luck, bad luck," the farmer replied. "Who knows?"
>
> The next week the mare returned, bringing with her two wild stallions. "With three horses you are now a rich man," the neighbors said. "What good fortune this is."

"Good fortune, bad fortune," the farmer replied. "Who knows?"

That afternoon the farmer's only son tried to tame one of the stallions, but he was thrown and broke his leg. "Now you have no one to help with the planting," the neighbors said. "What bad luck this is."

"Bad luck, good luck," the farmer replied. "Who knows?"

The next day, the emperor's soldiers rode into town and conscripted the eldest son of every family, but the farmer's son was left behind because of his broken leg. "Your son is the only male in the province who has not been taken from his family," the neighbors said. "What good fortune this is...."[9]

Cindy, a thoughtful and articulate woman with multiple sclerosis, depicts in an essay the dramatically contrasting view our culture characteristically holds regarding vulnerability and change.

I suspect that we all, at some level, would like to be reassured that the painful, ugly, and seemingly abnormal in life — as exemplified in illness and death — are transitory, or better yet, simply do not exist....

Recently, advertisements have appeared in magazines giving the story, and even picture, of an automobile crash. Not to worry — there is a happy ending! The victim, who is otherwise young and healthy, was driving a Volvo! Whether armored with visualization to overcome illness or the right automobile to overcome death on the road, we want to feel that we are invincible...if only we have the right equipment.[10]

About eight months after Cindy wrote those words, she was seriously injured in an airplane crash. She fractured three vertebrae and spent many months of a slow and painful recovery in a body cast. Her account of the event bears a striking similarity to the tale of the Chinese farmer: "Miraculously, we lived and had the good fortune to be rescued from the wreckage in very short time."

In addition to the injuries from the crash, Cindy was contending with the ongoing challenges of her multiple sclerosis and possible exacerbations due to the trauma. She said to me shortly after the accident, "If I can just get back to the level of health I had before the accident, I will be pleased." Many of us struggle with "what ifs," our worst fears about the complications and consequences of illness. Yet *if* those dreaded changes, or others not anticipated, should indeed come to pass, we would, like Cindy, give anything to return to our current status.

The "what ifs" that plagued me during the year-and-a-half between the onset of my symptoms and a final diagnosis actually helped me accept Sjogren's syndrome as, if not the good news, at least not so bad. The strange symptoms manifesting in various parts of my body, along with the dramatic decline in my general health, indicated I had a serious illness. My imagination filled in the rest. I tried on every disease I knew, including metastatic cancer and feared the unknowns of rare disorders I couldn't name. Melancholy thoughts about last-time experiences and final days were ever present. When I received the news of an illness that is potentially though *not necessarily* progressive, and that is not life-threatening, I was filled with a profound sense of gratitude which still remains.

Yet the illness I live with daily also remains, the reality of my limitations as well as more periodic bouts of "what if" regarding complications or a rapidly progressive course. Although the gratitude does a great deal to quiet my fears, it never quite puts them to rest.

The fact that we live in vulnerable bodies means not only that we can become ill or injured, it also means that we have the capacity to heal. Each of us has to our credit a lifetime of recoveries from small bruises and minor illnesses. And since those of us currently living with ongoing illnesses haven't succumbed, we are evidently healing from the impact of our illnesses on a daily basis.

Cindy wrote another essay while she was recovering from her accident and made these observations:

> Now, with little else to think about, I am awed by the healing powers of my body.
>
> At first it was watching the scratches and bruises fade from my arms and legs as I lay in the hospital and rehabilitation center. Then it was finding movement returning to my inert left leg — at first, just the toes, then the ankle, the thigh and knee, and now the

entire leg, although it is still quite weak. Concurrent with the return of life to my leg has been my growing ability to stand, then walk with a walker, and now with a cane — for a few steps, unaided.

The body heals itself in a silent, mysterious way. All this mending must surely represent much activity going on in my body, but I am unaware of it: it lies somewhere beyond my consciousness — like my digestive processes or breathing.

The other day, as we were driving...to my physical therapy session, I saw a stand of trees with pale gold leaves. When did that happen — and how? I was startled, just as I was when I found I could stand up safely in the shower, even with my cast on.

The natural order of things prevails in this world, and I feel grateful that my body in its healing is part of that natural order. That same order will prevail when the time comes, as it inevitably will, no longer to heal, but to die. Even as those golden leaves will someday soon wither and drop to the ground.

Miraculously, that time has not yet come for me, although I thought, as the plane crashed, that it had. And there is time to take for healing.

Healing and Curing

The capacity to heal physically in small, gradual ways naturally fuels hopes and expectations about total recovery. But the grace of a cure, remission, or prolonged life doesn't always accompany the non-physical but profound healing that people often experience in the course of an illness. Uncoupling healing from curing allows us a wider arena in which to live life and participate meaningfully.

A cure involves a longed-for return to a previous state of health, and we naturally aspire to the most complete recovery we can achieve. But if the only acceptable evidence of being healed is a symptom-free body, the sense of being a whole, healthy person will never be secure. If we live our lives as though we'll live forever, then no matter when illness or death approaches us, we'll be caught up short. Indeed, the only thing we can count on with absolute certainty is our mortality. Our sense of self, our goals and values, have to allow for it.

Devoting all available time and energy to finding a cure can lead to a preoccupation with monitoring symptoms, which, in turn, reinforces a self-image as "sick" or "broken." Illness becomes who we are rather than something we have. The following essay, included in *How Can I Help? Stories and Reflections on Service* by Ram Dass and Paul Gorman, illustrates the consequences of exclusive concern with the body:

> I've been chronically ill for twelve years. Stroke. Paralysis. That's what I'm dealing with now. I've gone to rehab program after rehab program. I may be one of the most rehabilitated people on the face of the earth....
>
> I've worked with a lot of people, and I've seen many types and attitudes. People try very hard to help me do my best on my own. They understand the importance of self-sufficiency, and so do I. They're positive and optimistic. I admire them for their perseverance. My body is broken, but they still work very hard with it. They're very dedicated. I have nothing but respect for them.
>
> But I must say this: *I have never, ever, met someone who sees me as whole....*
>
> Can you understand this? Can you? No one sees me and helps me see myself as being complete, as is. No one really sees how that's true, at the deepest level. Everything else is Band-Aids, you know.
>
> Now I understand that this is what I've got to see for myself, my own wholeness. But when you're talking about what really hurts, and about what I'm really not getting from those who're trying to help me...that's it: that feeling of not being seen as whole.[11]

Healing extends beyond physical condition and focuses on quality of life in terms of mental, emotional, and spiritual health. As the dictionary defines it, the word health is derived from an Old English word that means "whole" and refers to "an organism's ability to perform its vital functions." As human beings, our vital function is not to exhibit perfect physical health, despite daily media messages to the contrary. A sound body is a means to an end; it allows us to pursue our larger purposes with greater ease.

Because illness brings us so close to the edge of our knowledge and capabilities and to the threshold of our ultimate concerns and deepest fears, it often evokes a growing awareness of our vital function, of what is essential and enduring. It puts an individual life in the larger context of an interconnected world, a world distinguished by shades of gray rather than boundaries between black and white. People often comment that they have learned a great deal from their illnesses and have made long-overdue changes. They talk about a renewed appreciation for simple things, a focus on the present, an increased ability to give and receive love, and a comfort with — and trust in — the mysteries of the unknown. Many say that by facing squarely the issues of illness, pain, loss, and death, they have discovered in themselves an underlying strength or spirit that enhances their lives. These people feel that as they transcend physical challenges and changes, they transcend dark and deep-seated fears as well.

Diagnostic labels, abnormal laboratory reports, and physical limitations may indicate ongoing deficiencies within our bodies. But they don't diminish our capacity for wholeness or impair our ability to heal in the fullest sense: to be complete, intact, to live with a sense of meaning and connection, with feelings of aliveness and peace of mind.

Shortly before she died of breast cancer, Treya Killam Wilber, co-founder of the Cancer Support Community in San Francisco, emphasized the sustaining power of healing when a cure is uncertain or unlikely:

> I suddenly thought, if I do become well for long periods of time, will I lose this deliciously keen, knife-edge awareness I now have, this satisfyingly one-pointed focus, this motivation to explore, to question, to meditate, to read, to visualize, to write, to create? ...Then I realized, the possibility of death will never be far from me. I will always carry with me this goad, this spur, this thorn, reminding me to stay awake.[12]

Nancy Mairs, author of *Plaintext*, has also achieved a soul-satisfying existence, despite multiple sclerosis. She voices this remarkably pragmatic attitude toward a cure:

> ...if a cure were found, would I take it? In a minute. I may be a cripple, but I'm only occasionally a loony and never a saint. Anyway, in my brand of theology God doesn't give bonus points for a limp. I'd take a cure; I just don't need one.[13]

I personally find the position of not needing a cure an appealing one, a perspective I try to maintain. It seems to get to the heart of the nature of healing: to live with illness without a sense of lack.

But the experience of lack is a relative one; our ability to overlook the losses and limitations connected with illness is easily influenced by circumstance. There are times when the desire for relief from symptoms can test any ability to discriminate between want and need.

I began writing this section on healing and curing in the middle of a flare of symptoms. It was a day I had set aside to write, so I kept at it. About mid-day I remarked to my husband Larry, "I think I'm having trouble writing about this because I'm not sure I believe it. When you're feeling awful, the idea of healing without a cure seems ridiculous."

"Are you going to include that in your book?" he asked.

Writing a book about illness is, to some extent, a "yes, but" endeavor. Attitudes toward illness vary enormously among individuals and can fluctuate erratically for any given person. Just as I need to keep track of my thoughts on the bad days if this book is to be an honest account, we each derive our overall sense of illness from both the highs and lows that punctuate each day. I prefer a "yes, and" approach — to represent life with illness not as fragmented episodes which cancel out one another but rather as a composite that reflects an underlying wholeness.

Even when a cure is within reach, for many people it evolves within the broader context of a life-encompassing healing rather than as the endpoint of a linear course from illness to health. Mickey reflects that his "list of acceptable losses has grown" as a result of his diagnosis and successful treatment for vocal cord cancer. Since his condition was not life-threatening, his original aversion to surgery and radiation was overshadowed by the prospect of a cure. The possibilities of a weakened voice, and even of losing his vocal cords entirely and speaking through an artificial device, became by degrees, imaginable, tolerable, acceptable. Mickey didn't lose his voice, nor has he lost his elastic perspective that seems to accommodate to everything short of losing life.

Bob also had vocal cord cancer but, unlike Mickey, his cancer was widespread at the time of diagnosis. Bob's "cure" involved extensive surgery that required not only removal of his vocal cords but major rearranging and re-routing of the organs within his chest. He takes a somewhat jocular attitude toward his structural changes. Bob says he talks more freely now, with his speaking device, than he did before; he explains that it holds people's attention, and he demonstrates how he can, by gesturing toward a "malfunctioning" device, end the conversation when he's ready. In describing the care he needs to exercise because of surgically inserted openings on the surface of his upper body, he jokes that he's at risk of drowning in the shower.

Bob makes light of his limitations because he is grateful to be living with them. Before he became ill with cancer, he was struggling with alcohol and drug addiction; he expresses gratitude — and surprise — that he didn't die then. Bob sees his life now as an opportunity for "redirection" and signifies this in his characteristically playful style: he fulfilled a dream of owning an electric train set, which gives him hours of pleasure and keeps him "on track."

The process of healing is often enhanced through symbolic expression. By representing the experience of illness in a personal and authentic way, we interact with it, reshape it, determine its position and proportion in our lives. And we make tangible the energy we still have available, to move, to create, to heal.

Renée's talent for orchestration didn't end with the interruption of her conducting career. As a way to keep her gift alive, she made a "healing bracelet" by beading onto a band of cloth an elaborate three-tiered design representing the cycles in nature. Renée tries to see illness, too, as cyclical rather than chronic, and finds the implicit order in the natural world a grounding influence. Each intricate element of her bracelet blends gracefully into a unified whole — like a well-performed symphony.

The symbol chosen for healing the wounds of illness is sometimes expressed quite directly, literally. Rachel Naomi Remen, the medical director of the Commonweal Cancer Help Program, recalls an experience she had during the time she was working as a pediatrician. A young child pointed with pride to the needle puncture where her blood had been drawn and announced, "Look, this is where I was brave."[14] Because of the way this child chose to see and understand the mark on her body, it was transformed from a wound into a badge of courage.

As adults in this culture, we tend to treat our bodily imperfections, and certainly our wounds, not as marks of distinction but as signs of our inadequacies. As a tattoo artist, Karren has had some unique opportunities to participate with people who choose instead to respond to the loss of a body part without a loss of self. Like the young child, they draw attention to the places that are working the hardest to heal. Andrée came to Karren for a tattoo several months after surgery for breast cancer.

> To have a tattoo of a rose put over the scar was partially an aesthetic decision: it balances my remaining breast. Although something negative happened, it's now something beautiful that I am proud to show people....
>
> I chose a rose, a single rose because the rose is sacred to the goddesses. Temple priestesses always carried a red rose. They are a symbol of love, passion, life, vitality, and spirituality. Their colors, red and green, are emblematic of the fairy people in Ireland, and of magic. The thorn is seen in their folklore as the place where the little fairies climb up the rose. The beauty of the rose has a dark side, the thorn can wound. The rose is the perfect thing to do with my missing breast. It is not just a decorative tattoo, it covers my scar. A transformation has happened from a breast into a rose.[15]

Karren spent nearly a full day creating a long and elaborate "snake arm" for a man who had lost his hand. The man is a singer and slide-guitar player in a rhythm and blues band, and all the band members came to witness the tattoo session as a ritual of beautification and renewal.

Reaching that vantage point usually involves major disappointments and adjustments, painful losses and episodes of grief, and infinite patience. When someone emerges from that process feeling strong and hopeful, it is the culmination of an heroic effort. When people share those kinds of personal experiences with one another, it is inspiring. That is quite different, however, from someone else trying to convince a person who feels devastated by an illness that things could be worse, that there are lessons to be learned, that good things will come from the experience. People become strong by being supported as they go through their unique version of the necessary steps through illness, not by having the depth of their struggles discounted or minimized.

One of the most painful aspects of the experience of illness is that, along the way, it can and often does leave people feeling broken, lost, separate — alienated from others and from life as they knew it. Usual roles and ways of making contact may be disrupted, and the overwhelming implications of illness can topple even the firmest sense of purpose and most solid set of beliefs. At such times, the distinction between healing and curing can easily blur, especially when physical symptoms seem to eclipse any other dimension of life. Because it interferes with the basic human needs for meaning and connection, many people define illness as a spiritual crisis as well as a physical one. It is a question of faith for each of us, regardless of the presence or absence of particular religious affiliations or spiritual inclinations.

As people sort out these issues, they inevitably wonder what other people with illnesses do, how they live, where they derive their strength. Loneliness and desperation often bring people to support groups, but there are usually some elements of curiosity and hope as well. People find in gathering with others an opportunity to address, along with other practical matters, these broad existential concerns that give shape to the experience of illness and to the rest of our lives.

Wounded Healers

The first days after I closed the preschool were a dark, empty time. Without the familiar framework around which to structure my life, and support my self-esteem, I searched for something to fill the void or at least provide a direction. I found a small degree of comfort in the garden, where I recognized that I was rather like a plant that had been pruned. I wondered whether I too was gathering nourishment during my dormancy, preparing to branch out, set new buds. I recalled a line from a poem written by my friend Kate, about "roses blooming under your skin." Maybe that was happening too.

Mainly I drifted around in my own thoughts, at first as disorganized as the scraps of paper on which I scribbled them. At the end of a week, I gathered up the rapidly accumulating notes, sorted through them, and to my surprise, discerned some order in the jumble.

The ideas clustered around illness and healing, loss and grief, acceptance and transformation. What I wrote reflected quite a shift from the way I had approached my illness up until that point; at the beginning I had been trying to paste the leaves back on the tree. Now I was more open to acknowledging change and to trusting that renewal and growth could emerge from loss.

Although my outpouring of thoughts reflected my personal life experience and unique circumstances, I imagined that other people must also feel that they were being sculpted in unanticipated ways by their own illnesses. I felt I was a member of an invisible community of individuals who could benefit greatly from joining together, both to validate each other's struggles and absorb each other's strengths.

With little idea of how to proceed, I developed my notes into an essay (which later was published as a small booklet) and shared it with a few people, one of whom was Susan, the director of the Adult Day Program at the local senior center. Susan and I became friends through an intergenerational program we had developed between the children in my preschool and her elderly clients. Susan also received a yearly grant from the Northern California Arthritis Foundation to lead various educational programs. She invited me to come to one of the meetings to talk about some of my ideas and facilitate a discussion about the emotional aspects of coping with illness. As an outgrowth of that meeting, Susan generously offered to include in her next yearly grant proposal a weekly support group for people with illnesses and their families/loved ones, with me as the facilitator. Over time, the group attracted people of various ages with a variety of illnesses, and became an ongoing program sponsored by the local hospital and a community medical center. Eventually, there were three separate groups, to accommodate increased attendance and to cover a wider geographic area.

In the meantime, I enrolled in a training program for hospice volunteers. I kept gravitating toward people and experiences that offered a perspective different than the one more commonly held in our culture: that illness, pain, loss, and death are somehow alien to normal existence. Befriending vulnerability, revealing limitations, exposing wounds — these are, by conventional standards, signs of weakness and passivity.

In other cultures and earlier times, however, illness, pain, disability, or wounds have been recognized as paths to wisdom, as connections with the spiritual world. In the belief systems of these traditional societies, healing is a spiritual transformation, and a profound illness evokes a profound understanding of healing and therefore the capacity to heal others as well. A shaman, which literally means "the one who knows," receives the initiation or calling through an encounter with illness or in the throes of acute physical distress. Personal healing becomes the vehicle for knowledge, power, and the special ability to move fearlessly between the worlds of human suffering and sacred mystery.

The wounded healer concept may appear off in the distance historically and geographically, and certainly seems far removed from modern medical approaches. But it defines the very essence of the kind of relationship that encourages people to uncover their own natural healing abilities, and to recover the sense of meaning and connection with others that is so crucial to our well-being. The growing popularity of self-help groups attests to the power of peer support and the bond created by sharing firsthand experience.

Sara is an archetypical wounded healer. Her "initiation rites," the diagnosis and treatment of breast cancer, occurred against the backdrop of an alarming unfolding of events in which cancer played the dominant role.

> My mother and brother had recently died of cancer, and my father was diagnosed with cancer three months after I was. Cancer had overwhelmed my life at this point, and I needed to get my life back. I was searching for someone who could understand.[16]

As part of her search, Sara started to attend our weekly support group meetings, later became a member of a monthly cancer support group, and eventually volunteered to counsel newly diagnosed breast cancer patients as a "Reach to Recovery" worker for the American Cancer Society. These structured activities are the surface manifestations of a much more encompassing life focus that Sara has defined for herself. In the aftermath of the succession of deaths in her immediate family, Sara continues to shepherd many other people, including those gravely ill, through the cancer experience.

Sara at first wondered about this strange "cancer connection" she was establishing, the growing number of friendships that took root in hospital rooms and oncology clinics, by simply making herself available to someone in need.

With time, Sara has found that when she accompanies others through their own ordeals with cancer — each time she stares cancer in the face — "it takes away a little more of the fear."

> I was very afraid and felt very alone, in spite of all the love and support I received from my family and friends in the early stages of my treatment.... When you are first diagnosed, it is like being in cancer kindergarten....
>
> I met my dear friend Nancy in the hospital after both of us had undergone surgery for breast cancer. We had cancer to connect us at the beginning. We now have a fast and true friendship that reaches way beyond the bonds of this disease. Through this initial friendship with Nancy, I was able to relate to her my fears, and by

doing so, gained strength and courage. I no longer felt isolated....

With each new friendship through cancer, I was gaining a better sense of myself and my strengths. I was meeting these women and they were STRONG — and through them I was becoming strong.

...The heartfelt bonding we've shared has touched a place deep within me — a place that is quiet and healing.... It is all part of the unbroken circle....[17]

Unfortunately, several of the people in Sara's "unbroken circle" have died. In each instance, Sara has been present, steady, and intent on making their transitions as easy as possible. And each time she finds some healing for herself in what she witnesses:

I saw in Laura such grace and dignity in her dying. Laura's heart was truly open to her death, and through that, more power came to me and *my* heart opened more.[18]

A few months ago Sara was recounting to me the last moments she spent with a member of her cancer support group who was dying. They were in the hospital, and the woman was feeling quite agitated. Sara told me about a guided meditation she read to her from Stephen Levine's book, *Who Dies?* It calmed the dying woman considerably, and Sara was quick to credit the comforting words on the page for the transforming effect. I agreed that the passage from the book was a useful one, but something more was involved — the attention and love with which it was delivered. I remarked, "Sara, *you* could read to someone from the *Wall Street Journal* and it would have a beneficial effect."

In the role of wounded healer, one is both the agent and the recipient of healing, and as Sara's example indicates, rather than shift back and forth between the two positions, we offer and receive healing simultaneously. This ability to support healing in one another is not based on some magical power or special expertise. It derives from our humanness, from the compassion and trust forged by exploring together the continual cycle of wounding and healing through which we all move.

The decision to attend a support group acknowledges our common role in sharing the human condition and all of its unknowns.

It reflects a willingness to be present with each other's pain and uncertainty, and to expand personal boundaries to include others into our awareness and concern. The opening lines of a poem entitled "The Friend," written by the Sufi poet Rumi, captures the solidity of relationships founded upon such a caring commitment:

> Friend, our closeness is this:
> Anywhere you put your foot, feel me in the firmness
> under you.[19]

A group member expresses the same sentiment in even more earthy terms: "sitting together in the mud." I see the group as a safety net, ready assistance when we are thrown off balance, reassurance of a soft place to land.

Like many other members who eventually begin attending the meetings, I originally considered my illness a private matter. It was something I barely admitted to myself and was certainly not ready to share with others. When people tell me their reasons for not coming to the group sooner, I hear echoes of my own list: I am not really ill; if I were, I could handle it myself; I'm not a "group person"; I don't want to sit around and talk about my health, I just want to get on with my life. At some point, for all of us, the isolation and the need to talk with others having similar experiences outweighed the initial resistance. The transition is made easier for some when I explain that it is a group for people who hate groups.

The opportunity to "come as you are" is itself healing. The mutual understanding and unconditional acceptance create a sense of communion, a surprising level of intimacy among recent acquaintances. Personal human experience, simply and honestly expressed, and sincerely and openly received, is the most natural and available form of help we can provide. People find it healing to know that their own struggles and responses not only elicit a deep level of empathy but also bring clarity and guidance to others. Individual suffering feels less like an isolating, meaningless ordeal when we are greeted weekly with expressions of concern — "I was thinking about you this week and wondering how you were doing," or expressions of appreciation — "Something you said last week really helped me; how you handled your difficulties encouraged me to see more choices for myself." We feel heard, understood; we know that we matter.

Comedian Gilda Radner wrote about her experience with ovarian cancer in *It's Always Something* and shares the following thoughts about meeting with others:

> If indeed God created the world and then left us on our own to work things out, then getting together with other people to communicate is what we should be doing. I learned at The Wellness Community that that is the most magic thing we have, our ability to open our mouths and communicate with each other.[20]

The Buddha described compassion as the trembling or quivering of the heart in response to pain, a very tender, open state of trusting in ourselves and knowing we can be present with whatever happens. Many people find that illness opens the heart in a way it has never opened before to other people's pain, especially the pain associated with illness. And with the growing compassion comes a sense of proportion about one's own suffering. I frequently hear someone comment about coming to the group "feeling sorry for myself" and leaving "feeling more concerned about others who have more serious problems." That comment, however, reflects the degree to which people care for one another more than the range of illnesses represented in the group. A woman with advanced metastatic breast cancer told me, "I feel so badly for those with arthritis who live with chronic pain. At least I feel pretty well between my chemotherapy treatments." For her, cancer and approaching death seemed to fade into the background of someone else's sorrow.

A sense of proportion about one's own suffering, however, does not mean discounting it. Cheri Register, in *Living with Chronic Illness: Days of Patience and Passion*, cautions against labeling as "self-pity" the natural and necessary range of emotions that are part of the "cycle of sick-healthy-sick-healthy":

> Yes, we all know that life isn't fair. Injustice is the great cosmic flaw that keeps us from experiencing life as truly good and beautiful. It is a fact to be mourned and decried. But how can we do that collectively if we don't do it individually, each time we experience

injustice ourselves? Imagine being unmoved by the senility of your aging mother because the loss of the human promise in a baby's brain injury is more tragic, or not grieving an accidental death because murder is more horrifying. Our own private afflictions, no matter where they rank among the world's horrors, are cause enough for grief.[21]

Compassion, on the deepest level, attunes our hearts to the collective pain, which *includes* our own, and at the same time, heals the pain of isolation that makes our individual burdens more difficult to bear. This is not to suggest that people feel better about their own circumstances by taking comfort in the misery of others: "I'm glad it's not me." Rather, as boundaries dissolve and connections increase, there is the sense of "It could be me."

"It *was* me" often provides the impetus to help others through difficult circumstances that have been personally endured. Rosie is the patient representative at our local hospital, a position created to formalize her many years of volunteer service as a seemingly inexhaustible reservoir of emotional support to the full range of hospitalized patients, including those terminally ill. Rosie's "been there" experience was a month-long hospitalization for polio when she was eight years old.

>One day I was sick, and the next day I was taken away from my parents. Because of the quarantine, my parents were not allowed to visit. I never knew they were downstairs; I assumed that I had been abducted and was being punished, but for what I didn't know. No one explained anything, and I didn't ask any questions. The treatments were so painful and the staff so uncaring, I was afraid to speak up for fear of being hurt even more by the "guards." The huge room, with bed after bed lining the walls, looked like a prison or the concentration camps I saw on newsreels; this was 1946.
>
>It seemed that I could be there for eternity, so I set about devising a rescue plan. This all happened right after my communion, so I decided to bargain with God. Looking back, that was consistent with my Sicilian upbringing, and I chose a good partner for my alliance.

I prayed continuously, day and night, becoming glassy-eyed and more withdrawn. When I was finally released from the hospital, I felt my bargain had worked. I carried away from that experience both a profound fear of abandonment *and* the sense that if you want to do something badly enough, you have some power or control.

Hospitalized as an adult for back surgery, I once again had that helpless feeling of being at the mercy of others who held all the control. Those painful, childhood memories came flooding back, and for the first time, I began to write about them.

I also started my work to help people who come into a facility as patients and feel lost, confused, and alone. I have an instant understanding of how painful experiences, with no explanations, can feel like a prison run by tormentors.

Nursing became my way to work out that issue — being lost and cut off from love. As a nurse, I broke the rules to get what I wanted for the patients; when I became patient representative, I *changed* the rules — and I love it!

Rosie appreciates the subtleties of the wounded healer relationship. She describes her work as "enabling the patient rather than charging in on a white horse in a dramatic rescue." We don't, in fact, heal one another; we support and encourage healing in each other through relationships that invite people to discover the strength that comes from knowing their own wounds. Sharing this process establishes a trust in healing as well as in each other. It inevitably becomes apparent that healing, as slow and elusive as it may be, is taking place in all of us. *Something* keeps us going, moving through the difficulties, engaging with life.

Judy, still struggling with the loss of her singing career as well as her health, met Katherine, who began coming to the support group upon being diagnosed with terminal liver cancer. During the last months of Katherine's life, these two wounded healers developed a relationship and provided for one another what no one else could.

Judy's father had died several years earlier of liver cancer. Because of her own health problems and the long distance between California and Kansas, Judy could make only periodic visits to see him. She often spoke of her frustrated desire to spend more time at his bedside, talking, being close and loving.

Judy had learned what she could about liver cancer in order to help her father and saw an opportunity to provide for Katherine a kind of "table of contents" for the days ahead. More than the information, however, the understanding and concern, the intuition and sensitivity, that Judy brought to the relationship enormously enriched Katherine's remaining time. Because of insight gained through her father's death and her other losses, Judy appreciated that Katherine didn't need to be "fixed," only to be loved.

Upon first meeting Judy, Katherine felt an immediate connection. She loved to listen to her perspective on things and also felt deep empathy for Judy's sadness and pain. They spent time in Katherine's home, and toward the end, Judy helped the family by staying overnight. They shared stories, and sometimes Judy read aloud. Katherine loved the idea that it was like a "pajama party" — and a respite from all the *doing* around her dying. During one of their final conversations, Katherine said to Judy, "Boy, if we had known each other when we were young, we could have turned this town upside down." Judy carries these parting words as a heartfelt expression of the vital relationship she shared with Katherine, and she also carries her own father's death with a bit more ease.

The wounds of illness often touch on other wounds, old hurts that predated the illness or sensitive areas of current concern. Attending to the issues connected with illness can penetrate other places we feel fragile or confused, angry or afraid. In our efforts to achieve wholeness in spite of illness, and even in the face of death, we often find the resources to heal those other wounds as well.

That was true for Katherine, who continued to attend the support group, in spite of overwhelming pain and fatigue, until her very last days. When I saw her pale, weak form approaching, I felt like death was walking through the door. But so was a sacred gift, an embodiment of the kind of goodness and strength of which human beings are capable.

Katherine came to the meetings as though her challenges were no more weighty than those of others, as if to say, "This is part of life too. Dying doesn't exclude me from the concerns of the living.

Let's talk." And when she spoke about letting go of past hurts and forgiving the people who inflicted them, *she* became a "table of contents" for the rest of us who still had the luxury of time.

During one meeting a woman talked about how insensitive her family and friends had been concerning her illness, and she went on to detail the many ways they had disappointed her in the past. Her accumulated anger almost filled the room. She declared her resolve to purge these people from her life, never to trust, to go it alone.

Katherine listened empathically and then described some recent experiences of her own. Her ex-husband, whom she had not seen for many years, came to visit her — and apologize: "He had much to apologize for." Her son, who had seemed so uncaring, was, she saw, struggling with his own grief. "It's all water under the bridge," said Katherine. "With so little time left, why stay angry? We can't change the past."

Katherine's words landed like a gentle bird on the anger of the other woman, for whom forgiveness seemed forever out of reach. Although Katherine never directly advised her, over the weeks I sensed a gradual but noticeable softening in this woman's attitude, an indirect acknowledgment of the healing Katherine brought to the group on the threshold of her death.

Chapter Two

Freedom and Choice

We must believe in free will.
We have no choice.
— Isaac Bashevis Singer[1]

A Semblance of Control

During the many months I continued to teach preschool despite the obvious strain on my health, I remember awakening each morning to the same disconcerting thought: In about an hour six people will be turning up my driveway and leaving their children here for the rest of the day. How am I going to manage?

Caring family members and friends who knew how difficult my work had become suggested the obvious: Stop doing it. Close the school.

"That's not a choice," I insisted. It's not that I, and the many other people who adjust to their illnesses in baby steps, don't appreciate the richness and range of choice wherein lies human freedom. It's just that the unavoidable changes imposed by illness are often test enough of our self-awareness and ability to adapt. Under those circumstances one doesn't necessarily leap at the opportunity for growth and change, toss out the old, and welcome the excitement of risk. We are already at risk.

Many of us eventually come to see more choices and make the changes that ultimately are best for our health and well-being. That, however, doesn't imply that sooner would have been better. A choice feels most authentic when it evolves out of the interplay of our accumulated experiences and a growing perspective, not when we are prematurely drafted into change. Unfortunately, for many people, rapid or dramatic physical decline precludes the option of clinging to old, familiar ways. Those of us who do have some margin tend to play at the edges of our boundaries and hold fast to whatever degree of influence we can exert over the timing as well as the direction of the changes in our lives.

In her book, *Living with Chronic Illness: Days of Patience and Passion*, Cheri Register recounts her own experience with liver disease and "easing gradually into a way a life compatible with illness":

> Most of us, healthy or sick, live out our lives on inconclusive evidence. To avoid being demoralized by the greater uncertainty that illness imposes, it is wise to hang on to normal expectations for all they are worth. I have never regretted sticking to my original plan to get a Ph.D., even though there were times when I doubted that I would live to complete it, let alone make use of it. Going to classes each day, reading assignments and writing papers, and measuring life one academic quarter at a time gave my otherwise chaotic existence a structure to undergird it. Getting involved in intellectual questions and the political questions of the day lifted me out of a melancholy preoccupation. In the end, it took only two additional years beyond the time I expected to complete the degree, and such delays are the rule in academe anyway. If changes do need to be made, the need will make itself known. One day you stop to realize that you will probably fare much better if you discontinue one habit and adopt a new one.[2]

We are understandably reluctant to break old patterns or separate from the life we have known if we feel broken and separate inside. Yet the longer we remain wedded to a self-image or way of life that is familiar but unmanageable, the more broken and separate we feel. This tug-of-war between feeling trapped and risking change reveals one of the most pervasive issues for people living with illness: the struggle to maintain control. Life, as is, often feels out of control, but so does a future of yet-to-be-tested unknowns.

A loss of control over the functions of the body can indeed feel like a global loss of control. Because an illness has an impact on all other aspects of life, our days seem to bend to the dictates of the body rather than the power of the will. And the dictates of the body often bestow more power on others: health care providers who possess an expertise we lack, family and friends upon whom we may become dependent, and able-bodied individuals who, unlike us, *appear* unlimited in the ability to shape their own destinies. Much of the anger people express over the impact of illness stems from fears about loss of control; the targets of the anger are often the people or events that represent or exacerbate that sense of powerlessness. Following a three-month hospitalization during the late summer months, a woman in the support group returned home to find that all the flowers she remembered in her well-tended garden had gradually withered and died: "It was devastating to think that a whole season had passed without me. It made me angry."

Taken individually, the choices we allow or the decisions we make might seem short-sighted, inflexible, unwise. It may appear that we have not fully considered our options or achieved sufficient clarity to choose among them. But these individual choices often have an underlying coherence, a strategy designed to maintain or regain a consistent direction within our lives.

To function as a participant in the life of our choosing rather than as a victim of circumstances beyond our control, we each must explore our long-standing, perhaps as yet unarticulated, sense of ourselves and of the world. We must clarify what we wish to express in life and how we feel most comfortable expressing it. A healthy orientation to illness is congruent with who we are and how we choose to live.

Joe's lifelong passion has been sports, and continues to be, in spite of ankylosing spondylitis. A form of spinal arthritis, his illness causes, at first, immobilizing pain — "like a toothache all the way down my spine" — followed by a period of less pain but a literal immobilization due to fusion of the spine. Few people with ankylosing spondylitis would turn to golf as their treatment of choice, but Joe uses it as an opportunity to hone his athletic skills. He has strong arms and has developed a control and economy of motion that more than compensate for the rigidity of his spine.

For Joe, who was a high school golf coach for several years, golf is more than a game; it keeps him engaged with life and feeling good about himself.

> It was hard and hideous to go from being a strong, athletic person to being stiff and rigid....
>
> But gradually the depression lessened as the pain lessened. I was able to begin getting around, and it took getting out of the house and doing something I liked. I love golf. So I started playing golf and met some people who appreciated what a good player I was, considering the inflammation of my spine. And they welcomed me and encouraged me and I started to get a little better.
>
> Just before I started my decline in 1984, I had won the club championship. And then in 1989, I won it again. It was like David and Goliath. Although I was one of the shortest hitters down there, I somehow managed to win. It was amazing, although I admit there was some luck involved. But it's a feat I'll take credit for anyway.[3]

In terms of both health care and lifestyle issues, many of the choices connected with illness look like the lesser of two (or more) evils and often involve varying degrees of loss. It takes time to decide which of the initially unappealing alternatives permits a sense of personal coherence and the sense of competence which derives from it. Like young children who are simultaneously getting used to their bodies and trying to express a growing identity, we may require an adult version of some stumbling around before settling on the most skillful way to utilize our bodies to fulfill our larger human needs.

A man who had two heart attacks responded to each one in an entirely different manner. He doesn't claim to know what the best long-term strategy is, but he does know that he has the capacity to choose — and then to choose the opposite.

> After my first heart attack, I exercised, stopped smoking, ate carrot sticks. Then I had a second heart attack. I figured I had nothing to lose. I eat what I want, started traveling — even a trip to Europe — and tried bungee cord jumping. I've always been a "Joe Lunch-Pail" kind of guy. Now, I don't know....

We all want to "do well" with our illnesses. But reconciling medical recommendations with an intuitive pull toward quality of life is rarely a straightforward, once-and-for-all strategy. Since we are mortal, no prescribed treatment can protect us indefinitely, and since we are each unique, few treatments offer universal effectiveness. The choices we make will always be based on our own evaluations of what is most essential for a satisfying existence. Each person's decisions reflect a personal method of balancing a unique combination of needs — which can never be "right" or "wrong."

Laoma's long decision-making process regarding treatment for breast cancer reflected her firmly-held belief that true healing requires a body and soul united. Over a number of years, she lived for extended periods of time on the Hopi reservation. There she cultivated a deep kinship with the natural world, drawing on it as the ultimate source of wisdom and healing. This abiding trust in a unifying force that animates all of life continues to provide the context of Laoma's existence. Her actions and interactions, down to the smallest detail, comprise a living web woven of heart, spirit, and intuition. For Laoma, choosing a medical treatment was less a process of elimination than inclusion.

> The first part of the path is absolute terror. After the biopsy I was bombarded with information about how large the tumor was, what the cell type was, there were all these names. It is really overwhelming at that time to make decisions. Some people's first impulse is "Just get the cancer out of me"; they get themselves on a surgical table. I decided to try to gather my wits about me and gather more information. It's very important in the midst of all that fear to slow down and not make decisions out of those first fears.[4]

The first fears were also Laoma's worst fears — that she was following in her mother's footsteps. Her initial distrust of surgery and chemotherapy were natural, as her mother had died of breast cancer five years after having a mastectomy and then chemotherapy for a cancer cell type identical to her own. Laoma remembered her mother's surgery as traumatic and her chemotherapy treatments as devastating — and they didn't save her life. In addition,

Laoma had been a dancer and in general has always been a physical person: "The aspect of myself in which I have always been most comfortable, through which I can most easily express who I am, is my body." Removal of a breast, for Laoma, was initially unacceptable and, based on her mother's experience, unnecessary.

The strength of Laoma's aversion to the standard treatments was apparent in her choice of words: surgery was "mutilation" and chemotherapy "poison." She and her husband undertook a thorough search for alternative treatments, which included some trips to Mexico and a three-month trial of a nutritional program.

Laoma was confident that the alternative treatments would enhance her overall health and long-term resistance to cancer. But over time, she also became convinced that the standard treatments offered the best chance of immediate survival.

> By following the Gerson diet, I was building up my immune system and getting myself as healthy as possible on a cellular level. My skin was radiant and shining. I think anybody who saw me at that time probably thought I looked the picture of health. I felt healthier than I ever had; I felt energized.
>
> But we couldn't find a test that really measured whether the cancer was disappearing. That was a big problem, and I was finally convinced I needed to start including Western treatments. I didn't trust enough to stick just with the alternatives.[5]

Laoma found a surgeon who understood and honored her reluctance to lose a breast. He performed two "wide excisions" around the lump in an attempt, an unsuccessful one, to find clean margins and thereby avoid a mastectomy.

Almost six months had elapsed since Laoma's diagnosis. During that time, she shaped and reshaped her own healing program, creating a context into which she could comfortably incorporate a mastectomy and chemotherapy. While others might have felt fragmented with such an approach, Laoma trusted the interplay of the treatments she put together in her own way.

> I feel that doing alternative treatments, using Chinese herbs and teas and lots of vitamins and antioxidants — all of these things put my body into a state of health. When I finally did go to a Western

doctor, I was able to handle chemotherapy, which originally I saw as a poison. Down the line, I saw it as something that was going to help me. I was able to take the chemo and handle it in a way where I wasn't sick at all.[6]

Laoma is one of my dearest friends. I watched, with a combination of apprehension and awe, as she choreographed the complex series of moves and shifts that took place over the many weeks. Because of our deep connection, I experienced my own distressing version of her shock, disbelief, and profound sadness. I imagined that, facing the same choices, I would be equally fearful and conflicted. I also realized how much Laoma's guiding faith and flexibility gave her both the confidence to choose and a sense of peace about her decisions. She not only transformed the cancer experience for herself but enlightened those around her.

During the inevitable times we lose sight of where we are headed, we may find the disorientation of the man in this Zen story uncomfortably familiar.

> A man is riding a horse, which is galloping very quickly. Another man, standing alongside the road, yells to him, "Where are you going?"
>
> The man on the horse yells back, "I don't know. Ask the horse."[7]

We don't have to leave it to the horse. Illness may limit our range of choices, but it doesn't eliminate our freedom to choose. Although we may not have a choice about making the journey or about which horse we get, we can still keep hold of the reins and determine which path to take.

Staying in Charge

With or without an illness, none of us has unlimited control over the circumstances we encounter during a lifetime. How we respond to those circumstances, however, is completely within our means. Frequently this distinction is blurred; the freedom to choose, according to some, implies the power to change things that are truly beyond our influence. When that expectation is superimposed upon life's enduring difficulties, it contributes to a sense of failure, suggests a lack of sufficient will.

I have found it helpful to differentiate between staying in charge and being in control. Staying in charge emphasizes the freedom we do enjoy, without feeding either unrealistic notions of total control or, conversely, a sense of powerlessness in the face of overwhelming challenge. Viktor E. Frankl, in *Man's Search for Meaning*, describes his experience in a Nazi concentration camp and his observations about what helped people survive the most repressive conditions imaginable.

> We who lived in concentration camps can remember the men who walked through the huts comforting others, giving away their last piece of bread. They may have been few in number, but they offer sufficient proof that everything can be taken away from a man but one thing: the last of the human freedoms — to choose one's attitude in any given set of circumstances, to choose one's own way.[8]

Few would argue that the difference between those who were rounded up and imprisoned in the concentration camps and those who were not was simply a matter of sufficient will. And few would also fail to applaud those who, under such circumstances, exercised the freedom "to choose one's own way." Yet currently some people regard the presence or absence of disease or disability as universally subject to individual control; they additionally fail to appreciate the freedom we express by choosing how we will live within the confines of our health.

There is no question that mind, emotions, spirit, and lifestyle are factors in illness and health. They interact in significant ways with factors of heredity, environment, and some degree of luck. The causes of an illness and the course it takes are always a mix of these factors, but it's not a straightforward equation, nor is it always possible to "solve for X."

Allowing for personal influence over our health and well-being is empowering; oversimplifying illness as avoidable and fixable under all circumstances merely comforts those who are well and diminishes those who are ill. Treya Killam Wilber tackles this issue head on in her article in *New Age Journal,* "Do We Make Ourselves Sick?"

In trying to understand my own cancer and in working with others, I have come to see that the causes of cancer are many and varied, that they are different for each person and each situation.... It helps me to picture the causes of the disease on a pie chart where the various wedges represent genetics, lifestyle, diet, environmental influences, past medical treatments, social factors such as strength of social connections, and so on. We don't know how large each wedge might be — we don't even know how many there are — and the chart will look different for each individual and each type of cancer.

Research indicates that one of these wedges should represent personality factors — ways of responding to stress is the favorite example. I certainly have found it helpful to be aware of this dimension, because it is one place my actions and my conscious choices can clearly affect my health. What is not helpful, and actually is harmful, is when I oversimplify a complex situation and believe the personality slice is the whole pie, ignoring the role other factors play....

I have come to see that life is too wonderfully complex and we are all too interconnected — both with each other and with our environment — for a simple statement like "you create your own reality" to be literally true. In fact, a belief that I control or create my own reality actually attempts to rip me out of the rich, complex, mysterious, and supportive context of my life. It attempts, in the name of control, to deny the web of relationships that nurtures each of us daily.

As a correction to the belief that we are at the mercy of larger forces or that illness is solely caused by external agents, this idea that we create our own reality and therefore our illness is important and valuable. But it goes too far. It is an overreaction, based on an oversimplification. In fact, I have come to feel that the harm caused when this idea is taken to its extreme — as it frequently is — negates what benefits it otherwise may offer.[9]

People who live with illness have abundant examples of "this idea...taken to its extreme." One, however, will suffice to illustrate how a blanket application of a pet theory about disease can smother the individuality we always bring to any situation, including illness. A support group member, just diagnosed with breast cancer, described how she had found herself speechless in the wake of this observation offered by a friend: "Myrtle, I just finished reading a book, and I know why you got breast cancer. You nurture too much."

Myrtle is indeed a caring and generous person toward those around her, but she is also an accomplished artist and gifted teacher who has received numerous awards and widespread recognition for her work. Clearly she is not suffering from a lopsided existence where the needs of others have dominated her life. Another group member commented, "So if this connection between nourishing others and breast cancer is such a tidy one, why doesn't Mother Teresa have breast cancer? Is it just a matter of time?"

Staying in charge does include an honest look at our attitudes and behaviors, and a determination to make needed changes. It means gathering information about oneself as well as about the illness and possible treatments. A popular interpretation of this perspective encourages self-reflection but with an unhealthy dose of self blame: Illness is a "lesson" we bring upon ourselves, and we are both responsible for its onset and capable of eliminating it. A more enlightened approach suggests that we are responsible *to* an illness, not for it; that although we are not giving ourselves lessons, we can learn a great deal from having an illness; and that although not everyone can cure themselves of anything, there is probably no disease from which someone hasn't recovered, so there is always the possibility of cure.

As Treya Wilber pointed out, we don't literally create our own reality. We create our *emotional* reality and can *affect* reality, rather than manifest or eliminate certain givens in life. When people refer to the glass as half full or half empty, the implication is that it depends on how we perceive it, not that we can raise or lower the level of liquid with the power of our thoughts.

Research has shown that when people feel they are fully participating in decisions over the course of an illness, there are better psychological and sometimes medical outcomes. The belief that we cause illness and its progression, however, is associated with confusion, anxiety, and guilt. The best of the alternative approaches to health care emphasize lifestyle and the mental, emotional, and spiritual factors that give people the opportunity and tools to maximize this sense of participation. The theory of self-induced illness, on the other hand, does little to instill confidence and, in fact, has the opposite effect.

Larry Dossey is a physician, longtime researcher in the field of mind-body health, and former co-chair of the Panel on Mind-Body Interventions of the newly established Office of Alternative Medicine, National Institutes of Health. A strong proponent of the emotional and spiritual dimensions of healing, he also emphasizes that "spiritual achievement and physical health do not always go hand-in-hand."

> There are people who break every commonsense rule of health and never get sick. They go to bed drunk every night, smoke four packs of cigarettes a day, live to be 100, and they're physically healthy to boot. I bet everyone knows somebody like that. Flip that over, though, and what you get are the unhealthy saints and mystics. These are the God-realized Olympic-class spiritual achievers, leading irreproachable spiritual lives. They do everything right spiritually, yet frequently their health histories are miserable.

> If you don't think there are lot of these people in history, read the lives of the saints. Three of the holiest people I've known in this century have died of cancer. Krishnamurti: cancer of the pancreas; Suzuki Roshi, who brought Zen Buddhism from Japan to the San Francisco Bay Area: cancer of the liver; the most beloved saint in modern India, Ramana Maharshi: died a horrible, grotesque death of cancer of the stomach. And then there's Saint Bernadette, who saw the Virgin at Lourdes: dead at 35 with what's been variously called bone cancer or disseminated tuberculosis....

> Now what's going on here? Is there a correlation between your thoughts, emotions and attitudes and your level of physical

health? I've spent most of my adult life trying to demonstrate just that correlation. The correlations are there, they're strong, and we would be foolish to ignore them. But are they invariable? No. Profound spiritual achievement is no guarantee of physical health. Any model we make about the relationship between spirituality and physical health has to account for the large number of anomalies like those quoted above. We cannot ignore them. They are central to our model. The point is really very simple: It is possible to be highly spiritually realized and yet get awfully sick.[10]

Among the many studies that have investigated the mind-body connection and its potential influence on health, a few have recently gained particular attention for their impressive results and promising implications: University of California cardiologist Dean Ornish, M.D., has developed a lifestyle and stress management program for people with coronary artery disease. Stanford University psychiatrist David Spiegel, M.D., has conducted support groups for women with metastatic breast cancer. And University of Massachusetts professor Jon Kabat-Zinn, Ph.D., has been directing programs based on meditation techniques for people with a wide range of chronic medical conditions.

All of these researchers have demonstrated dramatic and measurable improvements in terms of both psychological and physical variables, but they are each hesitant to draw sweeping conclusions or make wide-ranging claims about prevention or cure. Dean Ornish acknowledges "an element of mystery and the unknown and, perhaps, even destiny in all of this."

I don't pretend to claim that this is the final answer here. In many ways, we have raised more questions than we've answered, but it is of interest that across the entire spectrum of our patients, there was a strong correlation between the degree of change they made in all of the intervention components and the degree of change in their underlying coronary artery blockages. Now for any given individual, there are always exceptions to that, but those are not the people we can identify in advance. So the advice I would give to a patient would be based on what is the strongest likelihood, what is the most they can do to improve.[11]

Even though the women who participated in David Spiegel's support group lived, on the average, twice as long as the women who had been assigned to the control group, he says, "We can't save lives." Among the members there was a "confrontation with dying [that] became an occasion for mastery and problem-solving...."

> It's one thing to help patients cope as effectively as possible with a serious and usually fatal illness. It is another thing to make them feel responsible for either giving themselves the disease or failing to cure it. We die because we are mortal, not because we have the wrong attitude. [12]

After achieving remarkable success with over four thousand patients who have completed his eight-week stress reduction program, Jon Kabat-Zinn emphasizes both the unavoidable nature of stress, pain, and illness in life and also the skills we can develop to cope.

> Since all the evidence we have looked at is only statistically valid, we cannot say that a particular belief or attitude causes disease, only that more people get sick or die prematurely if they have strong patterns of thinking that way, for whatever reasons.... There will always be a flux of different forces at work in our lives at any given time; some may be driving us toward illness, others shifting the balance toward greater health. Some of these forces are under our control, or might be if we put our resources to work for us, whereas others lie beyond what any individual can control. [13]

These kinds of reports, as well as many firsthand accounts from people who are ill, offer compelling reasons to identify the areas of our inner and outer life which may have an impact on our health and over which we have some influence. Evidence suggests that by engaging with illness as something comprehensible, manageable, and meaningful, we enhance the quality of our lives and, in some cases, enhance whatever mechanisms may be factors in improvement or cure. We can become more active participants within standard medical approaches, or pursue alternative treatments, personal lifestyle changes, psychotherapy, or group support. In each case, the result is an increased awareness, confidence, and sense of direction — a richer involvement with life. By staying in charge, we are promoting our healing, whatever the outcome regarding symptoms or cure.

At the time I became ill — and for many years before — I had been eating a healthy vegetarian diet and exercising daily. Ironically my first symptoms were digestive problems and muscle and joint pain. Many well-meaning acquaintances told me with assurance that if I started eating well and getting some exercise, my symptoms would disappear. Very few people asked me anything about how I lived or what I thought before offering me their suggestions. Frustrated with the cosmic injustice of my situation and weary of these daily encounters, I concluded — temporarily — that, for all the good it did me, I could have been lying on the couch eating chocolates all those years, instead of steaming vegetables and working up a sweat.

As time passed, my illness precipitated many changes, and I made some life-altering decisions: I ended my career as a pre-school teacher, separated from my husband of twenty years, and became involved with hospice and illness support groups to face some difficult issues head on. And I continued to receive suggestions about what to do in order to regain good health. Frequently I was advised to break old patterns and think about needed change, before I could explain that my world had been turned inside out. Again I questioned the value of all my efforts at self-reflection and personal growth, in terms of any dramatic benefits to my health.

After struggling with "I'm doing the 'right' things but I'm still not cured" and "I'm not cured so I must not be getting it right after all," I came to another perspective: Perhaps my healthy lifestyle kept me strong and well and postponed the onset of Sjogren's syndrome, for which I have a genetically determined predisposition. Perhaps because I continue those health habits and give attention to my emotional and spiritual life, I am faring as well as I am, heading off a rapid progression or complications of the disease. And in the here and now, I derive a strength and peace of mind from making some choices and living by them.

We can't evaluate how we *could* be doing, only how we *are* doing; it's impossible to determine whether our current state of health qualifies as a relative success or failure. We make the decisions we make and do as well as we can. By constant comparisons with a theoretical — better — outcome, we can diminish the validity of our choices and the gains we have achieved. Since we can never know all the theoretical outcomes, or causes, of an illness, we would do well to live by the "Rule of Six," a Native American tradition that teaches about choice and flexibility in the face of the unknown. Paula Underwood, an educator of Oneida descent, explains how she was taught this "long process of self-discovery."

> One of the attitudes taught in my tradition is the Rule of Six. The Rule of Six says that for each apparent phenomenon, devise at least six plausible explanations, every one of which can indeed explain the phenomenon. There are probably sixty, but if you devise six, this will sensitize you to how many there may yet be and prevent you from locking in on the first that sounds right as The Truth.
>
> But your task isn't over yet. Because you can't just float on a multiple option basis. Now your task is to apply your life experience, which is unique to yourself, and use it as a base to evaluate each of those options. Now you assign a probability factor. That probability factor can never be 100%...and absolutely never zero.
>
> You keep a floating attitude toward life, but you constantly know where you are in that context. [14]

To maintain a floating attitude toward life requires a significant amount of trust. It assumes an underlying source of support that keeps us buoyant and moving safely, purposefully, along the current. Lacking that trust, we imagine ourselves to be aimlessly adrift, at risk of being caught in the undertow. Whether our painful experiences are imbued with hope and meaning or fear and futility depends to a large extent on our conception of the unknown.

In Light of the Unknown

Recently a friend passed on a greeting card to me that comically portrays the human need to bring enduring meaning or universal significance to our otherwise overwhelming individual dilemmas. My friend recognized the card as "right up my alley" and correctly assumed I would want to show it to people in the support groups. The drawing on the front depicts a cat backed up against a fence and surrounded by five large dogs, closing in and barking ferociously. The cat looks terrified, and the dogs are ready to pounce. Beneath the picture the caption reads, "They say you learn the most from your most difficult experiences." The message inside counters with "What a stupid system."

At the meetings we laughed heartily and decided that both statements are true, but the discussion didn't end there. It raised some important questions, like "Who are 'they'?" and "Does the system just look stupid from here?" Before long, we were back to our favorite topic, the search for a link between meaning and suffering.

To some people "meaning in suffering" implies cause, some unifying principle that poetically accounts for personal misfortune. Others find meaning in the act of transcending their hardships, extracting significance from human response rather than divine intention. In her book, *Burst Out Laughing*, Barry Stevens recounts a dialogue — one that easily could have taken place at our meetings — among three people who each take a different position regarding the allegedly "stupid system":

> ...one person said, "You get what you need."
>
> Another person said, "You get what you deserve."
>
> Person three said, "You get what you get."[15]

People address questions of cause, fate, cosmic order, and ultimate meaning as individually as they handle their illnesses. But most of us connect survival with "spirit," however we each define that term.

Many turn to organized religion; they find in its tenets and traditions the assurance of a supreme being upon whom they can unquestioningly depend for wisdom, guidance, and support. "The structure of religion is like guardrails on the bridge," says the wife of a clergyman. "You might make it across without them, but all of your energy would go into feeling safe."

Others draw their strength from human connections rather than a higher power. As one woman put it, "My spiritual life unfolds in my relationships with others, day to day; as far as 'up there' — well, personally it's my sense that help is *not* on the way." Another advanced a less guarded view: "The universe has ears."

My own spiritual search is not for answers as much as for help in recognizing and remembering the questions to live by: How can I stay grounded in love and compassion? How can I soar above my personal circumstances? I look to the divine spirit not for solutions to my dilemmas but for the clarity and courage to respond to them wisely.

A Seventh-Day Adventist who attended the support group enjoys a close — very human — relationship with God. She treats him like a good friend with whom you share both the good times and the bad. At one meeting, she was updating the members on her efforts to give up cigarettes: "When I decide to stop smoking, it's because of the Lord. And when I get angry at the Lord, I start up again."

"Why not just leave him out of it?" was the suggestion offered by a religious skeptic (and non-smoker) in the group.

For many, a soulful connection with something that draws them in deeply becomes a personal source of healing and a private form of prayer. This sense of communion is captured by the Sufi poet Rumi in "The Ground."

> Today, like every other day, we wake up empty and scared.
> Don't open the door to the study and begin reading.
> Take down the dulcimer.
> Let the beauty we love be what we do.
> There are hundreds of ways to kneel and kiss the ground.[16]

For Joyce, beauty has always been an expression of the divine.

She made it part of her daily life through painting, gardening, designing greeting cards, and especially creating centerpieces and decorations for gatherings of the church and other community groups in which she had played an active role. Now in her seventies, arthritis, osteoporosis and dizziness due to low blood pressure have severely curtailed her activities. Except for attending the support group meetings, she rarely leaves home. Church and planning for church functions are what she misses most.

Shortly after Joyce began coming to the group, she found a way to express what she feels is her God-given role: to enhance the world with beauty. The meetings are held in an old community hall, and the room where we gather is definitely in need of enhancement. The drab metal table around which we sit inspired Joyce to revive her practice of bringing centerpieces. She arranges each element with deliberate care — almost reverence — as if preparing an altar.

No matter how we define spiritual and no matter what measure of authority we attribute to a holy presence, most of us have spent a good deal of time pondering the question "Why?" It is the initial and inevitable response to sorrow. Jerry, who has had nine heart surgeries, skin cancer, diabetes, and high blood pressure, as well as a host of non-medical crises in her pain-packed life, frames the question quite graphically: "I wonder why God keeps rattling my cage."

The familiar "Why?" questions start in childhood. They begin a lifelong search into our relationship with the world, a playful investigation undertaken with a fresh innocence and trusting curiosity. We continue to ask "Why?" throughout our lives. We try to transform various unknowns into facts and to weave them into some sort of "truth" within which our own place is clear — and safe.

Illness, pain and loss can propel us into a wild and confusing chase with "Why?" ("Why me?" "Why anybody?"). We don't know if we are pursuing the question or if the question is pursuing us. We fear that our encounter with "Why?" will lead to only frightening conclusions: that the world moves in senseless, chaotic ways against which we are helpless, that the power of evil has caught *us* this time, or that suffering comes into our lives only as punishment, a ghostly reminder of the past and an intimidating cloud over the future. The emotional responses to a world perceived as either chaotic, evil, or punishing are fear, anger, guilt, blame — and a global loss of faith.

Recently, I was walking along the ocean headlands and met up by chance with an acquaintance who had just learned her father died. She described him as a mean-spirited man and abusive father whom, nonetheless, she tried to forgive over the years. They had achieved some degree of reconciliation, but he remained distant and isolated, from his other children as well, until his death. "Do you think we pay for our sins?" she asked, trying to make sense of her confusing mix of anger and sadness.

It took me several minutes of rooting around in my accumulated beliefs and observations about life to form a direct response to her question: "I have the feeling we pay as we go."

I personally see no pattern of in-kind, timely payment for our actions. Perhaps the pattern is too deeply embedded in karma, the ethical consequences of our thoughts, words, and deeds across lifetimes, to be discernible to the human eye. Yet I believe we draw love and joy, or discord and gloom, into our lives with our daily actions in an ongoing way. We absorb what we surround ourselves with. We make our own brew; if the herbs we set in the water to steep are bitter, so will be the quality of the tea.

The explanations offered by structured religions and spiritual traditions provide a specific context and established community within which to bear our individual burdens. It is also possible to come to terms with the mystery and ambiguity inherent in life through lived experience rather than holy texts, through a kind of inner knowing whereby the sacred and the secular blend into one. Each of us comes to our own sense of a divine hand, the impartial laws of nature, an opposing dark force, or an interplay between or among them. And we settle on greater or lesser degrees of "don't know" or "just is." In his book, *When Bad Things Happen to Good People*, Rabbi Harold S. Kushner suggests a God who may not be able to keep bad things from happening but one who weeps with us when they do.[17] A similar perspective is offered by Unitarian minister Phyllis B. O'Connell in an article entitled "When Life Isn't Fair." In it she quotes a colleague: "You know, this is not a just world, this is just a world." O'Connell adds, "...and we choose to live in it anyway." [18]

"Words of inspiration" that validate a sense of injustice are usually more openly received by people who are ill than either scriptural passages or quotations from perennial wisdom that reduce personal suffering to a part of the plan. "Answers" about the unknown are ultimately based on speculation, and speculation by itself, no matter how consoling, cannot withstand the weight of real-life pain. For many no design feels grand enough to explain "the extra fees when I've already paid my dues."

Judy describes her growing up years in Kansas as infused with the church. However, the only part of it that held any personal meaning for her was the music: "Music became more of a religious experience for me than the traditional Bible teaching. It 'saved me' from at least some of the great inner turmoil — like an amazing imaginary cloak I could put on and feel myself safe and real."

A few years ago, Judy met with a caseworker who was reviewing her application for disability income. It had been initially turned down, in spite of the severity of her case of Meniere's disease. Anyone who has gone through the process of applying for disability benefits knows what a frustrating and often humiliating experience it can be. But Judy felt her caseworker brought something uniquely unkind to the encounter: he suggested she stop feeling sorry for herself and read the Book of Job.

Judy already knew about Job and found little in his story that was comforting. She needs something more immediate and tangible, moment to moment. In the midst of her vertigo attacks, instead of the Bible Judy reaches for a candle and rivets her attention on the flame. The steady intensity of the light keeps her grounded, somehow fuels her own flickering spirit. More meaningful to Judy than the Book of Job is the following quotation she brought to read at a meeting, from *You Can't Go Home Again* by Thomas Wolfe.

The tarantula, the adder, and the asp will...never change. Pain and death will always be the same. But under the pavements trembling like a pulse, under the buildings trembling like a cry, under the wastes of time, under the hoof of the beast above the broken bones of cities, there will be something growing like a flower, something bursting from the earth again forever deathless, faithful, coming to life again like April.[19]

Judy's "candle worship" is one example of a fairly common phenomenon among people who are ill. Many of us develop our own personal routines or rituals, perhaps originally born out of physical need, that serve as individualized forms of meditation or communion with the ongoing flow of life. Like many, I regard walks in nature as part of my spiritual as well as my physical program. I am fortunate enough to live in a very beautiful environment, a rural coastal town in Northern California, so walking as a form of meditation is a natural choice.

The contents of the mind claim little of my attention against the backdrop of ocean headlands, redwood forests, or fields of wildflowers in bloom. It restores me to be surrounded by things I *can* count on: the sun rises and sets, trees continue to grow, the birds always have songs to sing. And I am reminded regularly of the enduring yet ever-changing nature of life and my corresponding place in its cycles and seasons. Being *able to walk* presently is also something for which I am eternally grateful, given the nature of my illness and my close relationships with others who don't enjoy that luxury.

Daily life with an illness is itself a meditation practice. Being aware of moment to moment sensations in the body is not a learning technique confined to twenty-minute periods, morning and evening. Awareness and acceptance of discomfort and pain are givens of daily life. So is contemplating that the future holds no guarantees and all that we have is now. I personally am drawn to Buddhism because I find in its teachings both a source of peace and an accurate description of my life, especially life with illness: vulnerability, change, impermanence, and the importance of transforming suffering through mindfulness and compassion.

It is frightening that the world as we know it is filled with such suffering and despair. We universally agree that it doesn't look good on paper. How can we reconcile, in human terms, what is so overwhelming, senseless, unfair? Many regard illness as a form of cosmic injustice experienced as personal betrayal. The familiar comment, "My body has betrayed me," reflects a peculiar kind of loneliness — a disembodied spirit at a time when we still need our bodies. Sometimes this sense of betrayal extends to a generalized loss of trust: "I feel disconnected, as if everyone has hung up on me, God included." Similar comments that express this deep disillusionment are made by the devout and the irreverent alike. Never having a relationship with God in the first place doesn't preclude feeling abandoned, wondering where he or she is *now*.

We are challenged to discover the force of love operating despite uncertainty and tragedy, and to retain in our questioning the elastic quality of the childhood "Why?" that stands in awe before the unknown.

Years ago I saw a movie called *Lies My Father Told Me.* It was about the tender relationship between an elderly Orthodox Jew and his young grandson. A conversation from the movie that I always remembered (at least an approximate version) took place during a Sunday outing together. The boy inquired, "Zayde, do you really believe in miracles?" The grandfather, who always answered the child's questions honestly, responded with a sigh, "No, but I *rely* on them."

The following Christian story concerning divine intervention has a slightly different twist. It tells about a pious man living in a small town where a big flood occurs.

> As the water rises in the town and begins to fill the houses, a rescue boat comes to take the pious man to safety. However, the man waves the boat away, saying, "Don't worry about me. I believe in God and He will save me." Later, as the water rises higher, the man is forced to climb up onto the roof of his house, and once again, the boat comes by. Once again, the pious man waves the boat away, crying, "Don't worry, I believe in God and he will save me!" Finally, just as the waters reach the chimney and the man has to stand on tiptoe to breathe, a helicopter flies over and throws a

rope down to him. However, the pious man refuses to grab the rope and a few minutes later is swept away and drowns. When the pious man reaches heaven, he gets an audience with God, and after bowing, he says with consternation, "My Lord, I was your faithful servant, who worshipped you daily, loving you and trusting in you, but when the flood came, you would not save me. Why, Lord, why?" God looks at the man with a puzzled expression and says, "That's odd. I was sure that I had sent you two boats and a helicopter."[20]

Or as the Indian sage Sri Ramakrishna put it,

> The winds of grace are blowing all the time,
> you have only to raise your sail.[21]

If we attribute a linear quality to the elements of the unknown, we wonder where we will next land on the various continuums: joy/pain, love/loss, health/illness, life/death. Imagined as distinct points on a line, we each exist in a static, lonely position with a limited view, aware of only the small segment of experience that immediately surrounds us. "Is this as good as it gets?" fears a woman with emphysema when she contemplates the future.

On the other hand, we can incorporate the cyclical form of the natural world into our understanding of life. We can see our suffering as enclosed in the ongoing cycle of universal experience, a point in relationship to other points that together comprise a whole. By including human events within the circular flow of night/day, dark/light, winter/spring, we retain the faith that even in pain we can move toward joy, that out of loss we can rebuild hope. I'm not sure how this life force determines our individual destinies, but it links us with one another.

It is no surprise that a garden is a source of faith to many people. Day by day and season by season, the natural order of things is readily apparent. People gather helpful metaphors from their gardens and bring them to the support groups like colorful bouquets: "Seeds never blossom the day they are planted." "Nothing blooms all the time." "With healthy roots, a struggling plant can make it back to life." A woman in the depths of depression described how her outlook on things began to change when both her orchid and gardenia started blooming "when they weren't supposed to."

People also do things they aren't supposed to do. After numerous life-threatening complications following her sixth bypass surgery, Jerry was barely alive. Her family gathered to make a decision about removing the life support which had sustained her for many weeks in the intensive care unit. They didn't reach a decision, but some out-of-town relatives had to return home. Just as they were preparing to leave the hospital room, a nurse temporarily disconnected Jerry from the ventilator to drain the fluid that had accumulated in the tubing. From her comatose state, Jerry stunned everyone present when she declared matter-of-factly, "See you at Thanksgiving." Although Jerry has no recollection of the incident, she is pleased that she came up with the deciding factor. She did indeed see her family at Thanksgiving, which was a huge gathering to celebrate Jerry's recovery.

Terrible things do happen. That doesn't mean the world is a terrible place. Wonderful things happen as well, and because they do, we can heal. Whether we build our faith on the strength of God, grace from the universe, or the power of human love, we are sustained by the belief that living is worth the effort. And the effort need not be undertaken with a sense of resignation but rather as a healthy accommodation between human freedom and an abiding trust in the unknown. Within that relative harmony, the full range of human experience can unfold, and suffering can be endured.

Suffering becomes unbearable when the oppressive nature of external circumstances overwhelms both the human resources to cope in the present and the spiritual resources to hope toward the future. In that hope dwells not only the possibility of improved circumstances but the prospect of a growing personal strength or shift in perspective that can furnish a dimension of meaning. Pointless suffering is a dreadful existence, for all of us our darkest fear.

Without purpose, without hope, we barely survive. We endure hardship because life is worthwhile. We transcend it because life is sacred.

The following story, "The Three Stone Cutters," takes the form of a hypothetical interview with three men who are building a medieval cathedral. Although each of the men is faced with the identical task, the meaning they derive from it is entirely different. (I heard the story from Rachel Naomi Remen, M.D., but the original source is psychologist Roberto Assagioli.)

Question: What are you doing?

First Man (with bitterness):

Can't you see what I'm doing? I'm cutting stones into blocks, 16 inches by 14 inches. I'm cutting this stone, they'll take it away, they'll put another stone in front of me, I'll cut it into a block 16 inches by 14 inches, they'll take that stone away and put another stone in front of me. Day in, day out, I cut stone, and I'll be doing it until the day I die.

Second Man (with contentment):

I'm making a living for my beloved family. With this work, I'm going to be able to buy clothes for my children, food for my family, create a home to contain our love.

Third Man (with joy):

I'm building a cathedral to God, where people who have lost their way can come and find their way home again, and it will stand for hundreds of years.[22]

Ultimately our freedom resides in the attitudes and responses we bring to our current circumstances, however those circumstances may have originally come about. Looking backward at "Why?" is tempting, natural, human. The question is as persistent as the answer is elusive. But the pursuit of "Why?" is most instructive when it sheds some light on "How?" "What now?" "Where do I go from here?" If we are to keep hold of the meaning in life, we need specifics about how to get from one day to the next, how to find moments of comfort and reasons to try.

Chapter Three

An Evolving Perspective

We cannot do great things in this life,
we can only do small things with great love.
— Mother Teresa[1]

Assumptions and Expectations: A Reassessment

The Quakers refer to "the still small voice within." Although the form it takes and the message it conveys are unique for every person, this quiet intuition or inner presence counsels us to trust our direct experience rather than societal norms. It links us to the essential nature of life that underlies and transcends what is culturally approved and therefore conditional and transitory.

The din of the modern world makes it increasingly difficult to hear that small voice. Against the background of bold, rapid-fire messages from the media, a quiet whisper becomes barely audible. It is easily drowned out altogether. In a documentary on the Hopi Indians, an elder spoke of the consciousness required to maintain traditional ways in the midst of mainstream society: "I figure if something comes flying by at ninety miles an hour, I don't have to jump on. If it is something of lasting importance, chances are it will come by again."

Because we live in and participate in society, the assumptions and expectations by which it operates inevitably influence how we evaluate ourselves. The attitudes generated by society and the attitudes that we adopt as our own weave around each other, like voices in a fugue. For people with illnesses, an uncomfortable dissonance develops between these commonly accepted fast-paced, competitive standards and the reality of ever-fluctuating personal limitations. Contact with the still small voice becomes increasingly important if we are to maintain a sense of harmony.

Becoming better acquainted with the vitality of the person inside is what ultimately releases us from long-standing, automatic, and unexamined assumptions and expectations. Self-imposed or externally imposed, we often come to accept certain criteria as positive and then judge ourselves according to our fit with the mold we've chosen. Some of the "growing pains" of an illness result from the effort it takes to extract ourselves from that mold, which over time can harden and become a confining cast. The rewards for the effort are an extended sense of self and increased flexibility, a more solid self-image that is less reliant on external standards.

I correspond by mail with another woman who has Sjogren's syndrome. In a recent letter she introduced me to the idea of "self-basting," a means of cultivating inner sustenance rather than outside approval. The ability to be self-nurturing is indeed critical when living with an illness; the little, everyday occurrences that qualify as landmarks or turning points for us may go unnoticed or unappreciated by others.

People who are in good health often develop some notion of how they would respond *if* they ever developed an illness. They imagine a model of remarkable inner strength and exceptional resilience. Many of us have heard people speculate about "what I would do if I had six months to live." The scenarios frequently include exotic travel, completion of unfinished projects, the decision to pursue a lifelong dream.

When illness is no longer theoretical, the reality of physical limitations and emotional upheaval can easily sabotage those preconceived notions and lofty personal standards. Noble ambitions become less important than the routines and interactions of daily life. Those who live with illness are usually delighted when they are able to pursue normal activities and ongoing relationships; they would consider it a blessing to spend their last days doing just that.

Societal messages about pain are mixed. On the one hand, we seek immediate relief from our own pain and often tend to distance ourselves from the pain of others. The retreat from other people's pain frequently stems not so much from lack of concern as from fear. It is frightening to stay in the presence of pain if there is nothing we can do to alleviate it. And seeing ourselves mirrored in the struggles of others can trigger fears that "this could happen to me."

At the same time, we are told that pain can be ennobling, build character, add a deeper dimension to life. At the very least, one can learn to live with it, be creative about working around it. Those who live with chronic pain often find some truth in these statements, but only after a difficult and lengthy period of adjustment. People who are in good health frequently offer this perspective from a pain-free zone, a safe distance away. The intention is to comfort and inspire hope; the result, however, can be offensive and alienating unless such counsel is tempered with the humility appropriate for someone lacking firsthand experience.

Most people in the support groups agree that if anyone had predicted, before they became ill, the specifics of their diseases and all the ensuing losses and changes, they would have found it unimaginable. Yet each of us has managed to cope in ways we never thought we could and to find inner strength we never thought we had. That perspective is an important source of self-esteem, and also a source of courage for the future.

Our society, by and large, is grounded in an analytical, mechanistic approach: the gathering of objective facts into systems of information that are categorically applied to effect a desired change. This may be a useful strategy in certain areas of life. When, however, it is indiscriminately applied to human concerns, such as illness and health, it results in serious oversimplifications and misconceptions. In the context of a society that strives toward a model of comprehensive knowledge and attainable results, an ongoing illness becomes an aberration, connotes failure, occurs outside the course of normal human events.

Because this image of illness is so pervasive, people tend to discriminate between those who are "sick" and those who are "healthy," as if these labels are permanent or reveal very much about a human individual. We are each a unique person with a fully developed life and a rich personal history before we develop an illness. Unless we invest it with such power, a diagnosis cannot suddenly change any of us into a different person, erase our significance, or consume our life-sustaining energy. Rather, it may kindle some hidden aspects of it.

Part of the erroneous assumption that every illness is fixable is the "*quick* fix" mentality that characterizes much of present-day culture. People with illnesses say they receive little encouragement for taking time and space to collect their thoughts on what has happened or to reflect on possible changes. Rather they are encouraged to *do* something, quickly, to cure their bodies so they can go back to being exactly as they were before. Many of us have been advised to sign up *for* something, *with* someone, and to *go* somewhere to do it.

Certainly we all welcome and appreciate any information and encouragement that can guide us toward improved health. However, we need to maintain hope not only in our capacity to recover physically but also in our capacity to live in a meaningful way, whatever the circumstances of our health.

Encouragement of this kind often takes the form of stories about others, frequently public figures, who are exemplary in their achievements despite physical shortcomings. These accounts are inspiring, but they also can be intimidating to those of us who are healing privately, quietly, invisibly. It is important that we not shadow the results of our own efforts behind the impressive feat or string of accomplishments that captures public attention. In the words of Dostoyevsky, "He who masters the gray everyday is a hero."[2]

Daily interactions highlight the ingrained attitudes we hold regarding productivity and its assumed connection with an individual's worth. To an ill person whose health is not improving and whose activities are significantly curtailed, the questions "How are you?" and "What have you been doing?" can feel like probing inquiries rather than innocent greetings or habitual variations on "Hi." When those questions truly are requests for information, we would like to report that we are "better" and that we have been "busy" in recognizable ways. Cindy describes the myriad emotions that lie beneath the surface of such an encounter:

An Evolving Perspective

Recently I met an old friend who asked me rather intently how I was doing. I wanted to honor my friend's obviously sincere interest, but I wasn't sure exactly what that interest was. Was she interested in my health, the status of my multiple sclerosis?

Many of my friends and acquaintances seem to be. I think that behind this concern is, in part, the hope that I will tell them that somehow, miraculously, this incurable, untreatable disease no longer afflicts me....

Well, perhaps my friend meant not so much *how* I was doing, but *what*. Perhaps she was hoping to hear that I was leading a productive, creative, and fulfilling life, writing great poetry or prose, painting pictures, helping the less fortunate, or discovering the meaning of life.

In any case, I answered her from the emotional point of view, saying cheerfully, "I'm really quite happy except when I'm depressed." We both laughed at this self-evident statement and went on to chatter about other things.

The truth of the matter is, of course, that I'm not *doing* much of anything. And I am working hard to value myself in spite of that....

And each day I expect a miracle. However, I know that while I may share in the power that shapes miracles, it is only in an incidental (often coincidental) way. And it's that which adds surprise and wonder to my life. I wouldn't have it any other way.[3]

The strong link between self-worth and productivity usually takes root when we are young. I remember my elementary school report cards; the conduct section had a category for a behavior called "Does Not Keep Profitably Busy." A check in that box reflected not whether your work was completed, only that you didn't *look* busy. Thinking was chancy; sharpening pencils kept you safe.

During the years I taught preschool, I enjoyed reading to the children the story *Frederick* by Leo Lionni. It offers validation and support for those who manage to make important personal contributions without looking profitably busy. The tale is about some mice who were gathering corn, nuts, wheat, and straw to prepare for winter. One dreamy-eyed mouse named Frederick sat silently in the meadow while everyone else diligently worked. When the other mice reproached Frederick for not doing his share, he explained that he, too, was gathering supplies for the cold, gray winter ahead: sunrays, colors, and words.

The store of supplies and friendly conversation sustained and amused the mice during the first days of winter. But after a time, the food was dwindling and so was their patience with the long, cold days. They turned to Frederick, in the hope that his supplies would bring them some comfort.

Frederick asked them to close their eyes. He stood before them, and much to their surprise, they could feel the warmth of the summer sun as he described its golden rays. They encouraged him to go on, to show them the colors he had collected.

> "Close your eyes again," Frederick said. And when he told them
> of the blue periwinkles, the red poppies in the yellow wheat, and
> the green leaves of the berry bush, they saw the colors as clearly as
> if they had been painted in their minds.[4]

Frederick ended with a charming verse about the seasons, and all the mice applauded. They deemed him a poet, which he acknowledged as he shyly took a bow.

Still, there is little reinforcement in our society for being like Frederick. Early on, and throughout life, we learn that what we "do" or produce in a concrete, measurable way is more noteworthy than acts of integrity or expressions of creativity that cannot be counted or weighed. What if we asked children, "What do you want to be?" and actually *meant* be, not do? What if we encouraged them to think about the kinds of personal qualities and relationships they wanted to cultivate, rather than just the societal positions they wanted to occupy?

Standards of excellence are usually derived from comparisons — with past achievements, with other people, or with some distant model of perfection. These standards and comparisons can be particularly painful to a person with an illness. Sometimes others imply that not continuing with usual activities is giving in to an illness, becoming self-absorbed: "Perhaps a more positive attitude would help." A positive attitude involves discovering pursuits that are *currently* appropriate, not clinging to past endeavors, no matter how difficult and frustrating the effort. In our youth and health obsessed culture, a do-or-die approach has become more fashionable than a graceful adjustment to inevitable physical change.

Comparisons can also be self-generated; we understandably grieve for the things we can no longer do. But for many of us, those things become a basis on which to judge ourselves in the present. JoAnne LeMaistre, who has multiple sclerosis and has authored *Beyond Rage: The Emotional Impact of Chronic Physical Illness*, calls this phenomenon the "phantom psyche, that is, the composite image of how life would be without any limitations."

> The phantom psyche is usually not far from consciousness. It is the self-punishing mechanism whereby the chronically ill person continually erodes his sense of competence or self worth. "If only I didn't have arthritis, I could still be mountain climbing." "If only" statements are the bread and butter of the phantom psyche. They contain harsh judgments of worthlessness. In a happier mood, you might experience the same feeling of loss but say to yourself, "I really miss mountain climbing, but at least I can take a walk today."...
>
> Idealization of the past occurs even in the absence of illness, but illness seems to crystallize the past — when one had better physical function — into an image of perfection.[5]

Few of the support group members would consider their pre-illness lives as perfect. Yet we share the childlike wish that someone could "make it like it used to be" at least in terms of our health. Joe voices the bittersweet emotions many of us feel upon making new acquaintances: "I want to say, 'You should have known me before.'" Joe, at the same time, acknowledges that he feels he has become a more likable person as a result of his illness, "more human." Like Joe, most of us would like to have it both ways, to pursue the active life that comes with good health and retain the perspective and wisdom that come with illness.

Comparisons with other people are no less undermining than the phantom psyche. A focus on unfulfilled personal goals, combined with a preoccupation with the accomplishments of others, can create a building resentment and diminished sense of self-worth. In a society that glorifies competition, it takes courage to avoid comparisons, to move to the sidelines, leave the race by choice. It takes work to remember that the accomplishments of a former self or healthy friends are not an appropriate gauge; the true measure is the sincerity of the effort.

The strive for excellence is an admirable human quality, but it is different from the perfectionism which is endemic in our culture. Like the preoccupation with youth and health, the search for perfection denies the ever-changing nature of life. Eternal youth, optimal health, the perfect outcome — all suggest a fixed condition or static quality, which is a misplaced goal for anything that is alive and evolving. Cindy managed to retain her sense of humor when a friend, well aware of her multiple sclerosis, showed her his list of the qualities he was seeking in his "perfect woman." To meet his requirements, this theoretical woman would have to be young, healthy, energetic, athletic — and remain that way. Cindy and I shared a laugh over the following Sufi tale that exposes the futility of the search for perfection.

> One afternoon Nasrudin and his friend were sitting in a cafe, drinking tea, and talking about life and love.
>
> "How come you never got married, Nasrudin?" asked his friend at one point.
>
> "Well," said Nasrudin, "to tell you the truth, I spent my youth looking for the perfect woman. In Cairo, I met a beautiful and intelligent woman, with eyes like dark olives, but she was unkind. Then in Baghdad, I met a woman who was a wonderful and generous soul, but we had no interests in common. One woman after another would seem just right, but there would always be something missing. Then one day, I met her. She was beautiful, intelligent, generous and kind. We had everything in common. In fact, she was perfect."
>
> "Well," said Nasrudin's friend, "what happened?" "Why didn't you marry her?"
>
> Nasrudin sipped his tea reflectively. "Well," he replied, "it's a sad thing. Seems she was looking for the perfect man."[6]

Clocks and calendars are predominant fixtures of daily life. Both long-term and short-term goals are invariably anchored to time. The degree to which we can structure our time, use it efficiently, and adhere to schedules becomes the indicator of a successful life — on time, on schedule, on target. Efficiency and schedules are, however, only tools, means to an end. Sadly, in our culture they have become ends in themselves.

Time takes on an added urgency for people who are ill. Sometimes the fear that time will run out, either because of a shortened life or increased disability, impels people to accomplish as much as they can in the time that remains. Others find that time itself is precious; these people choose to devote more time to a few things they identify as truly important. Whatever we choose to do, illness inevitably slows us down and also requires that a certain amount of time be allotted to medical treatments or health-care-related routines.

We may not be able to measure up to the rest of society in terms of its recognized standards of efficiency, productivity, and perfection. We can, however, develop other personal criteria, for which speed and endurance are not prerequisites.

> To know even one life has breathed easier
> Because you have lived,
> This is to have succeeded.
> — Ralph Waldo Emerson[7]

At one of the support group meetings we tossed around some possible responses to the ubiquitous question "What have you been doing?" "I'm working on leaving the world in a little bit better shape than I found it. And it's a full time job." That self-confident statement may never reach words, but as long as we believe our unique presence is a significant contribution, we can somehow devise appropriate forms of expression. That is far more rewarding than holding on to erroneous assumptions and misguided expectations.

Thich Nhat Hanh, in *Being Peace*, explains that in Buddhism it is said that "for things to reveal themselves to us, we need to be ready to abandon our views about them." He goes on to recount this story told by the Buddha:

Finding the Way Home

A young widower, who loved his five-year-old son very much, was away on business, and bandits came, burned down his whole village, and took his son away. When the man returned, he saw the ruins, and panicked. He took the charred corpse of an infant to be his own child, and he began to pull his hair and beat his chest, crying uncontrollably. He organized a cremation ceremony, collected the ashes and put them in a very beautiful velvet bag. Working, sleeping, eating, he always carried the bag of ashes with him.

One day his real son escaped from the robbers and found his way home. He arrived at this father's new cottage at midnight, and knocked at the door. You can imagine at that time, the young father was still carrying the bag of ashes, and crying. He asked, "Who is there?" And the child answered, "It's me Papa. Open the door, it's your son." In his agitated state of mind, the father thought that some mischievous boy was making fun of him, and he shouted at the child to go away, and he continued to cry. The boy knocked again and again, but the father refused to let him in. Some time passed, and finally the child left. From that time on, father and son never saw one another. After telling this story, the Buddha said, "Sometime, somewhere you take something to be the truth. If you cling to it so much, when the truth comes in person and knocks at your door, you will not open it."[8]

In Search of the Authentic: Values and Beliefs

Shortly after I closed the preschool, I enrolled in a training course for hospice volunteers. I suspected that both the principles of hospice work and the people involved would embody values and beliefs that were now assuming greater importance in my own life. I also hoped that the growing awareness of my own vulnerability and mortality could be put to some useful purpose, that it might enhance my ability to help others in pain and those facing death.

One of the sessions of the training was devoted to sensitizing the participants to the experience of dying. We were led through an exercise to simulate the gradual process of letting go of life as death approaches. Strips of colored paper were passed around the group; there were five colors, each color signifying a category, and we received five strips of each color. The categories represented the major areas of life: material possessions, jobs or other roles, hobbies or interests, relationships, values or beliefs. We were instructed to write on the strips of paper the items, activities, people, and inner resources that we hold most dear, then to arrange the strips of paper in a stack according to relative importance, mixing categories as we wished.

There was some lighthearted joking at first, as we each considered the range and degree of our attachments. As I wrote "my blue down comforter" on a colored strip that represented beloved material possessions, I reflected that a warm, soft blanket might, in fact, provide one of the few physically comforting experiences still available to a person close to death.

The second part of the exercise was a guided visualization that began with the initial discovery of a small, suspicious lump. The imagery led us personally through a biopsy, cancer diagnosis, surgery, radiation, and chemotherapy, then along a painful and rapid decline toward death. At various points in the progression, the instructor told us to remove one of the strips from our pile and discard it. Since the items had been originally prioritized, we each reached for the bottom of our respective piles. But all of the items had been included in the first place because they were important. Many of us had trouble tossing out the bottom one and tried to reorder them. It was with great reluctance that we each began stripping away the elements of our lives.

Once this portion of the exercise began, the mood of the group noticeably changed. The chatting ended, and each person slipped into a silent and solitary encounter with loss and death. The experience was extremely painful. It made me face unacceptable losses, an unimaginable existence: one by one, everything secure and familiar, everyone cherished, disappeared.

By the end of the exercise, one strip of paper remained. Most of us saved the same "color" for our final moments, the color that represented values and beliefs. As difficult as it was to relinquish established roles, treasured possessions, and especially loved ones, we felt compelled to hold on to "perspective," "equanimity," "faith," "cosmic love" as our indispensable allies. Several people said they had never before identified their core beliefs; others remarked that, until then, they had not consciously ascribed much importance to them.

It is difficult for most of us to clarify and articulate the personal framework around which we structure the total of our life experience. The contemplation of death is the cornerstone. Of the many things that claim our attention, that which supports us through our last days has important implications for all the days between now and then.

For Jan, contemplating death was no mere exercise. Upon a recurrence of lung cancer eighteen months after her original diagnosis and treatment, Jan was told she would probably die within a year. That was six years ago. Jan currently has emphysema, which causes her to scale down her activities considerably, but her courage and confidence seem to grow proportionately. When people question her about the source of her strength, Jan explains by way of her personal axiom: "Since I didn't die after all."

> In so many ways, I "do it now" and feel I no longer put off living while I'm getting my act together so I can do it right....These past years have left me with such peace and new wisdom about living in the moment. I have grown spiritually beyond my greatest expectations....
>
> The enlightenment that came out of that terrible trauma — the surgery and recovery, and later the radiation — was a new sense of self-esteem. All that self-effacing stuff — how silly that was — I've no time for that now. After surviving such a terribly difficult ordeal, there came a sense of dignity and pride in myself, and I made a promise to stop the sabotaging and get on with loving who I am.
>
> And then I found out how much I am loved, by so many, and I thought, "This business of doubting whether I'm lovable is just silly nonsense, a waste of energy. I am loved and this certainly shows it."

Since I didn't die after all, I had a great 60th birthday party, no longer whimpering about growing old but delighted to be around to grow wrinkles.[9]

The resolve to live more fully in the present is a common response to illness. For some, the humbling realization that the present moment is all that we can truly count on is disturbing; it is a perspective that is adopted reluctantly, with a sense of resignation. Living feels confined to a small area, inserted between an irretrievable past and an uncertain future.

For others, developing a moment-to-moment relationship with life brings a sense of freedom rather than restriction. Individual experiences are separated and savored; days are no longer simply mass impressions or just a brief intersection of past and future. Longings or regrets about the past, and expectations or fears about the future, are recognized as just that. Put succinctly by a friend, "You can't change the past, but you can ruin the present by worrying about the future." From this perspective, the present moment is all that we have, but it is also all that we need. Our current circumstances and relationships offer ample opportunities to apply our insights from the past and to take actions according to our vision of the future.

Whether we welcome, or accept reluctantly, life in the present, we all want to utilize the time well. For many people like Jan, an illness brings a heightened awareness of time spent in habitual self-criticism and self-doubt. Some respond by committing to personal changes they identify as prerequisites for self-acceptance. Others reassess their personal standards and, finding them unreasonable, no longer blame themselves for not meeting them. But as Mark Twain pointed out, "Habit is habit, and not to be flung out the window...but coaxed downstairs a step at a time."[10] Many of us, in spite of valuing the moment, do spend some of that precious time devaluing ourselves. The personal limitations imposed by illness constitute an ongoing test of self-acceptance.

There seems to be a chicken-or-the-egg phenomenon involved in forgiveness: Some people find that forgiving themselves makes it easier to forgive others. It is also common to hear people say that self-forgiveness was possible only after they learned how to forgive another. Either way, many people with illnesses identify nurturing and, where necessary, healing their relationships with others as an important focus; it is something they are no longer willing to postpone. After attending a weekend workshop on relationships, a support group member passed along the following question that was proposed to the workshop participants: If you knew you were going to die tomorrow, would you need to use the telephone?

Some relationships can be healed only from a distance. In situations where abuse has occurred, it may not be psychologically possible or realistically advisable to cultivate a relationship that feels unsafe. At best, we can forgive the person, not the deeds.

Honoring limitations, our own and others, forges a common bond, an increased awareness of our interdependence. We each feel so alone in the knowledge that no one else can fully comprehend our personal experience, but even in that we are like one another. A heightened connection with and compassion for others engenders a broader perspective. Stephen Levine, author and counselor to the terminally ill, says, "It's not your pain or my pain but *the* pain."

For most of us, it is a challenge to maintain that kind of equanimity. Yael Bethiem, in his essay, "The Unhealed Life," displays a remarkable ability to place his own personal suffering in a larger — indeed global — context. Like Joe, he has ankylosing spondylitis but, unlike Joe, his rapidly progressive case has left him bedridden.

> In the silence of this room, I have begun to understand the power of an unhealed life.
>
> Even here, I am not alone. This silence is alive with the unfolding of other lives and with the turning and movement of the Earth. I began to sense my connection to the world's pain and my part in healing it. I realized that my transformation of pain into love was an act of service for humankind. By embracing my existence, I could bring courage to others to face their own pain....
>
> In the pain of an unhealed life is the pain of the world's heart made manifest....An unhealed life is a statement of our need to work together to heal the whole.[11]

In the sense that I use the term "heal," Yael Bethiem has definitely found a way to heal his life, despite the lack of a cure for his disease. In the same essay he describes another compensating aspect of living with illness that is familiar to many of us: an increased ability to celebrate the ordinary, to appreciate what's *not* wrong.

> Essentially bedridden for three years, I have invested a great deal of energy in teaching my body to move again. I have worked for a year to be able to stand outside for ten minutes at a time beneath the trees. I live in a town full of hills and old Victorian houses. Outside my door, on one of the few flat spots in town, I practice walking. Under a stately oak tree that has become my friend, I struggle with the limitations of this body. At times, when I cannot walk, I stand in silence. Never before, when my body was well and I rushed to and fro in the world, did I see the beauty of the sky in such bold relief. I didn't understand the whisper of wind against my cheek. Nor did I realize the nourishment I received from the world of nature — not until it was denied me.
>
> When I go outside each day, my cats rush to meet me; they know this is a special event. My time with the sky has been dearly earned, a shimmering victory that disappears like a mirage when held up against the easy movement of someone else's life.[12]

Our precious human capacity to feel emotion is the source of both our joy and our suffering. If, along with our other losses, we lose the capacity to appreciate whatever love and beauty are still available to us, we compound our suffering. The pain crowds out the healing effect of other emotions.

Illness, pain, loss, and death often seem to sit solidly in the middle of life, resisting our best efforts to move them aside, negotiate around them, or shrink them down to a manageable size. And the closer we stand to our suffering, the more of our attention it claims.

Stepping back gives us perspective. It affords a larger view, a glimpse of those things on the periphery of the pain that are still within our range of vision — and therefore still within our grasp. As we increase our awareness and ultimately our relationship with the things in life that can still make us smile, the pain, still there, yields a bit. It becomes less solid. We can work with it, reshape it, transform it through the presence of other influences.

A man who lost both a stepson to suicide and a lifelong friend to AIDS within a few short years is now accompanying his wife through a recurrence of breast cancer. In his poem, "In the Desert of My Soul," he touches a warm human presence beneath the layers of hardened pain.

> In desperation
> Not unlike an archaeologist,
> I find myself digging furiously
> Through layers of pages of letters and poems
> From old lovers and friends and family
> Digging, digging through lifetimes
> Of experiences and feelings...
> Looking for a glimmer of truth
> To shed some light into this seemingly dark age
> Of lost love and confusion.
> Dead friends, warm hearts and ancient wisdom
> Slowly float up to the surface,
> Their faces shining with a warm glow
> Their eyes ever so softly
> Speaking the tongues of the ancient ones
> Simply saying
> Love
>
> — Richard Yaski [13]

The Buddha used the example of putting a spoonful of salt in a small container of water. Because of the size of the container, the water becomes very acrid. If, however, a spoonful of salt is dropped into a river the size of the Ganges, it's not going to have the same effect. Enlarging our perspective does not get rid of the salt in our lives; we just learn to dilute it, create more space around it.

Our values and beliefs furnish the context of our lives: To what and to whom do we direct our attention, and guided by which principles? Whether a formal, conscious commitment or an informal reflection on the choices we make, we each construct a set of values or body of beliefs that links our experiences and locates us in the larger world.

At a support group meeting, Cindy was discussing an upcoming move, one of several in a fairly short time. She wondered if any place would ever feel permanent. After joking that an awareness of impermanence is, in a spiritual sense, an element of enlightenment, we had a serious discussion about "home," the place we put our roots, feel safe, find peace of mind. Another member described finding — and then having to leave — her ideal home many years ago. She said that after searching for another house that could provide her with the same sense of comfort, she realized, "*I* am my home. It's what I carry inside me, wherever I go."

Values and beliefs have to be flexible if they are to provide adequate housing for the circumstances of life and especially of illness. Like the home we return to daily, our perspective, if large enough, functions as a respite. It is the framework we use to sort out our accumulated experiences and within which we set the personal priorities and specific goals we take into the world.

Priorities and Goals: A Question of Balance

Recently my husband Larry offered a perceptive observation about my characteristic pattern of making/resisting change. He said, "You tend to wait so long before letting go of what has become difficult, you experience very little conflict by the time you finally decide." His comment was prompted by my totally unexpected (even to me) solution to the increasingly difficult task of maintaining our flower garden: "What do you think about replacing the garden with ground cover and maybe a couple of flowering trees?"

Gardening has always been a passion of mine. It remained near the top of my list of priorities, in spite of the toll it took on my body with each passing year since my illness began. I made some accommodations — low maintenance plants, smaller areas to cultivate — and was convinced that, somehow or another, I would always be gardening. I used to put on a recording of Vivaldi's *Four Seasons* to sustain me through autumn plantings; working chilly days in the damp, November soil, I would listen for the approach of spring.

At some point, the balance shifted. The joys of digging in the earth, planting, and pruning were outweighed by the pain and exhaustion that inevitably followed a day among the flowers. As my husband accurately pointed out, I continued to work in the garden until I no longer wanted to be there. I was, in fact, working in the garden when the suggestion about the ground cover popped out of my mouth. I had no idea I was going to say it, no conscious understanding that I had turned the corner.

My timing in giving up my work as a preschool teacher was similar. After I closed the school, people would ask, "Don't you miss the children?" Had I given up teaching at an earlier point in time, I'm certain my answer would have been yes. That's probably why I didn't make the decision sooner — too much of a loss. By the time I did close the school, I mainly felt relief. My physical needs were, by this time, stiff competition even for my strong emotional attachments.

This strategy of "waiting too long" is a common one among people living with illness. It illustrates the power of identified priorities and goals, the degree to which we cling to what we love or deem worthwhile. Certainly we wish to carry on as before for as long as possible. It makes sense to hope that we can find some happy accommodation between our established activities and current health. We each define, in our own unique style, the point at which the prospect of continuing in accustomed ways poses greater problems than shifting priorities and setting different goals.

Changes are not linear; we rarely can go directly from A to B. We are reluctant to relinquish A when B is nowhere in sight. And because we sense our self-esteem is at stake, we hold on with tenacity.

Many people have found that when they allowed some emptiness into their lives, they didn't descend into an abyss. Often, to their surprise, they came to prefer a life with space and time over tightly scheduled routines. As one person put it, "I now live with peace of mind, instead of with my mind in pieces." Another person pointed out that nobody on a deathbed says, "I wish I had spent more time at the office." When people begin to handcraft their lives according to their individual characteristics and needs, their former ready-made existence often looks bland and hollow by comparison. To consider whether present goals and day-to-day priorities are in fact congruent with personal values and rhythms seems like an essential ongoing task for all of us. Yet few of us undertake that task until we are shaken loose from our normal patterns.

When Kay first started attending the support group meetings, she stated with certainty that, if she could, she would like to go back to the life she was leading before the onset of her heart disease: perpetually busy with activities and responsibilities involving family, friends, and community. She had been feeling content and fulfilled and would gladly pick up where she left off. Several months later, she reported she was no longer depressed that her current life was slower, quieter, unplanned: "I do a lot in my head now," said Kay to describe the synthesizing and self-reflecting that has helped her adjust to her illness. "I no longer blame myself, either for getting sick or for not being the way I used to be. In fact, I think I like myself a little better." Taking time with things, rather than completing a project as quickly as possible, has been one of the noticeable changes. "It took me a whole week to paint the bedroom, whereas before I would have finished in a day. And that's okay; it takes as long as it takes."

"A corollary to 'it takes as long as it takes' is 'one thing at a time,'" suggested another group member.

"The one I would like to master is 'less is more,'" bemoaned a man plagued by a room in his house, the repository of accumulated chaos. He labeled this room "the collective unconscious."

By paring down unmanageable piles, people often clarify for themselves what truly matters most and focus their attention in those directions. Vietnamese Buddhist monk Thich Nhat Hanh tells this story about the inverse relationship between clutter and peace of mind.

One day the Buddha was with a number of monks in the woods. They were about to have a dharma discussion when a farmer came by who was very upset. He asked the monks whether they had seen his twelve cows that had run away. He said, "Monks, I think I am going to die. I am the unhappiest person on earth."

The Buddha said, "Gentleman, we have not seen your cows. Maybe they went in the other direction. Go look for them there." After the farmer left, the Buddha turned to his monks and said, "You monks are very lucky. You don't have any cows."

If we want to have peace, we have to learn how to release our cows, the ones outside and the ones inside. So look deeply to see how many cows you have outside, how many cows you have inside, how many things you think are indispensable for your happiness. See your projects, ambitions, worries, anger. Try to release them one by one. Practice letting go.[14]

An uncluttered mind that can embrace the pure and simple opens to the grace at hand that many of us seek in the exotic and remote. There is a stability and satisfaction inherent in small, everyday things; a sense of gratitude for feeling well enough to participate lends particular meaning and joy. Savoring the moment doesn't mean indulging in only short-term pleasures at the expense of long-term commitments or enduring values. It means focusing attention on where we are now rather than on how quickly we will reach our destination. When Jan was told her lung cancer was terminal, her garden "started looking great."

I wanted my "last spring" to be lovely. I said, "Before I die, I'm going to grow sweetpeas and get those strings up *before* the plants sprawl." I did, it was a marvelous crop, and I shared the blossoms with friends all over town. The garden continues to look pretty.[15]

Joe has three children. A son and daughter, now young adults, grew up during the years before Joe's ankylosing spondylitis became severe. Another daughter, Elizabeth, was born much later. Joe feels he is a better parent to Elizabeth because of the quality and quantity of time he spends with her, which is his highest priority. Joe says this wasn't the case during the years he raised his older children; he was busy with other things.

Elizabeth is a wonderful, happy, beautiful child. In a way this disease has been a blessing because I've been able to spend much more time with her than most fathers can spend with their little daughters....

I started going to Head Start with my daughter. It made me feel like I was doing something significant in the world, helping all the kids down there. Then I began helping in kindergarten, and it was great!

...enjoy your children, they'll bring you up, make you laugh.[16]

As a child I adored spending time with my grandfather, especially staying overnight at his house. I remember few of the particular things he said or did, but I carry with me a vivid impression of his quiet gentleness, his patience, his reassuring presence. He made me feel special because he listened and had time for me; he made me feel included. I loved to do ordinary things with my grandfather. We shopped for groceries together, and he would let me help feed the clothes into the old-fashioned ringer washing machine. It didn't really matter what we did. I just liked being around him.

Children often enjoy grandparents who share their delight with small occurrences and have time to hear what's on their minds. At one of the support group meetings we agreed that, as adults, we also find it most satisfying to spend time with people who are patient, attentive, agenda-free. Yet, ironically, our culture would lead us to believe that if we achieve a given status, accomplish particular goals, maintain a certain physical appearance, others will somehow like us better. Clearly, these external measures are not the necessary credentials for establishing meaningful relationships, which come from a quieter, softer, "grandfather" kind of place. People with illnesses know how much comfort a caring presence can provide, and the desire to provide the same for others makes us cherished friends.

Much can be gained by shifting from an "all or none" attitude to "I'll do what I can." In *Plaintext*, Nancy Mairs says that with the onset of her multiple sclerosis, "...although they were not over, the nature of my adventures would have to change."

I admire the grand adventures of others. I read about them with zest....With wonder I contemplate the actions of these rugged and courageous figures, who can strike out on trips of miles — two, two hundred and fifty, three thousand — ready to endure cold, fatigue, human and natural hostility, ready not just to endure but to celebrate.

But as for me, I can no longer walk very far from the armchair in which I read. I'll never make it to Tibet. Maybe not even to Albuquerque. Some days I don't even make it to the back yard. And yet I'm unwilling to forgo the adventurous life: the difficulty of it, even the pain, the suspense and fear, and the sudden brief lift of spirit that graces — unexpectedly, inexplicably — the pilgrimage. If I am to have it too, then I must change the terms by which it is lived. And so I do. I refine adventure, make it smaller and smaller, until it fits into this little toad that struggles through the jungle of clover under my bare feet. And now, whether I am feeding fish flakes to my bettas...lying wide-eyed in the dark battling yet another bout of depression, cooking a chicken, gathering flowers from the garden...meeting a friend for lunch...I am always having the adventures that are mine to have.[17]

I believe that my own transition to living with illness was made easier because my sense of adventure, my excitement and pleasure, have largely occurred in the dailiness of life rather than atop a distant peak. I characteristically focus on a few ongoing pursuits with a passion. I am fascinated with small changes over time, with the subtleties and nuances inherent in natural cycles. In addition, I have always enjoyed solitude, periods of quiet, unscheduled time for reflection.

The Greek poet Archilochus wrote in the seventh century BC, "The fox knows many things, but the hedgehog knows one big thing."[18] The implication is that foxes do a little of this and a little of that. They are unconcerned with the connection those things have with each other, variety being the guiding principle. I, obviously, am a hedgehog, who finds meaning by digging down to the bottom of experiences and discovering that, at their core, those experiences are indeed related in significant ways. This hedgehog quality also probably helped me integrate illness into my life. My need to find added meaning in my own situation drew me to connect with others who are ill — through support groups, hospice work, and writing. My illness became part of my "job description."

My new line of work seemed to have little in common with teaching preschool, but shortly after I began facilitating the support groups, I found some unexpected parallels. In each case, it was a small gathering of about six people, individuals often very different from one another and often having very immediate needs and concerns. In both of those situations, it was of critical importance that each person felt safe, supported, and respected as unique. I also recognized among the support group members the same refreshing vulnerability and honesty that I have always found so appealing in young children. And I observed in myself an initial tendency to be overly concerned with an agenda or focus for the meetings, reminiscent of elaborate lesson plans from my early days of teaching. In both situations, I quickly learned that human beings bring the "relevant material" with them through the door. The most heartening experiences in the preschool often happened when I felt most ready to put aside my agenda in favor of what was actually engaging the children at the time. Similarly, at the support group meetings, any topics written on my piece of paper inevitably and organically arose through discussions of real life situations that people faced daily.

These realizations helped me appreciate that what we do, the priorities and goals we set, are particular manifestations of an underlying essence that can be expressed in a variety of ways. When I remember that (and I often do not), it is easier to trust that I can find a rewarding replacement for the things to which I am attached and to which I attach my self-esteem.

Many of the support group discussions concern not only the reevaluation of goals in the present but the possibility of greater limitations and losses in the future: What if things get worse? Those who have lived with illness for many years sometimes can provide a reassuring perspective.

Cindy said that at one time she felt that not being able to continue her work as an editor was the worst possible thing that could happen; she loved her job and depended on the income. "It did happen, and it wasn't nearly as important as I thought," she says with a laugh. Cindy found she could manage well financially: securing disability payments, eliminating expenses connected with work, and generally living more simply, which she enjoys. And with the free time, she began to pursue other interests that have become meaningful and rewarding. However, Cindy is quick to point out, as are many people who make similar adjustments, that *at the time* a great deal of pain accompanied the changes and losses. Although blending with adversity is possible and potentially enriching, it is rarely pleasant initially.

Now, because of the current status of her multiple sclerosis, Cindy is considering a wheelchair. So is Rosie, because of delayed complications of polio and also an inoperable spinal tumor. Both women agree that it is difficult to transcend the stigma attached to a wheelchair, but they are trying to see it as something enabling rather than as a symbol of disability. Rosie looks forward to riding to favorite places that she no longer visits because walking there has been too difficult. She says she is tired of finding a spot to sit and read while others go off walking: "I want to move with them, feel the breeze against my skin."

We can feel competent, secure, and independent only if the standards and tasks we have set for ourselves are reasonable. By adjusting our level of activity to what is manageable, we can minimize the daily reminders of our limitations. Loss of function does not diminish our ability to make choices or adapt in creative ways. Although *things* may get worse in terms of physical condition, the ability to cope psychologically and to compensate in practical ways can prevent us from feeling that *we* are worse. For many people with illnesses, self-esteem rests not on particular accomplishments but on the ability to be flexible, clarify options, and make wise choices. The long-term goal is to utilize all of life's experiences and, in so doing, live well with illness. Other goals, subsumed under that larger purpose, are subject to change.

In her book, *We Are Not Alone: Learning to Live with Chronic Illness*, Sefra Kobrin Pitzele includes numerous practical suggestions for adapting to illness, emphasizing the importance of planning, pacing, and conserving energy. She suggests going into each day with a clear sense of priorities: "What *must* be accomplished? What *should* be accomplished? What would be *nice* to get done? Have you allotted time for *yourself*?"[19]

We often underestimate the significance of the last item on this list. During a lifetime most of us are drawn to certain experiences in which we "lose" ourselves, activities that leave us feeling focused and whole. The project or pursuit can vary from something as personal as praying or watching sunsets to something as expansive as creating a work of art. The value of these outlets increases when faced with illness and loss. A sustained interest keeps us invested in life; there is something we've chosen to make important; we care.

It is easy to put aside enriching activities that meet our higher needs when basic physical concerns and daily living tasks are sapping limited energy. But we often can grab more moments than we think. Even a small amount of time spent on a nourishing experience in an ongoing way is restorative. And losing oneself in a process often results in surprising self-revelation, as if playing a solo game of hide-and-seek.

An illness demands reordering priorities, restructuring life, discovering one's enduring uniqueness and finding ways to express it under changing circumstances. These tasks can be wrenching even for those of us who ultimately feel that some of the adjustments are changes for the better. Jan jokes about her alternating feelings of equanimity and feelings of deprivation. "In my meditations I try to stay peaceful and calm with whatever is happening, but life with illness is sometimes too damn overwhelming — and sometimes too damn boring."

Sue Bender, an artist and family therapist, wrote an elegant book called *Plain and Simple* about her sojourns with two Amish families. In it she describes her life in California as a "crazy quilt.... Hundreds of scattered, unrelated, stimulating fragments, each going off in its own direction, creating a lot of frantic energy.... I valued accomplishments. I valued being special. I valued results.... I never asked, 'Success at what cost?' "[20]

Bender went to live in the Amish community to consider, "Is there another way to lead a good life?" There she found a world where clutter and hurry were replaced with inner quiet and calm ritual. "No one rushed. Each step was done with care....No distinction was made between the sacred and the everyday....Their life is their art."[21]

Upon returning home, Bender concluded, "...I don't want to be Amish, but I had a chance to observe a way of life that nurtures contentment." Similarly, those of us who have grown in wisdom by way of illness would still not choose illness as a way of life. Bender's ongoing conflict between doing and being is also a struggle familiar to many of us. "The need to be special and stand out, the need...to be one among the many — these equally competing, conflicting values are all part of me....To reconcile these seeming opposites, to see them as *both*, not one or the other, is my constant challenge." And Bender again could be speaking for many of us with the goal she identified for herself: "It's time to celebrate the life I do have. Piecing together the paradox — making peace with the paradox, to find a balance in some larger sense so that a life can feel whole — with the pieces I have."[22]

Part Two

On Individual Terms:
Responses to Illness

A bird does not sing because it has an answer —
it sings because it has a song.

— Chinese Proverb[1]

A crisis or sudden loss affords little time for reflection. We move swiftly to reach safety, restore stability, implement whatever measures are necessary for survival. Rescue teams may come to our aid with well-rehearsed protocols, and we are grateful to have others in charge to act decisively and direct us accordingly.

The onset of an illness and its ensuing course often comprise a series of crises and losses. But unlike the death of a loved one, a raging fire, or highway collision, illness is not a time-bound event with a particular endpoint. The cyclical, recurrent, or progressive nature of illness requires that we develop a personal strategy for accommodating the unpredictable changes and losses. Otherwise we experience each episode as acute, identify every disruption as chaotic, and repeatedly perceive ourselves as helpless in the face of overwhelming circumstances. To live in a continual state of crisis is a terrifying existence.

Most of us turn to those in the health professions and related fields for information and techniques to care for our bodies and adapt our lives in practical ways. But we each go on to develop our own prescriptions for understanding illness, responding to crises, grieving the losses, and resuming life.

The loss of the body's integrity triggers fears about a host of other losses: loss of familiar roles, loss of control, loss of connection, loss of meaning, loss of hope. These aspects of life are, of course, the underpinnings of our self-concept, our very identity. The collapse of self-esteem is among the most pervasive of the losses associated with illness.

During a crisis or period of grief, often a pale, diminished self-image emerges. One's own palette renders an incomplete picture, one that captures few of the distinctive features that characterize each of us. But a crisis also tends to accentuate our typical patterns and unique ways of responding. The process of adjusting to illness may highlight the lifelong identity that remains vital and intact despite change and loss.

Grief is a hard grace. It invites us to pay attention to hints of truth, to trust our intuition — "Is this really right for me?" — and to rely on our creativity — "I will find my own way." By becoming better acquainted with ourselves, we can each fashion a new self-portrait: a reflection of wholeness and well-being that transcends the physical level; a shining presence that integrates all levels of experience, including illness; the embodiment of a wisdom that befriends vulnerability. This is no easy task — to witness life at the same time we are living it. In the words of philosopher Alan Watts, "Trying to define yourself is like trying to bite your own teeth."[2]

It helps to understand the context of the confusing emotions and overwhelming adjustments associated with illness: We are responding to crises, we are grieving for losses, often in an ongoing way. There is no "normal" response to the demands of illness, and there is no one approach to healing that suits everyone. Two people may receive the same diagnosis or suffer the same symptoms, but their illnesses are experienced as individually as any other of their life circumstances. Like the birds in the forest, our voices blend with others of our kind, but we each have our own song to sing.

Chapter Four

Crisis and Loss

Every year
everything
I have ever learned

in my lifetime
leads back to this: the fires
and the black river of loss
whose other side

is salvation,
whose meaning
none of us will ever know.
To live in this world

you must be able
to do three things:
to love what is mortal;
to hold it

against your bones knowing
your own life depends on it;
and, when the time comes to let it go,
to let it go.

— Mary Oliver
from "In Blackwater Woods"
American Primitive [1]

On the Threshold of Change

The word "crisis" conjures up frightening images. We visualize
our deepest fears, our most alarming nightmares, coming to life

and raging out of control. In meeting the force of such events, we are roused to action, stretched beyond our usual limits, and challenged to respond with all of our resources. The full implications of a crisis include not only the power of the threatening external event but also the potential responses to that event and the ultimate outcome resulting from those responses.

The dictionary definition of crisis reflects this hidden potential inherent in life's critical junctures: the turning point for better or worse in an acute situation, an emotionally significant event or radical change of status in a person's life, a decisive moment. And the Chinese symbol for the word crisis has two characters: one means danger, the other means opportunity.

This is certainly not to suggest that any of us would ever choose pain as the path to insight, justify unbearable grief in the name of growth, or discount or diminish the panic we feel when we fear that our world is crumbling. Rather, it is to recognize that the human spirit can hold fast to life in all of its manifestations, even the most difficult. If we are to survive our crises, it is because we believe in this sacred possibility.

"As long as you have your health" is an often repeated phrase. It implies that good physical function guarantees our ability to handle any of life's circumstances and potential difficulties. But many of us don't have our health to draw upon routinely, let alone in emergencies. Frequently the state of our health *is* the emergency. Since we cannot summon up physical strength and stamina at will, many of us learn to garner other resources.

Sometimes the very fact that we have survived past hardships gives us confidence to face current and future challenges. "I am a survivor" is the foundation upon which many of us erect our lives, and each new episode of survival provides additional fortification. These kinds of events are usually etched in the memory, vivid in terms of specific details as well as the accompanying emotions. We remember and somehow mark the "anniversary" of a hospitalization or diagnosis. Such stories are told and retold many times, often testing the patience of those who don't appreciate the significance of these recitations. Sharing these experiences with others, and to some extent reliving them, is a method of taking stock, calculating one's assets. The support group members understand the value of telling these survival tales; they reinforce their own level of confidence by relating their personal stories to others who can deeply empathize, and they find inspiration in hearing how others have endured.

Pain and loss can also be experienced as cumulative, and many of us feel our coping methods have been exhausted rather than enhanced by our past experiences: "Being stretched hasn't made me stronger or more flexible; if anything else happens, I sense that I will break." This perspective assumes that if another setback occurs, it will occur in isolation, that the larger context of life holds no unforeseen possibilities for support or compensation. It sets a finite limit on our own potentials and the strength of our connections with others and with the world.

Like most people I have talked with, fears about the limits of what I can handle float in and out of my life. Also like many others, I value my autonomy and enjoy being independent. An incident occurred many years ago, while I was still in good physical health, that serves as a reminder to me of how a seemingly overwhelming situation can become manageable. I had made an appointment with a therapist to discuss some frustrations with my job at a residential treatment center for autistic children. Like many residential centers, the facility always seemed to be on the edge of crisis: a shortage of funds, a high rate of staff turnover, and the physically and emotionally demanding nature of the work. I had been employed there several years and was discouraged, exhausted, and yet committed to staying. I described to the therapist that I felt like I was in quicksand. He encouraged me to explore that image, and all I could come up with was a sense of being trapped. Whichever way I moved, I just sank in deeper. "Isn't there anything you can do?" he asked. Quicksand, to me, left no options. Once you're in it, you're stuck. The therapist kept asking his same question, and I continued to explain that no matter what you do, you continue to sink. Finally, he threw up his hands in exasperation and said, "You could call for help!" He was amazed that the possibility of relying on others hadn't even crossed my mind.

Now that I live with an illness, asking for and accepting help definitely cross my mind, but they are still not usually the first options I consider. I work hard at balancing my lifelong pattern of self-reliance with my heartfelt joy at the solid trust and loving connections that emanate from offers of help freely given and openly received. So many of the losses related to illness cluster around the issue of self-sufficiency; so much of the healing lies in an appreciation of our interdependence.

Naming the Losses

Loss implies separation. "Lonely," "removed," and "cut off" are terms people commonly use to describe the experience of living with illness. The language of loss reveals the profound psychological dislocation that permeates the more visible physiological and functional disruptions. The discontinuity with previous roles and relationships is frequently experienced not only as a grievous change in circumstances but as a bewildering change in identity as well. Many people draw a clear distinction between who they "were" and who they "are," as if, with the onset of illness, a former portion of the self had been severed like an excised organ or amputated limb. And few of us who live with illness feel secure enough about the future to venture more than a guess about who we will "become."

Detaching from the aspect of self defined by work was particularly difficult for me; adjoining my home was the large room that once housed my preschool, now empty and silent. After saying good-bye to the last child on my final day of teaching, I left the room quickly and closed the door behind me. Wooden blocks stood in piles on the floor, like a building project halted midway through construction. The last few paintings hung on the easel to dry; the young artists, however, would not be returning on Monday to claim them. Mounds of orange playdough, molded into odd configurations, left a strange tabletop landscape that remained there for many weeks.

In sharp contrast to my previous habit of immediately cleaning up at the end of each school day, I avoided even stepping into the classroom, let alone putting things in order. Weeks stretched into months before I began to set things back on the shelves, rinse off the paint brushes, wipe the tables clean. And it was a few years before I was able to clear the shelves, pack up the supplies, and pass them on to other preschools. I acknowledged the losses connected with work slowly, in stages, in step with the small gains I was making in restructuring my life and reestablishing my identity. And I waited until another purpose for the space was overwhelmingly apparent before dismantling it as a schoolroom: an office to accommodate all the paperwork I was generating through my work with support groups, hospice, and my own writing. Until that point, I had literally closed off a part of myself, stored it away in a separate room where the pain of loss could be contained.

At the first support group meeting she attended, Jeannette expressed the lost parts of herself as "the many hats I used to wear that now just sit on the shelf." Diagnosed with Hodgkins lymphoma about two years earlier, she underwent multiple surgeries and an aggressive program of radiation and chemotherapy. The cancer, however, continued to spread, and at the age of thirty-five Jeannette was told she could expect to live another six months to two years. As a single mother, the two hats that Jeannette donned with the most pleasure and pride were that of parent and provider. She was a highly successful doll and puppet maker, sewing many hours a day, and an equally successful mother to her two teenage daughters — "a supermom."

> My business was doing gangbusters the day I was diagnosed. I had one large account that could have kept me busy indefinitely. For years I've been making these little people, turning out one after the other. I only made two "real" people — my daughters — and now it looks like I won't be able to finish the job.

It is traumatic enough to lose or anticipate the loss of the meaningful activities that nourish us in the most fundamental way. A terminal diagnosis, in addition, assigns the new and unbearably painful "job" of separating from life itself. There is, in truth, no clear demarcation between living and dying; from the moment of birth we are approaching death. But any such continuity is easily obscured by the jolt of a terminal diagnosis.

The sense of fragmentation connected with illness is often intensified when the mind, emotions, or spirit are at apparent odds with the body. Many of us attempt to employ the power of our thoughts, prayers, and creativity in the service of healing. If our physical reality repeatedly collides with our higher intentions, we are like a household thrown into turmoil by the futile efforts of a frustrated parent to control a defiant child.

Among the multiple selves that emerge during an illness, one of the most confusing is the dual role we assume as person/patient. Pain, discomfort, physical limitations, and the related treatments demand that we acknowledge we "have" something and that we devote serious attention to the care of our bodies. We are consequently labeled patients, according to the particular thing we have — cancer patient, diabetes patient, arthritis patient — and the labels tend to stick. Yet those free from ongoing medical problems who make occasional visits to health care providers are rarely referred to as patients once they leave the office. And terms such as arthritis "sufferer" or cancer "victim" are unfortunately all too common. Although the intention behind such language may be to acknowledge the person's distress, it does so by subjugating the person to the disease.

Several years ago I attended a gathering of individuals who had Sjogren's syndrome. People exchanged stories and experiences, and discussed both the limitations of the disease and the possibilities in terms of human response. A broad range of coping techniques were mentioned during the meeting. One woman present had a singular reply to all of them: "My Sjogren's won't let me." She personified her illness as an unreasonable, domineering individual who was possessive of all of her time and attention. I was touched by this understandable attempt to maintain an identity separate from illness, but this woman had externalized a central aspect of her existence, endowed it with a life of its own, and lost a sense of her own autonomy in the process. Cindy also personifies her illness but in a way that connects her to, rather than separates her from, her experience.

I was feeling especially bitter one day when I felt a sudden jerking in my leg. Oh yes, it's you, my old friend MS, I thought, *you're still with me* — you don't desert me. What a bizarre, sick thought: MS, my *friend*!

At that point something shifted for me. I realized I had been fighting MS all along, trying to ignore and defeat it — and losing the battle. What if I treated it with consideration and respect instead? Maybe it wasn't a friend, but it certainly was a constant companion, a part of me I could no longer ignore.

And so I began to honor my MS. I started to use a cane, to rest before and after every outing, to seek and use help whenever and wherever I can. When my eyes blur, I stop trying to read. When my memory slips or I become confused, instead of panicking I try to give up all mental activity for a while and rest, relax, or meditate instead. I mentally pat myself on the back for everything I do, no matter how trivial. I thank my legs when they support me; when they don't, I touch them with love and sympathy and give them rest. I ask permission of my MS when I want to try something that pushes my limits; I make bargains with it: If you let me do this, tomorrow we'll rest all day if you want.

By personifying MS this way — as my constant companion, neither friend nor foe, but a part of me — I have learned to accept it. Curiously, by giving in to its needs, I no longer feel as dominated by it. It is a part of me, but only a part; there is more to me than MS. There must be, because who else is that, talking to my MS?[2]

Independence is something we cherish, healthy or ill. It is something we celebrate, at Fourth of July parades and at children's graduation ceremonies. We universally prize the right and the capacity to assume personal responsibility and to act autonomously. The pain, discomfort, and compromised function resulting from illness threaten independence, engender feelings of helplessness, and raise concerns about loss of control. Like a country struggling for its freedom, many of us put up a vigorous fight over the issue of independence and suffer greatly if we lose the battle.

Independence means different things to different people. For many, it includes not only self-sufficiency but the ability to function reliably in relationship to others — as available spouse or partner, active parent, steady income provider, dependable friend. If illness necessitates revising expectations or requesting and accepting help, the changes may be bitterly resisted if perceived as a loss of independence.

Some people preserve their independence by becoming skillful at clarifying their limitations and utilizing resources when necessary. For these people, seeking assistance represents neither weakness nor failure but rather the ability to orchestrate their own affairs. Securing disability income bears no stigma, nor does acquiring a handicapped parking sticker or organizing the help of willing friends.

Each of us has a unique combination of needs and capabilities that we balance in order to retain as much independence as possible. Those needs and capabilities change over time, as do the terms by which we define independence. Personal boundaries and a sense of privacy, usually quite ingrained, may have to be overcome, often quite painfully, to accommodate to the level of assistance required. The issue of independence, and each erosion into it, figures large in the losses of illness.

A loss of connection with others often stems from the inability to participate fully in the same experiences or meet the same expectations. Unpredictable health ultimately keeps all plans tentative, and the need for assistance or special arrangements can lead to feelings of dependency and inferiority: "It's just not worth the effort to make plans with others; I wind up exhausted trying to keep up — and sometimes feeling just as lonely as if I had stayed at home." People grow weary of explaining their limitations and feeling separate because of them.

The deep gulf between those with health problems and others around them, however, has another source that lies beyond the adjustment to physical needs. Illness magnifies the conditions under which, as humans, we all must live: finite time in a vulnerable body in an unpredictable world. This powerful reminder of our common fate often creates the painful boundary between people who are ill and those around them. As a culture, we are uncomfortable with human frailty and don't know how to acknowledge it, in ourselves or in others. Those who are ill are reluctant to talk about their concerns — "I don't want to burden anyone" — and those around them are equally reluctant — "I don't know what to say." And so we lose one another in the process. When I ask people if there are others, outside of the support group, with whom they share their feelings, the answer is frequently a version of "Not really." "I try to keep things light," said a woman with terminal cancer. Kay has been writing in a diary since the first of her four heart attacks. She keeps it in a prominent place "for all to read," yet no one in the family has picked it up. "I guess they are not ready," says Kay.

It is as if we have eaten from the tree of knowledge; we learned about vulnerability and mortality, change and impermanence, and we sense we are no longer welcome in the garden. This loss of innocence is one of the most profound losses related to illness and also an irretrievable one. Even if a dramatic cure restored us to good health tomorrow, it is unlikely we could ever slip back into a complacency about our well-being or make casual assumptions about the future. This loss of innocence in many ways sets us apart and at the same time bids us to use the knowledge we have acquired — to recover the connection with others and to heal the losses within.

Healing the Separation

On my birthday a few years ago, a friend gave me a lovely quotation, transcribed in graceful calligraphy and artistically framed. The words were those of a Sufi sage: "When the body weeps for that which it has lost, the spirit laughs for what it has gained." I decided to hang the quotation in a prominent place in the hallway, where it could serve as a poetic reminder. Shortly after I positioned this thoughtful gift in its carefully chosen spot, a plumber banged into it with a toilet as he was heading toward the bathroom at the top of the stairs. The glass cracked into a large diagonal line that stretched across the quotation from one corner to the other. I looked at the crack and my heart sank, then I read the words and I laughed. How perfect, I thought. I decided to leave this piece of framed wisdom with the giant crack across it just as it was, without replacing the glass. Looking past the exterior imperfection lends a special irony to the message.

Distinguishing between form and substance is an essential part of healing from loss. Identifying our intrinsic nature, that which withstands changes in outward appearances or particular capabilities, is the most elusive and also the most fundamental task of grieving a serious illness. Yet, unlike the simple crack in the glass that hangs in my hallway, the losses in "form" resulting from illness can leave us feeling shattered.

We cannot grieve our losses until we acknowledge them, and it is only through grieving that we transcend them. Every loss represents a valued facet of life, and it is essential that we mourn each one. Naming and enumerating the losses can feel like a painful arithmetic at times — a continual process of subtraction and division — each change reducing the quality of life, each adjustment fractioning a sense of wholeness. A natural part of healing is the attempt to find something meaningful to replace the losses, especially to fill in the blank spaces that follow the statements that begin with "I am" or "I do."

The grief process, however, involves not only transcending specific losses but making peace with loss as an ongoing and inevitable part of existence. The difficult task of relinquishing attachments is aided immeasurably by the presence of appealing substitutes, yet any tidy one-to-one correspondence can only be a temporary measure. The resolution of grief, at the deepest level, demands not only that we heal the individual wounds of loss but the fear of loss as well.

It is common practice to obtain insurance policies, in order to be "covered" should something happen to our "belongings." We invest hard-earned money to buy peace of mind; we choose a company we trust will prove reliable when necessity arises. Illness alerts us to the need for a kind of inner insurance, a comprehensive and dependable source of protection for whatever life-altering losses we may encounter. Surprisingly, a large measure of personal security can be derived from investigating the nature of loss itself:

What constitutes a loss? Who is doing the losing? This hard-won wisdom furnishes the internal resources upon which we must ultimately draw if our "belongings" begin to disappear.

Every shift in life is accompanied by some degree of loss. But most of us have been taught to minimize the importance of the "small" transitions, to adapt quickly to a change in residence, job, relationship, or personal outlook without an appropriate farewell. We tend to lose sight of the sea of experience that comprises life, mistaking the waves of change for the ocean itself. Our identity seems to ride on each successive swell. To the extent that we are unacquainted with the expansive and fluid quality of our essential nature, illness or disability can threaten us like a tidal wave.

Or we can try to trust the natural ebb and flow, and attempt to move comfortably within it. When people explore their losses in this way, with patience and faith rather than aversion and fear, they are frequently surprised by a strange sense of freedom. This paradoxical feeling of release usually has something to do with giving up the struggle to maintain a certain identity, now perceived as transitory, limiting, isolating. Boundaries created by roles, expectations, material possessions, including our bodies, lose their solidity. They no longer separate us from life in the moment and from one another. I've often heard people who are critically ill say, "I've nothing left to lose" and then go on to describe how their lives have been enhanced by living more fully, consciously, and honestly in the present. When Jeannette received a prognosis that gave her less than two years to live because of her rapidly advancing lymphoma, she felt she was also given a "license":

> It's as if I received a document that says, "This grants permission to Jeannette to live her remaining days as she wishes, to do the things that matter most, to stop and smell the roses." What matters most is compassion and forgiveness, not my ego. I've come to understand the torment in the lives of those who've inflicted pain on me, and have tried to heal the separation.
>
> I was beginning to listen to the chaos inside of me before I become ill with cancer, but after my diagnosis things started really clicking. I've discovered who I am, what is true for me. My place is

at home, with my daughters, as it always has been. All the voices that say otherwise no longer matter. And the dolls and puppets I've made have touched many lives — thousands — the children, the teachers, the therapists. I know the ground of my own being, and now my search is a spiritual one — for more connections, not more ego. Ego keeps us separate.

I feel accepting of whatever comes. I'm as peaceful as I've ever been.

In his autobiography *Joys and Sorrows*, cellist Pablo Casals describes an experience that almost ended his musical career. His response to this seemingly tragic potential loss is a curious one.

> It was when we were making our descent on Mount Tamalpais that the accident occurred. Suddenly one of my companions shouted, "Watch out, Pablo!" I looked up and saw a boulder hurtling down the mountainside directly toward me. I jerked my head aside and was lucky not to be killed. As it was, the boulder hit and smashed my left hand — my fingering hand. My friends were aghast. I had a strangely different reaction. My first thought was "Thank God, I'll never have to play the cello again!" No doubt, a psychoanalyst would give some profound explanation. But the fact is that dedication to one's art does involve a sort of enslavement, and then too, of course, I have always felt such dreadful anxiety before performances.[3]

The doctors predicted Casals would never regain full use of his hand, but with constant treatments and exercise, his hand healed completely. During his recovery period he met Gertrude Stein, with whom he had the following conversation:

> Once when I was sitting with my injured hand in a plaster cast, Gertrude said, "You look like El Greco's *Gentleman With a Hand on His Chest.*"
>
> I laughed and told her, "Well, even if I can't play, my fingers are at least resting on the true instrument of all art and music.[4]

Loss carries us close to the core of our being, and that's not always a comfortable place. Writing this section on loss has been vexing, for as the title of Pablo Casals book suggests, joys and sorrows are inextricably bound. What we love and cherish today we may be grieving for tomorrow, and the raw emotions of grief engender a fuller heart and finer attunement to life. It is confusing to keep track of the dark and the light and the moving shadows. Reflecting on loss is somewhat like viewing a photographic negative, knowing that the dark areas and light areas will show up as just the opposite on the final print.

I've been trying to hold in my mind the broader context of loss, but as I write I also hold in my heart the specifics — the deep pain and sadness of illness, and the agonizing struggles of the individuals who live them daily. The interplay of loss and renewal is something each of us ultimately integrates in a personal way, as a result of direct experience rather than another's words. I had such an experience one spring, standing before Else Frye, a species of rhododendron growing in my garden. I don't write much poetry, but a flood of feelings about loss and hope collected into a poem around Else Frye, as she stood in full bloom.

> The rhododendron is covered with blossoms,
> each a perfect star,
> creamy white and fringed with pink,
> rich with the fragrance of nutmeg.
>
> Even now, branch and flower freely part.
> One by one, blossoms slip
> from balanced clusters,
> drift to the ground
> as branch tips welcome new leaves.
>
> Buds were set last spring,
> a full year preparing
> for this moment of glory
> — which gracefully yields to the next:
> foliage opening to the sun,
> anticipating next year's buds
> amid a carpet of white.
>
> Neither branch nor flower cling.
> Dare we part from the precious
> with such effortless trust
> in the next bloom?

Chapter Five

The Need to Grieve

Should you shield the canyons from the windstorms,
you would never see the beauty of their carvings.
— Elisabeth Kübler-Ross, M.D.[1]

To Weep and To Dream

A support group member was recently diagnosed with heart disease. During a meeting, as she reflected on the stresses in her life, she tossed out a most unsettling thought: "I realize I can't have emotions; they take too big a toll on my health." Imagine, if you can, a life without emotion. Would any of us truly reap contentment from a kind of emotional illiteracy, bereft of the capacity to read and comprehend the depth and complexity written into the human character? The issue for the woman with heart disease, as well as for all of us, is not *whether* we have feelings. We do. To be alive is to encounter the full range of human emotion. The issue is *how*. We can experience emotion without succumbing to it, and honor our feelings without granting them free reign over our actions. We are capable of fully experiencing a feeling without *becoming* it.

If, however, we attempt to wall off our emotions from awareness or block them from expression, they become exaggerated and distorted. Just as the juice of fresh apples, if tightly sealed and stored away, eventually sours into vinegar, stifled feelings ferment, take on a pungency. Time, by itself, won't resolve feelings that are unattended. I believe that much of the violence and addiction currently spilling across society are the toxic end products of bottled up emotion, pushing through the cork.

Confusing and powerful emotions surge through the experience of illness. Both the scope and the intensity of the feelings catch us off guard, and because the feelings are often unfamiliar and alarming, we may instinctively recoil. The internal pain of illness, however, is just as valid and in need of attention as the physical manifestations. When we short-circuit the psychological realities of illness, we interrupt the grieving process and ultimately impede our healing. The emotions that accompany loss may loom dark and threatening, but the attempt to escape them is self-defeating. An illustrative example is the man in "Flight from the Shadow," from *The Way of Chuang Tzu.*

> There was a man who was so disturbed by the sight of his own shadow and so displeased with his own footsteps that he determined to get rid of both. The method he hit upon was to run away from them.
>
> So he got up and ran. But every time he put his foot down there was another step, while his shadow kept up with him without the slightest difficulty.
>
> He attributed his failure to the fact that he was not running fast enough. So he ran faster and faster, without stopping, until he finally dropped dead.
>
> He failed to realize that if he merely stepped into the shade, his shadow would vanish, and if he sat down and stayed there, there would be no more footsteps.[2]

In the course of mourning the loss of good health, grief over previous losses may be revived or perhaps emerge for the first time. In addition, remorse over missed opportunities in the past, and despair over shrinking possibilities for the future, may surface. The griefs of a lifetime, including grief for the *unlived* life, may get hooked together into a tangled chain of emotion that seems impossible to tease apart.

Many useful frameworks have been proposed to help clarify and facilitate the grief process and the emotions that comprise it. Most correspond or overlap with the stages of grief outlined by Elisabeth Kübler-Ross, based on her work with people who are dying. These investigations into the human response to loss have alleviated a significant degree of suffering merely by acknowledging that grief has a purpose and that the emotions it elicits are natural and necessary. People are relieved to discover that they are not "crazy" on top of being ill. As writer Doris Lessing noted, "There are things which must cause you to lose your reason or you have none to lose."[3]

One of the critical functions of the support groups is to familiarize people with the grief process and its bearing on the adjustment to illness. The simple knowledge that others who are ill also mourn their losses is reassuring. People frequently employ personal imagery to access their own grief — a healing wound, an uprooted tree newly transplanted — and these symbolic representations are helpful to others as well. Grief becomes more of a "known," negotiable on human terms, rather than some alien, formless entity.

Many impart to their emotions a static, monolithic quality. At the root of *emotion*, however, is movement; we are aroused by our feelings, not encased in them. Even strong anger erupts and subsides, and inching through depression is not synonymous with being entrapped in it. Native American women symbolically acknowledge the grieving process by cutting their hair after a loss. Hair grows slowly, imperceptibly, at its own rate. But it does grow. In that we can trust.

Societal understanding of loss and grief leaves much to be desired. The right to mourn death is accepted, but when death is not imminent, grief over losses due to illness may be labeled as unwarranted, or worse, self-pitying. "At least it's not life-threatening," Grace has been told repeatedly by her doctor, who is treating her for a host of painful and limiting medical conditions. Jerry *has* a life-threatening heart condition and barely survived her sixth bypass surgery. Her doctor reminds her often, "You should be glad to be alive."

Both of these women cherish their lives, but that doesn't cancel out their need to mourn their losses. We grieve in order to acknowledge the significance of those things that have made us "glad to be alive," to affirm that life *is* worth living. When Judy was told by her doctor that she would probably never be able to sing again because of her inner ear disease, she expressed her grief openly: "I always thought singing was my sole purpose for being on the planet." Her doctor's response was brief: "Find something else." Judy wondered how easy it would be for him to "find something else" if he suddenly lost the ability to function as a physician.

Safety is the prime concern in determining how much of our grief to share, when and with whom. Illness itself tests our relationships; we understandably hesitate to strain them further by loading on our emotional needs. But concealing strong feelings interferes with meaningful communication and creates emotional distance, which can also jeopardize relationships. Among our family members, friends, and acquaintances we inevitably find a broad range of willingness and ability to offer unconditional love and support. We must balance all of these factors and be selective, sharing unbridled emotions with those few who can listen without judgment or fear. That may mean seeking out support groups or counseling, and also learning to edit, without deleting the essentials, in our interactions with others.

It is helpful to have the emotions of grief delineated as well as validated. Grief becomes comprehensible and therefore more manageable through an understanding of its component parts. Most often, it is portrayed as a series of stages — denial, anger, bargaining, depression, acceptance. Understanding the purpose of each of these feelings and the driving force behind them lends some meaning to what might otherwise seem a pointless, chaotic struggle.

Although these emotions may glare with unusual intensity during grief, they are also clearly visible along the normal spectrum of life. In an ongoing way, we get angry and forgive, depression descends and then lifts. Periodically we deny painful parts of reality, bargain to have things as we would like them, and struggle to accept things as they are. This continuity is important to note, as it places grief within the parameters of "normal" emotions; it also reminds us that, even as we grieve, grief isn't the sole source of energy fueling our feelings.

These "stages" of grief are descriptive rather than prescriptive. There is nothing predictable about grief, especially in connection with illness, where the changes are continual. Rarely a once-through process, emotional states are more likely to fluctuate and even be simultaneous than to follow any sequential or timely progression. The depth, duration, and order varies greatly, depending on the individual and the circumstances. A woman who accompanied her dying husband to the support group put it this way: "There's no user's manual.... More clear than not are those intuitive messages that say what NOT to do. Don't plan too far ahead; don't accept commitments you feel tentative about; don't wander too far from home; don't assume you're the same person you were."

The recurrent or cyclical nature of illness may spin us around repeatedly. New symptoms, exacerbations, related or anticipated losses — all may revive the emotional upheavals we thought were behind us. To many this signifies defeat: "I don't know if it's backtracking or going around in circles, but I seem to be back where I started."

During a severe inflammation of my hips and knees that lasted an unusually long time, my husband Larry made some thoughtful suggestions and generous offers. Given the situation, he felt his ideas were appropriate. Among them was the proposal that we replace the stairs in our home with a ramp. "Maybe it's time..." he said. "No! It's *not* time!" I retorted with uncharacteristic hostility, and vehemently rejected all his other suggestions as well.

I had, in many ways, "accepted" my illness, as the symptoms generally had been fluctuating in a fairly predictable manner. However, the severity and duration of the current flare was "new," and triggered a new round of denial, anger, and fear.

The inflammation eventually subsided, as did my defensiveness. With some distance from the incident, I concluded that a suggestion box might help. Larry could safely offer his ideas, and I could more openly consider them — by choosing a time I was emotionally capable of reflecting on my health. (We never did implement the suggestion box; just talking about it seemed to help.)

From my own experience and from the accounts of others, I sense that the adjustment to illness contains a vertical dimension as well as a horizontal one. When we find ourselves cycling back, we most likely don't arrive at exactly the same spot. Rather, we ascend an upward spiral, having accumulated some perspective and coping skills along the way. And even when we have major slips, there is a good chance we won't descend all the way back to the bottom.

Although most of us experience and express some measure of all the feelings commonly associated with grief, the manner in which we do so is highly individual. We each have an emotional style. Some scream their rage; the anger of others barely reaches a whisper. Some wear their sadness openly; others wrap themselves in it privately. Some try to filter their grief through the intellect, while others allow it to flow freely from the heart.

The booklet I wrote several years ago, early on in my illness and before I began sharing experiences with others, necessarily reflected my unique experience and personal perspective. It included a section called "Responses to Illness," which only later did I understand to be stages of grieving. On my own, I had come up with four, but information I gathered subsequently — through reading, talking with others, and hospice training — kept suggesting there were five. My own descriptions corresponded with surprising accuracy to four of the stages; the missing one — anger — I had left out entirely. I neglected to mention it because I neglected to recognize it in my own emotional repertoire, where angry feelings tend to masquerade as "frustrated," "overwhelmed," "upset."

Choosing a title for the booklet was also revealing. My original idea was *Healthy — Living Well With the Body You Have*. I realized at some point that the title might suggest the publication was about jogging and eating whole grains rather than living with *illness*. I found it curious that I was producing a publication about illness and yet avoiding any reference to it in the title. The dilemma over calling illness by its true name exposed the residual denial still floating beneath the surface of the manuscript — which eventually I entitled *Living Well With Chronic Illness*.

The grieving process unfolds erratically not only over time but also across the range of our losses. We may grieve deeply for some and minimally for others. We may be rebuilding bridges in certain areas of life and erecting barricades elsewhere. Marjorie Lyon describes in "How Are You?" the uneven nature of grief.

> To answer "How are you?" or "How am I?" seems to require that I make some judgment about myself. Am I good? Am I not good? Am I improving? Am I better than yesterday? Or last week?...
>
> I no longer feel the need to make those judgments. I am learning to acknowledge and accept my feelings whatever they happen to be. I've stopped trying to measure myself against some nonexistent or artificial standard. I try instead to accept myself as I am. I know I will always be different than before, but that's OK....
>
> ...It is difficult to know if we are "better" when we know we'll never be the same as before. It is difficult to know if we are on the road to recovery when we've not traveled this way before and aren't even sure where this road leads. Accepting the fact that recovery is a road to be traveled, rather than a destination to be reached, quiets the nagging question of how we are doing....
>
> If you meet me today and ask, "How are you?" my answer will probably be, "I'm OK." That says it well. It says that I accept myself as I am right now. I accept my feelings, whether I happen to be laughing or in tears. I accept where I am in the grief experience, even though I'm not sure just where that is.[4]

The natural expression of grief is not a luxury. It is work, demanding work, and perhaps the most significant job we can undertake. It demands courage and commitment, patience and flexibility, and the faith to probe the depths of our being and the edges of our awareness. It is fraught with risk: admitting the extent of our losses invites in pain, and expressing that pain may drive others away. But grief also holds promise. If we once cared so deeply, we can care again. We can, as before, cultivate something new from a seed of possibility. The capacity to care is expansive and the imagination to dream is transformative. I believe that the intense emotions of grief can arouse our spiritual yearnings and simultaneously ignite our creative spark. Through our spirit we recapture the eternal, and through our creativity we endow it with personal meaning.

Judy is no longer able to belt out her songs on stage, but she has written a few lullabies she sings in hushed tones to her grandchildren. And there's an unfinished song that keeps calling her back: "When really sad things happen and you don't know what to say — that's when I write a song."

And perhaps that is, after all, the grief work that each of us must do — compose our own lament.

Hope and Fear

Hope and fear are two undercurrents of life that pull at us with increased intensity during the process of grieving the losses of illness. Frightening possibilities carry us in one direction, and wishes and dreams draw us in another. The grief responses of denial, anger, and depression are, in many ways, reactions to overwhelming or unrelenting fear. Hope, on the other hand, moves us toward other responses — bargaining for a better outcome or accepting, with peace of mind, whatever outcome should occur.

Fear. Fear lives in the shadows. The language we use shrouds it — "my deepest, darkest fear" — and also silences it — "an unspeakable fear." If we do express fear, we may be admonished for "feeding" it, as if we could somehow "starve" fear by denying it a voice.

Whether or not we choose to speak about our fears, they speak to us, at times so loudly as to drown out all else. We need to listen to our fears, to hear and heed their message. We need to talk about them, to them, and share them with others. Fear becomes more threatening if we turn our back on it rather than face it squarely. Neither irrational nor morbid, fears of increased disability, pain, hospitalization, and death, as well as of financial strains and family disruptions, are natural concerns of those living with illness. Having those fears honored as valid, in and of itself, relieves some of the anxiety. People need to talk *through* their fears, not be talked *out* of them.

114

Worry can take form as vague anxiety — "I feel so vulnerable" — or as a specific fear — "I dread the thought of surgery." The apprehension may range from mild uneasiness to frank panic. Acknowledging fears about the potential losses of illness is a form of anticipatory grief. Just as with an impending death, imagining "the worst" allows people to prepare themselves in advance, both psychologically and practically. It is a way of adjusting to a difficult situation slowly and protecting ourselves from being shocked and overwhelmed at a later point. It helps us feel more in charge of our lives if we know what to expect and can think through possible responses. The energy bound up in fear can be utilized to gather information and also our inner resources.

Exploring our fears in order to problem-solve is different, however, from accepting them as truth. Sometimes people can become so preoccupied with their fears of the future, it alters the view of present reality. They perceive their fears as certainties rather than one possibility, and they lose sight of other possible outcomes. Investigating a consuming fear provides the opportunity for a realistic assessment. It may not always put the fear to rest but can at least provide perspective; rather than a thick, blinding fog, it becomes a cloud we glimpse floating in the distance.

An important function of the support groups is the opportunity they provide for people to verbalize their fears. As a former nurse, Jan is well aware of what end-stage emphysema can be like. And as a nutritionist, she watched one of her clients to whom she delivered meals become increasingly homebound because of his emphysema. Jan describes her battle with her fears about her own emphysema as "fighting to feel safe." When her frequent respiratory infections sap her energy and increase her need for steroid medication, she "grieves for the continual erosions into the quality of life." But Jan prides herself on her ability to use her feelings creatively and is continually devising ways to "feel safe" in spite of her fears. Her son and his family, including her beloved grandson, live a few hours away; they have begun to explore together the possibility of her moving in with them, if a decline in her health should necessitate that. "I'm great at building stories," says Jan. "I might as well use my imagination to solve problems as well as create them."

Thich Nhat Hanh explains that in Buddhism, "we say there are three kinds of gifts."

> The first is the gift of material resources. The second is the gift of helping people rely on themselves.... The third is the gift of non-fear. We human beings are afraid of being left alone, of becoming sick, and of dying. Helping people not be destroyed by fear is the greatest gift of all.[5]

Hope. Prayer is hope made audible. Just as we need others to listen to our fears, we want someone to hear our prayers. Most people in the groups say they pray, in one way or another. Some invoke the traditional prayers of their religious training. Others describe highly personal ways of affirming their belief in a spiritual presence — meditating, spending time in nature, doing something creative, connecting with loved ones, offering service to others. Whatever form it takes, most people, even the most self-reliant, have times that they look beyond themselves to sustain hope.

Prayer as *petition* awaits a concrete answer and reflects an optimism attached to a specific outcome — a cure, pain relief, an arrest in symptom progression. Prayer as *communion* consecrates our essential nature as inextricably linked with the larger continuum of life. It nourishes a peace of mind with whatever may come and reflects a faith in unforeseen possibilities — an increased ability to cope, renewed meaning in life, loving connections that heal the loneliness.

Hope in the form of optimism can easily merge with fear: Hope of achieving a certain result may translate into fear of not attaining it, hope of maintaining our current circumstances may engender fear of change. As one person put it, "I'm *afraid* to hope."

Hope as an open-ended faith, however, establishes and extends our connections with life and with others. It keeps our passion and compassion alive in the presence of fear, allows us to be brave and afraid at the same time. In this sense, there is no such thing as false hope.

Illness often initiates a disturbing chain of events. Many of us understandably take that as an omen. We have difficulty imagining that our luck will change, and assume instead the problems will only continue, intensify, multiply: "Bad things always happen in threes." When things are going smoothly, however, we may be almost hesitant to give credence to our good fortune, let alone trust that it will continue or even improve. We are suspicious that "it is too good to be true" and "knock wood," as if to appease some devious trickster who is playing with our fate.

When we attribute a momentum only to bad luck but not to good luck, we are carried into the future by fear, without hope. If, in addition, we assume that bad luck and good luck are mutually exclusive, we miss the grace that is often hidden even in a life fraught with problems.

Hope and fear are both focused on the future, and the future is always an unknown. It is helpful to be aware of the possibilities, both the frightening ones and the promising ones. But waiting — either "for the other shoe to drop" or "for my ship to come in" — postpones life until a future date. The interface between hope and fear is risk, and that is, in fact, where we do much of our living. Unable to predict which will be realized, we face our fears, dare to hope, and make our choices in the present.

The Faces of Grief

Denial

If we accidentally touch a hot burner, we reflexively pull our hands away from the stove. A built-in survival mechanism directs us to withdraw from painful circumstances. The example of the stove is uncomplicated. We don't avoid the fact that the burner is hot, we simply avoid the burner.

We cannot, however, physically avoid our bodies and the changes imposed on them by illness. Our inborn instinct to protect ourselves from pain may manifest instead as intellectual or emotional withdrawal. The facts and information surrounding a diagnosis, the reality of symptoms and limitations, the need for medical attention, the implications for the future — these are all aspects of illness that may overwhelm a person's usual ability to respond. Under such circumstances, we seem unable to comprehend or remember what we are told about our illnesses. We may question the accuracy of the information or the competence of the person communicating it. Or we may take exception to the prognosis and dismiss recommendations for treatment or ongoing health care. Many people initially make a statement to the world, and to themselves, that nothing has changed. They try to continue with all the same activities and to meet the same standards as before, in spite of the added strain that means for their bodies at a time when they need extra care.

There is much misunderstanding concerning denial. To many, it has an exclusively negative connotation. It appears to be a maladaptive response or a pathological break with reality. There are extreme cases where this may be true, but this does not describe the majority of people who need to establish their own rhythm in adapting to the overwhelming changes of illness. Like a rest in a musical composition, a period of denial provides a necessary break, to process what has gone before and to prepare for what is to come. In an odd sort of way, people who spend a period of time in denial are taking *good* care of themselves. They are administering their own form of anesthesia to avoid overpowering emotional pain, they are establishing a temporary refuge where they feel safe and protected. Denial is a survival strategy aimed at keeping fear in check and self-esteem intact.

Another misconception about denial is that it is a uniform entity. The pores of a filtering device, however, may be large or small. We can never really know what is going on inside others, we can't determine how much they are taking in. The denial of one person may operate as a solid wall, the denial of another may be tissue-thin. We can only trust that people who cannot swallow their illnesses whole will, with time, begin to bite off and digest what they can.

It is important to ask why denial around illness is so common. How can the mind and heart deny the reality of the body, and why do otherwise reasonable and responsible people seem stubbornly to resist the "truth"? My sense is that this respite allows time for a different kind of truth-seeking, often unconscious, and the search is an inward one. It is as if, in preparation for letting go of the physical self, we must first establish our true self, the one that transcends bodily changes and, unlike the body, can always be trusted. A person who seems numb and out of touch with their physical condition may, in fact, be engaged in a rich and fruitful inner journey that is necessary before embarking on the medical one. Looking back on my own long and confusing period of denial at the beginning of my illness, I remember a vague awareness that moved me to gather inner resources I wasn't sure I had. Without those resources, I sensed I couldn't handle the change in my health; therefore it must not be "true"....

The fact that my husband Larry is a physician did little to penetrate my denial. I didn't hear the information he tried to share with me, and I promptly forgot the bits (actually a surprising amount) of medical knowledge that I had absorbed through osmosis during our twenty years together.

As an internist in private practice, Larry was well-acquainted with denial as a standard way of dealing with health problems. Before I became ill, he would often tell me about patients who had ignored symptoms for long periods of time, before seeking treatment or before adjusting their lifestyle to their physical limitations. I found that hard to understand, I wondered about people who didn't cherish their life enough to take care of themselves. Naive and self-assured, I had yet to be put to the test.

I attributed my earliest symptoms to the flu and waited for them to subside — and waited and waited. After about a month of continual gastrointestinal problems and profound fatigue, I finally made an appointment with my doctor. (Larry was not my doctor; we found early on in our marriage that the relationship of doctor/patient is best kept separate from that of husband/wife.)

Based on clinical findings but inconclusive laboratory results, my internist suspected that I might have giardia. Common in rural areas, giardia is a parasite that contaminates drinking water. Satisfied with that diagnosis, I took the medication, started to improve, and declared myself cured.

The initial work-up included many tests and procedures that felt alien to my heretofore well-functioning body. Waiting for results that might reveal serious or even life-threatening conditions was agonizing. I was delighted to be recovering from giardia and have all that behind me.

Then my symptoms returned, initiating the now all-too-familiar pattern of coming and going that is characteristic of a chronic illness. (The improvement while taking medication for giardia was coincidental.) It was at that point that I turned to denial as my treatment of choice. I convinced myself that if the symptoms subsided at times, I must be generally healthy. I refused to return to the doctor, undergo more tests and procedures, or discuss my health even with the people closest to me, including Larry. I decided I only needed some "fine-tuning" and arranged regular acupressure treatments and paid even closer attention to diet and exercise than usual.

For the better part of a year, I struggled to keep my physical problems hidden from others, and from myself. As new manifestations appeared — eye symptoms, muscle and joint inflammation — it became increasingly difficult to continue my usual routines, including my well-practiced self-deception.

I began secretly looking up my symptoms in Larry's medical texts. By this time, I admitted to myself that I "had" something, but I wasn't ready to explore it fully and directly. Flipping through the pages of possible diagnoses and recommended treatments was my way of getting used to the medical waters before I jumped in the deep end. My private forays into *Principles of Internal Medicine* brought me up against distressing conclusions: Either I had an advancing case of a serious illness that the tests and examinations hadn't uncovered, or it was "all in my head." I was looking for *something* to account for my symptoms — but something minor and treatable.

Larry, of course, knew what his textbooks had to say about symptoms like mine. He, too, was reading and worrying. The very thing that was most on both our minds was the one thing we weren't talking about. The silence surrounding my illness only made it more imposing.

Initially, Larry encouraged me to see a doctor, to admit the reality of my symptoms, to acknowledge that it was significantly affecting my life. I, however, minimized my health problems to such an extent that he eventually gave up trying to convince me otherwise.

My denial finally gave way during a brief but poignant moment with Larry. He said, "I respect your right to handle this in your own way, and I honor your usual common sense and good judgment. You say that you 'feel pretty well most of the time,' but you are like a different person and you don't even know it."

Having Larry acknowledge my own way of doing things, and hearing his observation that it wasn't working, somehow impressed me.

He went on to make one more statement that turned out to be pivotal: "I'm wondering how bad you have to feel before you'll do something about it."

In that brief encounter, Larry had offered no advice, and what he said required no response. There was nothing to deny, react to, or resist. He simply held up a mirror so I could see for myself. It encouraged self-reflection, it was an invitation to reach inward to draw my own conclusions.

Shortly afterward, I decided to acknowledge my health problems and sought help — from both Western and alternative health care providers. It was a long and discouraging road toward diagnosis and treatment, and I had my moments of retreat back into denial. They provided, continue to provide, a respite now and then. It still takes time to reconcile myself to new symptoms or increased limitations, but my denial is neither as complete nor long-lasting.

The people who decide to attend support groups for those with illnesses are, of course, not denying their illnesses. But we all have *aspects* of our illnesses — new developments, treatment recommendations, long-term implications — that we are inclined to deny. As I learned from my own experience, with Larry, all we can do is be a steady and patient mirror for one another as we grow in self-knowledge and develop our own agendas for putting that knowledge to use.

Anger

If a thief invaded our home and stole our most precious possessions, any of us would likely be outraged. We would feel justifiably angry that our personal boundaries had been violated, and that we had been robbed of what is rightfully ours.

Illness intrudes into the structure of our existence in a painfully similar way. It violates our bodies, our notions of justice, our assumptions about the right to a long and healthy life. It disrupts our households, our relationships, and our plans for the future. With our safety and security in question, we fear future incursions into our sense of control, our clarity of purpose, our opportunities for meaningful connection.

The target of illness-related anger is confusing. There is no clearly identified villain to hunt down. Whom do we blame for our physical conditions — ourselves, God, people who have caused us stress, bad genes, toxins in our environment? And if there is nothing or no one responsible, then isn't living in a chaotic world maddening?

Anger is a natural response to feeling hurt. Illness hurts. It also hurts to feel abandoned or rejected, and misunderstood. Although people in the support groups express a great deal of anger at their circumstances — "this damn disease," "this unjust world" — the anger that seems to weigh the heaviest is directed at other people who "just don't care" or "can't seem to understand." Descriptions of humiliating treatment by health care providers, social service agencies, and insurance companies are commonplace. Insensitive reactions and thoughtless remarks from family members, co-workers, friends and acquaintances can sting deeply a person already feeling fragile and betrayed.

Anger thrives in an environment of poor communication and unrealistic expectations. I believe that much of the anger experienced by people who are ill is a reaction to the fact that physically healthy people can so easily miss the mark in their interactions with them.

Certain interactions are particularly charged. Medical examinations and treatments can exacerbate the feeling of being intruded upon, invaded, violated. It is important that those delivering health care communicate a respect for the dignity, comfort, and privacy needs of the patient. People have a higher threshold for the indignities of medical procedures if their emotional needs are attended to along with their physical ones.

Other charged situations arise over well-intentioned attempts to help. To a person with an illness, these may overstep boundaries that are important to maintain — the ability to make one's own decisions and manage one's own affairs. A woman in her sixties was enraged at her daughter who instructed her to "be sure not to take the clothes out of the dryer until they are completely dry." "I may be ill," said the woman, "but I do know how to do laundry!" The daughter had come by for the afternoon to help with household chores, but her mother was left with a great deal of anger along with a tidy house.

Angry feelings alert us that something is wrong. That has survival value. It moves us to resist, protest, register our indignation against what we perceive as undermining to our well-being. Anger is an experience that seeks expression. It is a feeling and a behavior, and it is important to distinguish between the two.

We have a right to our feelings but also a responsibility for how we express them. We cannot be faulted for having feelings any more than we can be blamed for having illnesses. Yet we must assume responsibility for dealing productively with both our illnesses and the anger they engender.

Anger is energy, and the way to release it productively is to transform it. Anger can be openly expressed in ways that are not destructive, injurious, or aggressive. In response to people who have truly violated us, we can use our anger to give us the courage to be assertive and direct in ways that will be heard. Retaliation usually just leads to counterattack and initiates a cycle in which both parties suffer. According to Stephen Levine, in *A Gradual Awakening*, "Buddha likened anger...to reaching into a fire to pick up a burning ember in our bare hands with the intention of throwing it at someone. Before the injury is done to another, it is done to ourselves."[6] A Zen story makes a similar point:

> A man is struck by an arrow from an unknown assailant. Rather than
> tending to the wound, he refuses to remove the arrow until the
> archer is found and punished. In the meantime the wound festers un-
> til finally the poison kills him. Which is the more responsible for his
> death: the archer's letting go or the victim's foolish holding on?[7]

Dealing with anger productively also means taking the responsibility for understanding its source. There is no question that people could be a great deal more caring and sensitive toward the
needs of those who are ill. If healthy people sincerely put themselves in the place of people who live with illness daily, they would
say and do things that are much less likely to provoke anger. Yet it
is easy to make others the target of anger that truly has nothing to
do with them. Pain, disability, and fatigue inevitably cause frustration, impatience, and irritability. At those times, there may be
nothing that anyone else can do that seems right or enough. The
mere fact that others are healthy and can move about freely may
lead to anger misdirected at them. And sometimes anger from the
past or a habitual pattern of blaming others gets funneled into the
encounters that occur around illness. This kind of global anger has
a far deeper source.

Some of the anger expressed by people who are ill lands on those
who "mean well." Although most of us appreciate the intention behind an inappropriate offer or suggestion, we still grow weary of
being misunderstood. People also find it demeaning to have others
scrutinize them, something physically healthy people are not inclined to do to one another.

We've talked at length in the support groups about the need to
transform that anger with understanding. Many people simply
don't know how to approach or help someone who is ill, and we can
utilize their good will as an opportunity for education. Anyone
who has been ill for any length of time can begin to predict the
kinds of comments and suggestions that people offer; they almost
fall into generic categories. Anticipating those comments and developing a straightforward but gentle response can salvage one's
self-respect and also defuse the anger. We can clarify to people
that we are indeed resourceful and capable. We can diplomati-

cally point out that a suggestion is obvious or theory simplistic, and at the same time, express appreciation for the show of concern.

It takes a great deal of understanding and creativity to deal with our anger in this manner, but it is a healthy way to transform it. The alternatives are lashing out at people who then feel confused and unappreciated, or passively letting them continue in their erroneous assumptions about us and the nature of illness.

The support groups are an appropriate place to ventilate this anger about those who are long on advice but short on — or entirely lacking — firsthand experience with health problems. By sharing these experiences with one another, the group members gain a perspective on how commonly this occurs and are less likely to take the remarks so personally. With enough perspective, we can even see some humor in the misplaced comments. There is a story Ram Dass tells that the group members particularly appreciate in light of their experiences:

> A mother brought her kid to Gandhi and said, "Please tell my son to give up sugar."
>
> Gandhi said, "Come back in a week."
>
> The mother left perplexed. A week later, she came back and Gandhi said to the kid, "Give up sugar."
>
> The mother said to Gandhi, "Couldn't you have told him that last week?"
>
> Gandhi replied, "No, because *I* hadn't given up sugar last week."[8]

If we try to push away our angry feelings, we merely feel anger at our anger. We lose the opportunity to gain some insight into our feelings and to achieve some mastery over them as we utilize the energy for problem-solving. Unexpressed, anger tends to smolder as bitterness and resentment or may explode into hatred or rage.

Once we experience our anger, we can begin the task of understanding it. When understanding reaches the level of compassion, then anger can be transformed into forgiveness. We all have difficult people in our lives, and they often do hurtful things, regardless of the state of our physical health or theirs. If we can muster up enough compassion to look deeply into the lives and hearts of those individuals, we often find people who are sad and hurting themselves. When the suffering is great enough, it spills over onto others. While there are some *deeds* that are unforgivable, it is still possible to forgive the *person*. It releases both people from being locked in anger and opens the way toward resolution.

We can also extend our compassion to the metaphorical thief who has stolen our good health. Continual anger toward one's own illness creates an internal conflict that only further jeopardizes our well-being.

Thich Nhat Hanh advises that we "take good care" of our anger. He speaks of his own experience in the poem "For Warmth." He wrote it during the Vietnam War as he watched his village being destroyed by bombs for the fourth time, the village he helped rebuild after each of the bombings.

> I hold my face between my hands
> no   I am not crying
> I hold my face between my hands
> to keep my loneliness warm
> two hands protecting
> two hands nourishing
> two hands to prevent
> my soul from leaving me
> in anger[9]

Bargaining

We live in a society that promotes the idea that more is better — success, money, good health, long life. Rarely are we encouraged to ask, "How much is enough?" and "At what cost are we doing all this accumulating?"

Living with illness requires that we become skilled negotiators with ourselves. We must not only weigh carefully the obvious risks and benefits of our decisions; we also need to consider the deeper questions: "How 'good' does my physical health have to be to live my life fully and with peace of mind?" "To what lengths will I go to satisfy myself that I have 'done everything'?" "Am I willing to make major changes that I know will enhance my well-being even if they don't rid me of my illness?"

How people answer these questions determines the kinds of choices they make about their health care treatment and also the priority they place on other areas of their lives. These choices, to a large extent, crystallize around the issues of healing and/or curing, and Western medicine and/or alternative health care.

Many people discover they have shifting "bottom lines." Long-held beliefs that "I would never take the medication doctors prescribe," or " I would never bother with all that alternative stuff," give way to the desire for improved health.

Other people's bottom lines can interfere with an ill person's need to be flexible and open-minded in his or her decision-making. When Laoma was trying to decide about treatment for her breast cancer, she found herself in the middle of two camps. The people in one camp tried to reinforce her own reluctance toward surgery and chemotherapy with assurances that *they* would never submit to those treatments either. From the other camp she heard warnings about the dangers of postponing the standard Western treatments while trying alternative methods: "I can't imagine taking such a risk!" Fewer were the people who proclaimed their faith in *Laoma* rather than in their own beliefs. I encouraged her to keep in mind that the issue was not Western vs. Eastern, it was Laoma vs. cancer.

Although people who share their own personal health care preferences are trying to be empathic and helpful, it isn't actually relevant what another would do. We are not them. Our decisions are shaped by the available choices *and* our unique life experiences. Additionally, none of us truly knows what we would do in a situation until we are faced with it. Like many of the people I've talked with, I had some strong opinions about health and illness until I developed my own physical problems. Reality has a tempering effect on even the most deeply held theories.

The fact that we *do* bargain for improved health reflects hope. We believe that we can derive benefit through some means we have yet to try. It is not always health care treatments that become the focus of people's efforts. Many pursue lifestyle changes or devote more care to the emotional and spiritual aspects of their lives. Bargaining may mean simply resurrecting hope, which in and of itself may enhance the environment for healing to take place. Jan isn't exactly sure why her lung cancer, diagnosed as terminal, disappeared six years ago. She suspects it had something to do with acting on her faith.

> I found out about an alternative healing method in Southern California involving a raw food diet and cleansing of the system. I hated that place but hung in for three long weeks because I believed that if my body was to be healed, I needed an act of faith for the healing to manifest through. When I got back home, the first X ray showed the "spot" shrinking. The following X rays showed that the spot shrank away in a few weeks. Was it scarring? Cancer? Who knows?[10]

Ultimately, the bargains around illness are made with ourselves but they include other people along the way. Elisabeth Kübler-Ross, M.D., provides an example in a story about a critically ill woman who was her patient in the hospital.

> The woman begged the doctors to help her survive long enough to attend her son's wedding. If she could just get to the wedding, she said, it would be all right to die right after that. So they infused her and transfused her to build her up. The day of the wedding all her intravenous lines and tubes were removed. She was dressed up and made up until she looked beautiful, and off she went to the wedding. When she returned to the hospital, everyone was expecting her to stagger onto the ward, lie down and die. Instead, she came back on the ward and said, "Don't forget I have another son."[11]

The person at the other end of the bargain may be unaware of the true nature of the terms. A few years ago I became close with an elderly woman named Helen who bargained for her death rather than for her life. She had advanced Parkinson's disease and felt the quality of her life was so minimal that she longed to die. She was frustrated that no one would assist her toward that end and that she couldn't come up with a workable solution for herself.

Helen took a fall at one point and was hospitalized with a broken hip. At first she refused to have surgery. She said she saw no point to it, as she was just waiting to die. Then Helen suddenly changed her mind and was eager to undergo surgery. She confided in me that she saw it as a solution to her problem: At her age and in her condition, surgery was risky. She could die from the anesthesia, from some aspect of the surgical procedure, or from pneumonia or some other post-surgical complication. The medical staff, unaware of all this, was pleased that Helen had changed her mind and that she seemed so eager to have her hip repaired.

Helen didn't die during surgery and was furious. She had a long recuperation in the hospital and was resentful and argumentative with the hospital staff throughout her stay. During that time, I had the feeling that Helen's anger was keeping her alive. Her daily altercations and attempts to control her surroundings with an iron hand seemed to energize her. And, in fact, two days after she returned home to the life she had so wanted to escape, Helen died.

Like the other manifestations of grief over an illness, the bargaining response is more predominant at certain points than others. The willingness to commit to promising treatments or programs waxes and wanes. On the surface it would seem that the worse we are feeling, the more motivated we would be to try. I've noticed the opposite pattern in myself; I have to be feeling relatively well to muster the necessary hope and enthusiasm. When my symptoms are most active, I find it difficult to handle *anything* additional. Also, those are the times my denial tends to resurface; therefore I am less likely to acknowledge the need to take action. In discussing this with the support group members, I learned that many have noticed a similar tendency in themselves. This is an understandable source of confusion to others who may wonder why we are not more willing to help ourselves.

I've often reflected that one would have to be in perfect health to investigate all of the available health care options. It would constitute a full-time job. I personally find it more tempting to expend my limited energy on nurturing a sense of wholeness than pursuing the elusive goal of a symptom-free body. A Sufi story about Nasrudin illustrates how easily we can lose ourselves in an exercise in futility.

Nasrudin...comes back from the marketplace with a huge basket of hot chili peppers. While he is sitting in his room eating one pepper after another, a student enters and asks why he is eating what are obviously burning hot peppers. His eyes are tearing, his lips are swollen and chapped, his tongue swells in his mouth. "How can you eat those awful hot peppers, one after another?" he asks. To which Nasrudin replies, "Well, I saw them in the market place and they were so pretty I couldn't pass them by." "But," his student asks, "how can you do that to yourself? How can you keep eating one burning pepper after another?" And Nasrudin answers, "Oh, I keep thinking I'll find a sweet one."[12]

A man in the support group summarized well the negotiated settlement we each, in our own way, seek to reach with our health. He says he "snacks" on various treatment options. "It's a matter of finding the balance between the Western medical message that you have to stay sick and the New Age message that you have to get well."

Depression

Feelings of sadness are a normal and inevitable consequence of illness and loss. Any significant disruption or disappointment in life cannot help but alter mood and outlook; the response to illness is no different. But if growing disillusionment surpasses our ability to sustain it, it hollows a depression into our daily existence. We slip into that recess, and if our sadness excavates deeply enough, it becomes increasingly difficult to crawl back to the surface. Depression is much like creeping through a subterranean world. We retain only a dim memory of life above ground and are barely aware of the light of day.

The relationship between depression and illness is a complicated one. Some illnesses affect biochemical or neurological functioning, causing mood and/or behavioral changes, including depression. Depression can also be a side effect of certain medications used to treat illness. Often a clinical depression that predated the illness can resurface or be exacerbated with the onset of a physical condition. And the physical symptoms that typify depression often overlap with symptoms characteristic of systemic illness: fatigue, musculoskeletal pain, gastrointestinal upsets, headache, changes in appetite and sleep patterns. Any of these factors can compound the depression that is a predictable response to the stresses and losses of illness.

The predominant self-image during depression is worthlessness, and the predominant mood is hopelessness. Changes in physical condition can leave people feeling inadequate to participate meaningfully in the world and with little reason to try: "Life seems a series of lonely, empty days, passing at a glacial pace. They have no purpose, and I have no purpose."

During episodes of depression, any personal shortcomings, real or imagined, become exaggerated. We draw ourselves in caricature and then supply self-deprecating captions to underscore our guilt, shame, remorse, and self-doubt. In the context of illness, we tend to magnify our physical limitations and diminish to microscopic proportions our other assets and capabilities. A support group member described a constant presence in her life that sits perched on her shoulder, chiding her with comments like "It's all your fault," "You could have done better." "It's there so much of the time," she laughed, "I decided to give it a name — Arthur."

In his book *When Bad Things Happen to Good People*, Rabbi Harold S. Kushner tells a story that illustrates the kind of scathing criticism we heap on ourselves during grief.

> I had an experience some years ago which taught me something about the ways in which people make a bad situation worse by blaming themselves. One January, I had to officiate at two funerals on successive days for two elderly women in my community. Both had died "full of years," as the Bible would say; both had succumbed to the normal wearing out of the body after a long and full life. Their homes happened to be near each other, so I paid condolence calls on the two families on the same afternoon.
>
> At the first home, the son of the deceased woman said to me, "If only I had sent my mother to Florida and gotten her out of

this cold and snow, she would be alive today. It's my fault that she died." At the second home, the son of the other deceased woman said, "If only I hadn't insisted on my mother's going to Florida, she would be alive today. That long airplane ride, the abrupt change of climate, was more than she could take. It's my fault that she's dead."[13]

I read this story at one of the support group meetings. When I finished, a woman, extremely depressed herself, posed the possibility that, in each case, the mothers might well have fared better if their sons had chosen to handle things differently. Perhaps the sons *were* responsible for their mothers' deaths.

I agreed with her premise but not her conclusion. The two men did the best they could with the information they had at the time. If they were guilty of something, it was the inability to predict the outcomes. When we are depressed, we even fault ourselves for not being clairvoyant.

Just as our self-image is distorted when we are depressed, so is our world view. It reads much like the daily newspaper. Our attention is selective and captured mainly by distressing events. That is what we headline, and we include ourselves in the stories. During periods of severe depression, the world appears uncaring, unsafe, even hostile. We assume we are all potential victims, and illness is counted among the dangers.

This lack of perspective is a hallmark of depression. Our own ills and the ills of the world appear out of proportion, and other aspects of life are dwarfed in comparison. Since we feel at odds with those who don't share this perspective, there is a tendency to withdraw from others. The alienation and isolation can further contribute to the shrinking perspective. With little outside input or feedback, the shadowy, interior world of depression looms even larger. "It's like a toothache of the soul," said an anguished woman at a support group meeting.

Depression is often discussed in terms of a cycle to reflect this relationship between isolation and lack of perspective. The pessimism and apathy characteristic of depression create another cyclical pattern. It takes will and energy to help ourselves, and a depressed person, by definition, has none to invest. So the pessimism and apathy grow more profound and further drain the person's ability to break the cycle.

So what is the way out? What brings people back to a functioning level, to the point where they once again can appreciate the full range of life experience? What moves people to care and to hope? I often ask people in the support groups to share with the other members their methods for handling depression. We all have idiosyncratic tricks, but a few common themes emerge.

Most people say they have been helped simply by learning more about the nature of depression and by talking with others who have experienced it. As one group member explains, "I know more than I want to about *what* depression is like, but having outside information somehow helps me to understand the hows and whys." Appreciating that depression is part of the grief process validates its purpose. Hearing that others successfully pass through periods of depression, sometimes repeatedly, restores hope that it is not an everlasting state. And realizing that everything looks bleak when we are depressed clarifies the disturbing discrepancy between our own perceptions and those of people around us. "Things still look gray to *me*," sighs a young woman with lupus. "But now at least I'm aware that if this veil of depression weren't hanging in front of me, I might see the world differently."

Anyone experiencing depression is only too familiar with the persistent self-condemnation that courses through it. Not everyone, however, is familiar with the theory that depression is anger turned inward. Few of us have mastered a graceful way of experiencing and expressing anger. It is, therefore, valuable to consider whether our anger toward others or towards "fate" has, without our knowing it, made a U-turn before it reached its target. In the case of illness, self-esteem is already punctured by our physical and functional changes. If we additionally blame ourselves for those changes, the self-directed anger can deflate our sense of worth entirely.

For some people, perceiving illness as punishment or self-generated is more acceptable than viewing the world as a chaotic place where we are helpless in the face of tragedy. (This either/or thinking is characteristic of depression.) Illness, then, appears "logical" and also within our control: If we caused it, we should be able to eliminate it. People often find this position, and the accompanying feelings of guilt, more tolerable than the fear that illness is an incomprehensible situation that leaves us powerless. A depressed person is rarely able to manage the ambiguity inherent in illness: There are always measures we can take to improve our health and well-being. But because we can have some effect, we can't conclude that we are also the cause of illness, which has multiple and interrelated sources. If we see a man repairing his home after a fire, we don't assume that he is also responsible for igniting it.

This theory — depression as anger turned inward — may or may not ring true for any individual. But it does alert us to the devastating assault depression wages on self-esteem. This insight often moves people to search out and salvage those parts of themselves, small parts, that they deem worthwhile. Although fully rebuilding self-esteem may not come until later, these initial efforts establish the foundation.

Acquiring information about the nature of depression helps put the experience in a larger context, but we need more than explanations to counteract the downward pull depression exerts on our motivation and ability to function. People have a variety of specific and practical things they do when they are trying to climb out of depression. In describing these personal strategies, people invariably emphasize the minimal nature of the goals they set and the monumental effort it takes to achieve them.

The first leg of the uphill climb consists of "at least not making things worse." People often refer to the tendency toward isolation and inactivity, so characteristic of depression, as "my worst enemies." (A distinction is being made here between the lethargy of depression and illness-related fatigue — often difficult to tease apart.) A woman with rheumatoid arthritis says, "I tell myself not to give in. I force myself to leave the house, get out and be with people, even if I don't feel like it." Ever since his vocal cord cancer, Bob closely monitors the dips in his mood. He is on the alert for signs that he is becoming idle and withdrawn. "I always have a lot of little things to do to keep me going. I push myself to keep active, involved, moving." Many use the image of "lying around on the couch" to represent the epitome of depression; it symbolizes that they are losing the battle. Too much time on the couch is Bob's "red flag," and it mobilizes him into action. Most agree it helps to do *something* and also appreciate the wisdom of choosing small, manageable goals that allow for some sense of accomplishment. Kay finds that "just making the commitment to try" lifts her mood.

No matter how small the task, getting started is difficult for people who are depressed. Many of us "talk to ourselves," summon the encouragement of an inner cheerleader to drown out the other undermining voices. I tell myself to *pretend* that I am not depressed and remember that the things I am finding so difficult are things I usually enjoy. In this "as if" mode, I don't try to talk myself out of my true feelings; I knowingly play the role of a more cheerful, energetic self. It helps me to reestablish a connection with the vital aspects of my life. In spite of the artificial manner in which I begin, I find that I am at least able to distract myself and often even lose myself in what I am doing. This strange self-deceptive maneuver, I've learned, is similar to techniques others use to overcome the inertia so characteristic of depression.

The statement, "I try to get out of myself," so commonly made by depressed people, expresses the prison-like feeling that depression imposes. People want to free themselves of their own limiting patterns, and they stretch to make contact with other people and other experiences. Jan cautions that "dwelling on the past, contemplating the future, any kind of introspection just adds to depression. The important thing is to get your thoughts off yourself. Find someone or something else to occupy your mind."

Attending the support group is one example. The members find that although each individual's struggle is profound, it need not be isolating. Discovering the depths to which our caring for another can extend is a major way of transcending personal suffering. One member says that the group helps alleviate his depression because it also reminds him that "good" people do get sick: "I judge myself less harshly for having an illness." As people become less depressed, they often extend their connections into the larger community, frequently in service to others in need — helping at the soup kitchen, volunteering with the hospice program. A harpist in the support group began playing for patients in the hospital. Jerry likes to feed the sea gulls when she is depressed: "It gets me out, and there are often a few that seem less hardy or even lame. Then I feel especially good about making things easier for them."

It would be reasonable to ask how an increasing awareness of the suffering in the world could possibly help someone who is already depressed. Ralph Waldo Emerson addressed this question poetically when he observed, "When it is dark enough, you can see the stars."[14] The long night of depression has the potential to bring an added clarity and dimension to our lives. It sensitizes us to what suffering means, and not just our own. The struggles of another touch a sympathetic nerve within us; vibrating with that pain, we are naturally moved toward understanding it and also alleviating it.

Just as our eyes gradually begin to discriminate objects after a period of time in a darkened room, we can develop the capacity to "see" into suffering. It becomes something other than undifferentiated blackness. Moments of joy, indeed even "ordinary" moments, shine brighter by contrast. We notice opportunities for understanding, compassion, love, and forgiveness that can change the complexion of suffering. And as we locate others who are also moving through the darkness, their own suffering as well as their vision provide added perspective.

While some depressed people find that reaching out to others in need helps to shift their focus, enhance their self-esteem, and restore their hope, this is certainly not true for everyone. Many people simply try to punctuate their days with small distractions, while others seek a sense of personal accomplishment through concrete tasks or creative pursuits. Jan keeps both her knitting and a good mystery novel close at hand. As an artist, Karren is sensitive to her visual environment and appreciates how she can alter it to affect her mood:

> Last summer I decided I had to cheer myself up, lighten my spirit, so I thought the color yellow would be appropriate. I bought a pair of yellow canaries and some yellow marigolds. Every day that

I felt I needed a lift, I bought another yellow plant that flowered.
Before I knew it, my deck was all abloom with yellow flowers.

The soothing effect of music was a topic of discussion at a recent support group meeting. I said that Bach in particular reawakens me to the beauty and tranquillity in the world. "Bach is predictable," added another Bach fan. That initiated an interchange among four other people that went something like this:

"Bach makes me feel healthy."

"Bach makes me feel healthy, but Mozart makes me feel joyous."

"So what about Beethoven?" I asked, curious where this would lead us.

"Beethoven gives me the energy to keep fighting."

"Now Mahler — he makes me feel crazy!"

In the effort to push through depression, it is important that we don't sidestep our feelings. Sadness is something to work with and transform, not deny. It is difficult for most of us to accept the intensity of our feelings and certainly to allow the natural expression of those feelings in the form of tears. If a person begins to cry during a support group meeting, invariably he or she fights back the tears and offers a string of apologies: "I'm sorry." "Please forgive me." "I'll be okay in a minute." What have we done wrong? Embarrassment over the public display of emotion, a taboo in our society, provides only a partial answer. For many people confide that they are loathe to cry even when they are alone. We devoted the better part of one meeting to stories of "buried" tears, some that remained buried and some that unexpectedly "leaked out" later. Judy described that as she was growing up, she imagined all of her unshed tears as the falling rain: "I always felt better after a heavy downpour, somehow cleansed."

Any serious attempt to write about a subject puts one on intimate terms with it. Like depression, this section of the book seemed like it would go on indefinitely. I submerged myself in the vastness of human suffering, a world beyond words. The voice that cried from inside the depression sounded hopeless and confused, the voice that observed depression from the outside sounded detached and irrelevant. This paradox goes to the heart of depression: we must somehow harmonize those voices. When life is resonating with sadness, we need something like a Greek chorus to stand aside and remind us that we are but a single character and only partway through the play.

Chapter Six

Exploring the Edges

For these few days
The hills are bright
    with
      cherry blossom.
Longer, and we
    should not
    prize them so.

             — Yamabe no Akahito
           Springs of Japanese Wisdom[1]

Acceptance

How well we *accept* the unfolding of our lives has a great deal to do with what we *expect*. The more elastic our expectations, the more room we have to incorporate unforeseen events. The more flexible our assumptions, the greater our repertoire of responses.

I recently had a conversation with a woman in her late seventies who enjoys remarkably good health. She has been extremely energetic and active her whole life and is accustomed to accomplishing what she sets out to do. She told me how distressing it was to find she was "beginning to slow down," how discouraging it was to see the same thing happening to her peers.

When is it acceptable to slow down, let alone develop an illness? When we are in the flush of youth, the fifties seems far enough away. At fifty, we experience those changes as premature, more appropriate for someone seventy. And at seventy, we feel cheated that we didn't sail through until — ninety?

Changes in our body always seem untimely if our expectation is perpetual good health and endless years. That is our *wish*, but it is too much to expect of a body that is mortal. It would also be the wish of most of us to die in our sleep at a ripe old age, at the end of a healthy, fulfilling life. Although that is ideal, all too often it is not the case.

There is much we can do to enhance our health and extend our longevity, but there are natural limits. Like the cherry blossom, we each have our precious time to bloom. Yet we live in a society that is enamored with technology and deifies human ingenuity. In the drive to maximize our human potential, we've become arrogant and irreverent toward the sacred source of that potential. Although the human mind can devise the artificial means to extend the bloom of the cherry blossom, doing so violates the nature of the tree.

The expectations of the seventy-six-year-old woman I spoke with made it difficult for her to accept her current level of functioning or appreciate her lifetime of good health. The natural changes of aging were traumatic for her, and I said what I could to be supportive. But silently I was asking, "How do the trials of aging measure up against an early physical decline or premature death?"

There was my own illness, which came on at thirty-seven rather than at seventy-six. Untimely? Yes — unless I consider Jeanette, dying a painful death from cancer at thirty-five. Imelda, now twenty, has been severely ill with lupus since the age of twelve. She told the support group how fortunate she felt after one of her hospitalizations. She met a young boy who had progeria, a disease of rapid aging. He looked like an elderly man and would die by the time he reached his early teens.

An awareness that things could be worse doesn't cancel out the realities of our personal struggles. Illness and death are always difficult to accept, whatever the age or circumstances. But expectations based only on what we want from life, rather than what we know of life, make acceptance that much more difficult.

Accepting hardships such as illness is not synonymous with passive resignation, stagnation, or defeat. Acceptance is an ongoing, active process, aimed at peace of mind and a sense of wholeness. It moves us through grief, drawing our attention and energy toward the positive side of what is, rather than what isn't, used to be, or might have been. It is a hopeful exploration of what is possible within given limitations. We shape our experiences and our relationship to them through the human capacity for transformation and transcendence.

True equanimity — the ability to bear with equal mind — rests on developing an ease with the nature of life. It is the ability to be "at home" with impermanence, change, loss, and periods of grief. Although unwelcome, we can acknowledge those inevitable aspects of life, along with the more joyful elements of human existence. In the words of author Flannery O'Connor, whose life was limited and shortened by lupus, "...you have to cherish the world at the same time you struggle to endure it."[2]

Striving to accept, one by one, the challenges and disappointments of life can be discouraging and exhausting, like lifting a series of heavy boulders, each one separate and formidable. The strain is somewhat eased if we can cultivate an acceptance of life as a whole, an uncharted road marked both by stretches of easy travel and unexpected obstacles.

Fluctuating emotions and episodes of grief also mark the path through illness. Equanimity gives those feelings space, so we can be "at home" with our feelings as well as with our circumstances. Even feelings of non-acceptance need acknowledgment; many people express this as "accepting the unacceptable."

The most profound level of acceptance is self-acceptance. Just as we tend to fall out of love with life when things are not going well, our relationship with ourselves suffers when we face our own shortcomings. Healing that relationship requires the kind of unconditional love we give to children. We encourage them to do their best but also allow them their limitations. When they fall short of our expectations, we may register disappointment, but we don't withdraw our love. As adults, especially ill adults, we are usually not so generous with ourselves. Many of us grow uncomfortable in our own company, no longer count ourselves among our closest friends. This self-estrangement is movingly conveyed in "Love after Love" by Derek Walcott:

> The time will come
> when, with elation,
> you will greet yourself arriving
> at your own door, in your own mirror,
> and each will smile at the other's welcome,
>
> and say, sit here. Eat.
> You will love again the stranger who was your self.
> Give wine. Give bread. Give back your heart
> to itself, to the stranger who has loved you
>
> all your life, whom you ignored
> for another, who knows you by heart.
> Take down the love letters from the bookshelf,
>
> the photographs, the desperate notes,
> peel your own image from the mirror.
> Sit. Feast on your life.[3]

How do we feast on a life impoverished by illness? How do we sit with the painful emotions that follow in its wake? How do we befriend a body that betrays us? There is no formula for transcending or transforming our experiences, nor is there an endpoint. It is an ongoing personal pilgrimage, along a road that may curve so gradually as to obscure the turning points. Renée says that any strategy for accommodating to her lupus has to continually change to keep pace with her fluctuating symptoms. Illness is a process and so, therefore, is acceptance.

Accepting illness is a way of making it our own. It is a creative act, unique to each individual. It requires all the curiosity, imagination, intuition, commitment, and faith necessary to any other creative endeavor. We work with what we are given and use whatever tools we can find, often discovering we have many more resources than we thought. The act of accepting illness changes not only the experience of illness; we undergo a metamorphosis as well.

Flying Without Wings is an account of Arnold Beisser's life since the onset of polio at age twenty-five. It left him paralyzed from the neck down and unable to breathe outside an iron lung. Beisser had just completed medical school and won a national tennis championship when "without warning, my body failed me. In a few hours I was transformed from a doctor to a patient, from an athlete to a cripple. Polio ravaged me so that I could not move. I could not stand, walk, sit, eat, drink, or even breathe by myself."

> My physical world had shrunk to the small room that contained my iron lung. My field of vision was limited to the ceiling and what was reflected in the mirror on my iron lung. In the evening, when the world grew darker, my world shrank further. I could no longer see the pattern on the ceiling, and the reflection in the mirror was dim. Not until two years later, in my fourth hospital, could I turn my head to the side enough to look down a corridor outside my room.
>
> One evening, lying there alone, feeling particularly hopeless and bored, I looked down the corridor wishing for, perhaps expecting, someone or something. But I saw only the darkened hallway with a few doors opening onto it. There was no activity, and there were no people to be seen. My despair mounted, and I felt as though I could no longer stand it. Then, slowly, I began to see variations, shades of gray and darkness, shadows and light. The doorways opening onto the corridor formed subtle geometric patterns according to the different ways the doors were ajar. I began to look carefully and wonder at this scene that only a few moments before had depressed me so. It now seemed startlingly beautiful. My perception had shifted, my eyes miraculously refreshed. This experience was full and whole. I looked down the hallway for a very long time. I think that at last I probably fell asleep, but I am not sure.
>
> I do not know how that perception arrived, or why it left, but from then on I understood that what I sought was possible. My task now was to discover how to change from the one state to the other.[4]

Change is inherent in any creative act. To adapt to illness is continually to invent, redesign, improvise. Self-expression is also inherent in creative work. To accommodate to illness is to imprint upon our circumstances our unmistakable mark. Anatole Broyard, author of *Intoxicated by My Illness*, says he "would advise every sick person to evolve a style or develop a voice for his or her illness.... Adopting a style for your illness is another way of meeting it on your own grounds, of making it a mere character in your narrative."[5] Broyard was an editor, literary critic, and essayist for *The New York Times* for forty years. His book chronicles his last months, as he was dying of prostate cancer. His own "style" evolved from his lifelong love of words.

> ...I am a critic, and being critically ill, I thought I might accept the pun and turn it on my condition. My initial experience of illness was as a series of disconnected shocks, and my first instinct was to try to bring it under control by turning it into a narrative....
>
> Just as a novelist turns his anxiety into a story in order to be able to control it to a degree, so a sick person can make a story, a narrative, out of his illness as a way of trying to detoxify it. In the beginning I invented mininarratives. Metaphor was one of my symptoms. I saw my illness as a visit to a disturbed country, rather like contemporary China. I imagined it as a love affair with a demented woman who demanded things I had never done before. I thought of it as a lecture I was about to give to an immense audience on a subject that had not been specified.[6]

Style, in any creative endeavor, evolves over time. It undergoes clarification, refinement, and becomes highly individual. Some of us make bold sweeps across a broad canvas, while others of us trace our experience in delicate lines and muted tones. Defining one's personal style for living with illness is essentially an exercise in self-awareness. It is the statement "This is who I am, this is how I do things." Acceptance of illness becomes easier if we believe we can fashion our lives around it in our own characteristic way.

When Judy stopped singing because of Meniere's disease, she spent a great deal of time reflecting on her singing career. Over the years, she had sung many kinds of music but all in her own unique style. As a gift to the people closest to her, Judy collected on one tape what she felt were some of her finer performances. She named the tape *Judy Mayhan: In Various Disguises*. Judy explained that she was just beginning the search for an offstage identity, a style that she could live instead of sing.

Style is reflected in everything we do. The small details of life, the everyday decisions and opportunities, are vehicles of self-expression. When Mickey was recovering from his treatment for vocal cord cancer, he decided to speak about it at his thirtieth class reunion. Being an outgoing person with a gift for storytelling, he had entertained his classmates at previous reunions with updates on his life. The reunion was a natural opportunity for Mickey to celebrate his voice.

Kay derives pleasure from making and keeping commitments. Her heart disease changed greatly the kinds of things she could commit to, but not the desire or ability to channel that energy elsewhere. Kay decided to adopt the Dean Ornish plan for reversing heart disease, a highly structured program of lifestyle changes involving diet, exercise, and stress reduction techniques. She also decided to go back to school and finish the requirements for her high school diploma and then go on to study computers.

My own style of dealing with the complexities of illness is to simplify the rest of my life. For me, highlighting what is truly important and eliminating what is superfluous or distracting brings peace of mind. Certainly there are practical advantages — fewer things to absorb my limited energy and an increased sense of competence over my daily affairs. Life dictated *only* by practicality, of course, can become dull and inflexible. My penchant for simplicity, however, has a grander purpose.

In the spaciousness of an uncluttered life, I feel a sense of freedom. Like many people who are ill, I have said that I feel "trapped" in my body. But I don't feel trapped by my life. Nor do I feel a sense of lack. It feels luxurious to devote care and attention, in an unhurried way, to my relationships, my work, and my daily surroundings. When I was more "active and productive," before I developed an illness, I tended to move through things quickly rather than connect with them deeply. I always wanted those deeper connections, sensed that I was out of step with my natural style. My illness brought me closer to a more mindful way of living, and for that I am grateful.

The spaciousness, sense of freedom, and mindfulness, how-ever, quickly evaporate into a whirlwind of activity when I for-get my limitations and add more into my life than I can reasonably handle. There is much in the world that is tempting. Although my natural inclination is toward simplicity, at times I still find myself stretching the simple life to see how much it can accommodate.

My husband and I recently redesigned our flower garden for practical reasons; the work had become too difficult for me. But looking out on the new garden, I am struck by how the change also symbolizes the internal shifts I've undergone in accepting my ill-ness. The original "pre-illness garden" reflected my life at the time: a mass of flowers and shrubs that filled every inch of the garden. In contrast to that congestion of colors and textures, the new garden looks stark, especially since the recently planted ground cover has yet to fill in. But the sparseness lends an order and elegance that I find appealing and satisfying, both to the eye and to the soul. Two well-placed trees, a Japanese maple and a flowering crabapple, grace the far corners of the garden. A beautifully shaped boulder sits about midway between the trees, and a few ferns stand quietly in their spots. These select things, complete in themselves, make a garden. If we choose well, we often need less than we think.

Not long ago, a friend identified my style of living with illness as "putting a good spin on a bad situation." Although that might sound like he was complimenting me for being adaptive, that wasn't the way he meant it. He was concerned that I wasn't ac-knowledging or expressing the difficulties I was having with a flare-up of my symptoms. I told him over the telephone that it had been hard, but I was actually managing fine. That didn't make any sense to him. How could something hard be fine? After we hung up, I thought for a long time about his question and the whole conversation. I realized that for physically healthy people, health problems represent something acute, a crisis, a situation that few would characterize as "fine." Living with an illness for over twelve years, however, I have had to distinguish between acute and chronic, discriminate between a crisis and an event, develop a higher threshold for a "bad situation." There are, of course, acute episodes within a chronic illness, and it is important to identify them and respond appropriately. But ongoing or fluctuating symptoms somehow have to be integrated into life if we are to perceive ourselves as whole.

This ability to coexist peacefully with our circumstances and our bodies, as they are, requires the quality of receptivity. To be in a receptive state is to be alert, attentive, and open to some degree of mystery. It demands heightened perception and a readiness to respond. Many people express concern that acceptance of illness is a life-denying act; on the contrary, accommodation elicits our full involvement and participation. It entails deep understanding, clarity of purpose, and wise action. To repeat the Oriental proverb stated at the beginning of the book, "If fate throws a knife at you, there are two ways of catching it — by the blade and by the handle."

Cindy captured succinctly the choices we have when faced with a difficult situation: "Fight it, flee from it, or flow with it." The third alternative clearly engages our ingenuity, vitality, and will. In our culture, however, receptivity is considered a feminine quality and, sadly, men are rewarded more for fighting difficulties than flowing with them. It is no surprise that the overwhelming majority of people who have come to the support groups are women. Someone who is battling with illness is unlikely to attend. Also, women tend to find comfort in discussing their problems with others; men are more likely to seek solutions in action rather than words. The men who have attended the meetings have been inspirational in their ability to successfully integrate the masculine and feminine aspects that reside within us all.

Whatever our gender, it is important to take a strong stand in regard to illness. That is different, however, than entering into an angry wrestling match with our own bodies. The Chinese martial art of Tai Chi suggests an alternative way of maintaining ground in the face of a threat. It consists of a series of slow, gentle movements that enhance energy, concentration, and balance. The goal is to understand and harmonize with an opposing force, disarming and transforming the advance rather than resisting it with brute strength.

Few of us can maintain a consistently stable and flexible attitude toward illness. Sometimes it is a distressing symptom or frightening complication that throws us off center, other times it is the cumulative impact of the struggles and losses that brings us to our knees. There is much we can do between those episodes, however, to cultivate a steady, peaceful center within ourselves upon which we can draw when we feel most threatened and alone.

Many ill people intuitively sense the need for something to ground them and turn to meditation or other spiritual practices that calm the mind and expand the heart. When we make a habit of consciously observing ourselves and our surroundings through moment-to-moment changes, we are practicing a different way of seeing; we penetrate more deeply, notice more subtleties, perceive more connections. In the quiet solitude of meditation, we are also practicing a different way of listening. We begin to hear our intuition, to attend to the voice within us that is wise and trustworthy rather than frightened and confused. We also hear more clearly messages from the heart, our own hearts and the heart of the world. Discovering the sacred in each day is healing. Our personal circumstances are more acceptable if we feel connected to some larger context. "I try to make every day Sunday," says a woman who lives with chronic back pain.

Of course, meditation can be pursued on many levels, some of them quite esoteric. But the essential practice is to become quiet and focused, and the ultimate purpose is to bring that peace and awareness into daily life. During a recent support group meeting, several members were describing the anxiety involved in trying to continue the lifestyles or activities that once had given them so much pleasure. We agreed that peace of mind had moved up several notches on our priority lists, displacing many of those once-loved but now overwhelming pursuits. We also agreed that in our busier days, peace of mind was hardly considered a goal; it was boring, the consolation prize. Peace of mind, however, is the sole — and soul — source of happiness in a world where things will continue to come and go. The ability to cultivate peace of mind serves us better than any other skill or talent or material resource we may acquire.

Peace of mind keeps us in the present, paying attention to what is
— what is important and what is possible.

I keep a short and simple verse by Thich Nhat Hanh on my desk
where I see it first thing in the morning. The meditation works for
me because it is direct and accessible.

> Breathing in, I know I am breathing in.
> Breathing out, I know I am breathing out.
>
> Breathing in, I see myself as a flower,
> Breathing out, I feel fresh.
>
> Breathing in, I see myself as a mountain,
> Breathing out, I feel solid.
>
> Breathing in, I see myself as still water.
> Breathing out, I reflect things as they are.
>
> Breathing in, I see myself as space,
> Breathing out, I feel free.[7]

A spiritual practice offers one way of bringing us closer to our
experiences, including illness. It is one method of self-reflection
which helps us appreciate our true essence and find the most meaningful way to express it. People have many other ways, however, to
nurture their connection with life and with themselves.

Some of us construct meaning around illness itself. If it is to play
a major role in our lives anyway, we might as well have it speak for
us the lines of our choosing. By making the *subject* of illness my
work — through the support groups, hospice work, and writing —
I've come to see my own illness as an unexpected catalyst rather
than solely a personal calamity. Against the shadow of illness, what
is essential in life stands out in bold relief. That is what I am learning, at an accelerated rate; that is what I am sharing with others. It
is the work of a lifetime.

After the removal of his vocal cords, Bob began "speaking" in
the public schools, acquainting the children with his artificial voice
and also with the most significant risk factors for developing vocal
cord cancer: smoking and drinking. Knowing that he is having
some impact on the health and well-being of the next generation is
an important element in helping Bob accept his circumstances with
such grace.

There are many examples of wounded healers who are openly sharing the wisdom they have gained from living with illness. The act of supporting, educating, or inspiring others is a powerful way of transforming suffering into meaning and enhancing a sense of personal worth. There are also many examples of people who prefer to draw as little attention as possible to their illnesses. For these individuals, illness doesn't enrich the meaning in life, it threatens to rob them of it. Under such circumstances, people, to the extent that they are able, direct their focus toward other aspects of their existence. They bring their passion and commitment to things that can compensate for, or overshadow, the presence of illness.

Fiction writer Flannery O'Connor found that her lupus condition so severely diminished her strength that she could work on her novels and short stories no more than two or three hours a day. Yet she wrote in a letter to a friend that she was "making out fine in spite of any conflicting stories."

> Lupus is one of those things in the rheumatic department; it comes and goes, when it comes I retire and when it goes, I venture forth.... I have enough energy to write with and as that is all I have any business doing anyhow, I can with one eye squinted take it all as a blessing. What you have to measure out, you come to observe closer, or so I tell myself.[8]

The kinds of things that we can pursue in order to "neutralize" illness span a broad range: writing, creating art, or making music; cooking, sewing, or gardening; exercising, communing with nature, or caring for a pet; volunteering, taking classes, or maintaining loving connections with family and friends. People who are still able to work often make a wholehearted commitment to their jobs. What is common to all of these activities is that they fully engage the heart and mind. They are individual ways of touching something universal; they rekindle our sense of joy and purpose and passion for living — even with illness.

Shortly before she died of breast cancer, Treya Killam Wilber settled on the idea of "passionate equanimity":

> ...to be fully passionate about all aspects of life, about one's relation with spirit, to care to the depths of one's being but with no

trace of clinging or holding…. And as for the task before me, it means to work passionately for life, without attachment to results."[9]

Treya's "journey without a goal" is the road of acceptance. Every point is a point of arrival; every step brings us closer to ourselves.

Death

As I awoke this morning, I considered my plans for the day: Make a quick trip to the store and the post office, take a walk on the headlands — and then write about death. Given my chosen line of work, this is not an unusual day. As the editor of the hospice newsletter, I am often writing about death. As the facilitator of the support groups, I have spent many hours talking with people facing death. And my own illness and middle age are constant reminders that I, and those close to me, are mortal.

Yet each time I write about death, I feel as though I am working on a mystery story, one that I can never wrap up with a tidy ending. At best, I can set the scene and provide a few clues, but the concluding chapter of life remains a sacred mystery until the moment we personally step into the narrative.

As I was paying for my groceries at the store this morning, I had a brief conversation with the check-out clerk which primed me for the task awaiting me at home. She said, "My mother died recently, and I've been carrying around the eulogy I wrote for her. I thought of you as a person who would be interested in reading it." Given my chosen line of work, this is also a typical conversation. In a small town it is readily apparent who does what; people I meet even casually often fill me in on any illness, pain, loss, and death that they are experiencing in their own lives.

I joked with the check-out clerk about my odd reputation. But I don't, in fact, consider these conversations odd; loss and death are inevitable aspects of life, not aberrations of it. I returned home, wrote "Death" at the top of a clean sheet of paper, and took heart as I recalled a quotation by Socrates: "...true philosophers make death and dying their profession...."

We know that death is inevitable; beyond that we can only speculate. We have medical expertise to describe the physical changes. As loved ones or friends, we use all of our attention skills and intuition to try and see inside the subtle shifts we observe. And accounts of near-death experiences, as well as the teachings of various spiritual traditions, give some shape to the otherwise formless unknown. Yet we are still left guessing about death — when, how, and to varying degrees, why.

This paradox — so much uncertainty around something so certain — brings us face to face with our human limitations. When we encounter the unfamiliar, and especially the frightening, we often try to find out more, in the hope that to know is to control. And in many ways our culture suggests that knowledge can be certain and control complete.

The death experience, however, defies this linear, problem-solving approach. It has more to do with how we are than what we know, a point Sogyal Rinpoche emphasizes in *The Tibetan Book of Living and Dying*.

> At the moment of death, there are two things that count: whatever we have done in our lives, and what state of mind we are in at that moment....
>
> ...relax completely. There is nothing new you need to learn or acquire or understand; just allow what you have already been given to blossom in you and open at greater and greater depths.[10]

To those who are with a dying person, Rinpoche advises, "Don't try to be too wise; don't always try to search for something profound to say. You don't have to *do* or say anything to make things better. Just be there as fully as you can."[11] In order to heed this sound advice, we have to be grounded by a trust in death as a natural process. We need to be humble and peaceful in the presence of the unknown, compassionate and patient in the presence of pain.

I became close with a woman named Carolyn during the last year of her life. My time with her taught me the importance of trying to sense the dying person's inner world of private experience and personal meaning. This is different from trying to imagine what one's *own* response would be in similar circumstances. Empathy for a dying person creates an essential and powerful link, but it can never totally illuminate the inscrutable process of the soul taking leave of the body. The living must defer to the dying in much the same way a child is urged to be patient: "You can't understand now, but someday you will."

A few months before her death from breast cancer, Carolyn called to tell me that her doctor said she probably had about six months to live. As soon as the wincing sigh escaped my lips, Carolyn responded in her typically straightforward manner: "You don't like hearing that, do you?" The honesty between us helped me distinguish my own grief at losing her, from *her* grief which was tempered by some degree of relief. Carolyn was weak and weary of the pain, ready to leave her body. She was fond of saying that "death is like taking off a tight shoe." Still another set of emotions stirred in me as I considered how I would respond to such a prognosis. Of course, my issues were different from Carolyn's; my shoes were not that tight yet.

A short time later, Carolyn called on a summer afternoon to ask me if I would come over that evening and stay with her for the night. Her regular caregiver was away, and she was too ill to be alone. "I called you," she said, "because you don't need anything from me. You can just be present with things as they are. There are others who would be willing to help, but I need to be free of their fear and sense of doom."

I was, of course, glad to help and also honored by the compliment. When the phone rang, I had been working in the garden, ruminating over how far apart to plant the petunias. When I hung up and returned to the petunias, I felt embarrassed at how petty my concerns were compared to Carolyn's struggles and impending death.

I later told a friend about all this, and she laughed and said, "That's why she called *you*. You care whether the petunias have the space they need. She knew that you wouldn't crowd her either."

Unless we live with a life-threatening condition, we take many things for granted — tomorrow itself being the most elemental. For a dying person, each day might be the last; ironically, the few remaining hours may become infused with renewed life. There is no time to wait to do or say the things that are important, or to waste on things that are not. This paradoxical enhancement of life during its final moments is at the heart of the spiritual teachings that link an awareness of death with contentment in life. Death becomes "the great healing." From this perspective, a life lived as preparation for death is a life fully lived.

"I've learned much of life / from impending death — /the blessing of a known disease," writes a man with AIDS who attends the support group. His poem continues:

> Something about knowing
> time's running out
> inspires a living more full,
> a cool protected heart burst free.
> Now I have my time to shine,
> my moment in the sun,
> So don't be sad for me.
>
> — Danny Ross [12]

Depending on their spiritual orientations and life experiences, people differ in their attitudes toward human mortality. Many are more fearful of the dying process, while others find the finality of death the most distressing. A painful, lingering, or lonely death is a frightening prospect to all of us, especially in view of the technological and impersonal approach that is characteristic of many modern medical facilities. End-of-life documents (living will and durable power of attorney for health care) as well as hospice arrangements (to help people die at home) add some measure of reassurance. But few of us have such solid internal resources or external support systems that we can embrace the dying process without significant concerns about our comfort and dignity.

Many people have strong feelings about the presence of loved ones at the moment of death. Some have fears about dying alone, for themselves or for those close to them; being together is important. Others may need freedom from the attachments of loved ones in order to die; solitude eases the transition. For those who want to be together and can't, or for those who have lost someone in a sudden death, Deborah Duda, in *Coming Home: A Guide to Dying at Home with Dignity*, offers comforting words: "We are no less loving or loved because of where we are...we know that love is not expressed only by sitting at the bedside."[13] And based on many accounts of near-death experiences reporting reunions with deceased loved ones, Elisabeth Kübler-Ross is convinced that "we never die alone."

Death means the end of life as we know it. The way we face the closing of the door depends on two things: how we feel about the life we are leaving, and what we imagine to be on the other side of the door. The end of life is especially poignant when death comes early, as was the case when Jeannette died at thirty-five.

Jeannette loved her life, yet seemed remarkably willing to let it go. She had a difficult life, yet seemed to grow in strength and love with each experience. And she saw her dying as a continuation of that process, adjusting gracefully to each change and loss. "The supermarket is too big for me now, so I just go to the corner grocery store," she described matter-of-factly. When her debilitating fatigue made it impossible for her to be up, she explained, "My bed has become a magnet." For Jeannette, somehow things were as they should be. I asked her what response from other people would be most helpful to her, and her answer reflected the same trust: "Just to be themselves." When others asked how she could endure the painful progression of cancer throughout her body, she seemed to have her attention elsewhere: "It's as if the body hides the truth." She adopted an image used by Elisabeth Kübler-Ross as her own metaphor, for her own metamorphosis: "like a butterfly emerging from a cocoon, shedding the body imprisoning the soul."

Jeannette had a near-death experience when she was fourteen and felt that any years she enjoyed beyond fourteen were grace. The experience she described was similar to others' accounts of near-death encounters. It reflected the commonly reported sense of peace, expansion, and well-being: an initial ringing or buzzing while floating out of the body; heightened visual and auditory awareness; rapid movement through a dark, tunnel-like space toward a beautiful, brilliant light or loving, compassionate being; a life-review in this luminous presence; and a gathering of relatives and friends who had previously died.

Also consistent with others' reports, Jeannette described reaching a barrier where she had to decide whether or not to return to life. The decision to return was accompanied by a great flood of love to share, a renewed meaning in life, and a fearlessness about death.

It was Jeannette's wish that there be no service for her when she died. She requested only that her family scatter her ashes on the ocean, from a point on the headlands known by locals as "The Cypress Circle." The Cypress Circle is a natural amphitheater of Monterey cypress, trees uniquely adapted to withstand the harsh oceanfront environment of unrelenting wind and churning saltspray. A sense of dark drama lurks among the twisted trunks and arching limbs, pummeled by the elements into a sculptural statement about survival. A mass of low tangled branches curve around an open space covered by a canopy of dense green foliage.

A few days after Jeannette's family had scattered her ashes, I went to The Cypress Circle to say a private farewell. As I sat in this mysterious place — part battlefield, part sanctuary — I felt Jeannette's presence, both her struggle and her peace. I understood why she chose this spot, this intersection between life and death, for her transition. There was a sense of timelessness there that felt comforting.

I walked to a clearing in the trees that created a portal to the ocean. It was a warm, almost windless day. As I watched the slow, steady rhythm of the waves washing ashore, I thought about the last time I was with Jeannette; how unlike the rhythm of the waves her breathing had been as she struggled for air in short, fitful gasps. Now she was absorbed back into the natural ebb and flow, floating and free.

I returned to The Cypress Circle and, in the hush of the bowed trees, read a quotation by Viktor E. Frankl that I had brought along for consolation: "We cannot, after all, judge a biography by its length, by the number of pages in it; we must judge by the richness of the contents.... Sometimes the 'unfinisheds' are among the most beautiful symphonies."[14] And then I burst into tears.

Although I try to make peace with death philosophically, I am still invariably shaken to the core over the deaths of those close to me. My reassuring beliefs about death exist alongside my emotional attachments; they don't override them, nor would I ever want them to. The price for loving is losing: caring for others means grieving when they die. It's a cost of living that exacts a great deal from us, in exchange for the inestimable blessing of life.

Kahlil Gibran, in *The Prophet*, said, "You would know the secret of death. But how shall you find it unless you seek it in the heart of life?"[15] Grace, who is approaching seventy, has undertaken that task. She looks back on her life as a series of "little deaths":

> I died as a single person when I married, I died as the mother of a household when my children left home. Life is a continual process of letting go. Appreciating that has helped me in life; I hope it will help me when the "big death" comes.

In his book *Meetings at the Edge*, Stephen Levine describes these periods of change in our lives as going "from one octave to the next."

> And dying is in many ways no different than any of these other transitions we have made. As one friend of mine used to say, "Death is just a change in lifestyles." With each of our changes, of our "movings on," we have always had to let go of the last stage before we could fully enter the next. It is like swinging on a set of children's monkey bars where you really can't go on to the next rung until you have let go of the last one. Sometimes when I am with my kids in the park, I will see how they trust the process of their momentum so much that they seem almost to fly across those bars without holding to any of them. But then I will see some of us old adults, so conditioned to distrust our natural momentum, and when they go across the bars, they refuse to let go of one until they have securely grasped the next. They hang there like herniated chimps grasping onto one but not letting go of the last. When the children go across, you see that there are moments when they have completely let go of the last rung and their hand hasn't quite reached the next, but it is the trust in their momentum that keeps them from falling. When we have that kind of

trust, we just move from bar to bar, or level to level, in a continuing movement that maintains itself effortlessly. In all growth we must let go of the last stage before the next can fully develop. In a sense, we are constantly having to die in order to be reborn. And here we all are, learning to let go and to move into the next unknown moment.[16]

The ease with which we move into "the next unknown moment" toward death depends, to a significant degree, on whether we see death as some sort of transformation, whatever that personally means, or merely as an end. "What is the purpose of life, given the certainty of death?" is a question that each religious tradition wrestles with in some form, and answers in some form by rituals or practices which reflect a concern for the journey of the deathless spirit.

Whether or not we choose to give specific or literal meaning to "the deathless" in the form of an afterlife or rebirth, our life energy continues beyond death. Each individual's unique presence undeniably alters the world and therefore what subsequently unfolds, especially in the lives of the people we touch. Whatever form it takes, our interdependence with other life energy constitutes the sacred aspect of our being.

Death gives shape to our existence as perhaps no other force in life can. It frames the picture, provides the last chapter, clarifies how each element contributes to the whole. Death is the time we encounter the human soul stripped to its essence, in all of its pain and in all of its beauty. In that intensity, that intimacy, we can discern something that endures through pain, through loss, even through death.

We all share a universal concern about death, regardless of our personal framework for the experience. It's the same concern we share about life — that we somehow make our experiences our own. We want to know that we matter, during life, during death. Ultimately, we want to be counted among those who "died the way they lived."

Unresolved Grief

An *awareness* of impermanence and death enhances life, makes it that much more precious. A *preoccupation* with loss, however, diminishes life, drains it of its vitality and meaning. Those who perceive loss not as a part of life but as the whole of it often describe their lives as "a living hell": "I might as well be dead." "What's the use of going on?" People unable to resolve their grief over the losses of illness live *in* loss rather than *with* it. Loss becomes constant, permanent, their total environment. It becomes home, and they become homebound.

"Code Blue" is hospital terminology for a life-threatening emergency that summons the immediate attention and full-scale intervention efforts of the staff. "No Code" is a term entered into the medical record of a patient for whom the quality of life is so minimal that resuscitation measures would be a disservice. It's as if people trapped in their grief have written a "No Code" into their charts for the future. They are saying no to "life support," rejecting the breath, heart, and nourishment that sustain our existence. They are convinced there is nothing worth reviving in a life enfeebled and scarred by illness.

Unresolved grief is different from the undercurrent or periodic bouts of grief that are inherent in life with illness. Grief helps us feel and move through our feelings. We venture forth, in spite of lingering sorrow. The inability to face the losses and experience the emotions, however, keeps people riveted to the past. They never come to terms with the "little deaths." Life-Before-Illness becomes enshrined, worshipped, visited in daily prayer: "If only I didn't have an illness."

A woman with inflammatory bowel disease moved to the Northern California coast after she became ill. She said she couldn't bear to stay in the surroundings that held so many reminders of the full and productive life she led before she became ill. Yet emotionally she never left home, in spite of her new physical address. She talked constantly about her previous way of life; the topic monopolized her thoughts as well as her conversation. An aspect of *healthy* grief is the attempt to keep alive one's characteristic and lifelong identity, while shedding the losses of the past — always a complicated task. But this woman, fearful and insecure, was convinced that her significance rested solely on her previous accomplishments which, paradoxically, provided both a sense of security and an obstacle to her stated intent to leave the past behind. After a short time in California, she moved again, the second in what was a series of moves. From the occasional letters she sends, I sense that she has been unsuccessful in the effort to honor her past without making it the centerpiece of her present.

The most deadly quality of unresolved grief is the perception that things will never change. People can't imagine a time when they *ever* will transcend their losses. With no hope of change or choice, loss prevails over life, becomes one's whole identity. Sadly, these individuals could state their metaphysical position thus: I suffer, therefore I am.

Unfortunately, while some people are transformed by their grief, others are destroyed by it. The statement "God never gives us more than we can handle" doesn't accurately describe the many people who buckle under the weight of their burden.

The magnitude of the load doesn't seem to be the determining factor. Certain individuals somehow develop the emotional muscle to shoulder the most incapacitating kinds of illnesses — and still retain a zest for life. They exemplify Nietzsche's statement, "That which does not kill me, makes me stronger."[17] Others, for some reason, crumple psychologically from far less dramatic symptoms and disabilities. I know such a woman; she feels perpetually defeated. She likens herself to Sisyphus, the figure in Greek mythology who was punished in Hades by repeatedly having to roll a huge rock up a hill only to have it roll down again as soon as he reached the summit.

How we perceive the task of grappling with illness can greatly affect our willingness to make the effort. Many people say they can never get *over* the losses, which amass into an imposing, impenetrable mountain. The apparent choices are an Olympic-style leap or an arduous, uphill climb, either one overwhelming to a person with an illness. Perceived in this way, losses erect a barrier; life dead-ends against a wall of grief, and there we remain stuck.

Over, however, is not the only route to the other side of loss. A willingness to investigate grief, to approach it directly and probe deeply, forges a pathway *through* it. Stepping into our emotions, moving through them, painful as that may be, allows us to gain understanding and build strength. Our energy remains vital, and although still difficult, life retains its continuity.

Unresolved grief prevents us from crossing that threshold. A major reason is fear — fear that intense emotion will drag us into deep, dark, lonely corners of our lives, forcing an encounter with issues we would rather not confront. Some of those issues are the hard human concerns: self-worth, vulnerability, control, intimacy, abandonment. Other issues involve personal history, including the painful or unresolved episodes which inevitably come under close scrutiny in the reckoning of a serious illness.

Those who choose to attend support groups are, on some level, participating in this archeology of illness. In order to better understand themselves and the nature of disease, they are willing to unearth the remains of past experience and to explore the terrain of the human soul and psyche. Those who keep their distance, from their emotions and from support groups or other paths toward self-reflection, often do so because they fear they will become lost. They are uneasy in the unfamiliar territory of emotions, and doubt that they could find their way back to safe ground.

There is good reason that many people prefer to tread lightly on the surface of their emotional lives. I've heard anguished personal stories from people who have endured the most unbearable losses, traumatizing abuses, and desperate circumstances. Why revisit these minefields of grief-laden, emotionally explosive memories?

A young woman with chronic pancreatitis came to the support group and recounted a lifetime of hardship and desperation that would seem impossible to survive. And she *was* barely surviving. She looked like a wounded bird, fragile and frightened, emaciated from her illness and debilitated by her struggles. She had been raised in a household where drugs and alcohol functioned as food would in a healthy household. From a young age, she and her brothers and sisters were "fed" the same substances her mother was using. While her mother was in prison for drug offenses, she was passed around to different "caretakers" where she was neglected, abused, and raped. At a young age she married — an abusive husband — and continues to struggle with her addictions that developed early on and are deeply ingrained.

This young woman is confused and overwhelmed by her medical condition and her pain. Because of the poverty of her upbringing, she has few coping skills and not the slightest notion of where to begin. The link between chronic pain and narcotic drugs makes it that much more difficult for her to begin to live her life instead of becoming numb to it. At this point in time, my personal efforts, along with the support of the group members, have had only a minimal impact in terms of helping her make changes and choices differently than she has in the past.

Avoiding the emotions of grief doesn't make them disappear. Unexpressed or indirectly expressed feelings surface in disguise and, ironically, assume greater authority as they go unrecognized. The anger and depression of grief can become distorted into blame and guilt. The charge of these emotions can become exaggerated, and may be displaced onto individuals and circumstances that are handy rather than responsible for the stresses of illness.

A man with rheumatoid arthritis attended a few support group meetings and never returned. He had come in search of a battalion, one that would back him up in his all-out campaign to expose every societal manifestation of insensitivity to illness. Many people naturally and justifiably express strong anger regarding unkind or indifferent treatment they have received from various quarters during an illness. His global outrage, however, had a distinctively different quality to it. He felt victimized by society generally and marshaled all of his energy toward building a counterattack. He consistently avoided any discussion of his own relationship with his illness; he never revealed how he, not society, viewed himself and his areas of vulnerability.

Social and political action can be a productive outlet for anger. It directs the hard-won wisdom gained from living with illness toward a higher purpose. This man, however, merely unleashed his anger, without harnessing it toward efforts to right injustices or implement change. Unable to attend to the inner world of illness, his emotional life became dominated by anger at society. Under those circumstances, any resolution, with his illness or with the world, seemed hopelessly remote.

The perspective of someone who is unable to process feelings of grief often becomes quite narrow, and the thought patterns that develop to support that perspective can become quite limiting. A certain rigidity characterizes the thinking of those trying to hold their emotions at bay; it functions like a gatekeeper, allowing entry only to that which does not disrupt the precarious standoff between life and loss.

Choices and decisions are restricted to an all-or-none, right-or-wrong context. The tendency to overgeneralize and jump to conclusions limits opportunities for understanding or change. The uncertainty and ambiguity that gives life its texture and depth are shunned in favor of a one-dimensional existence that, although dismal, is at least predictable.

Thought patterns that interfere with the ability to resolve grief also interfere with the ability to forgive; the two are closely connected. If we cannot forgive ourselves for having an illness, and forgive others and the world for falling short of our expectations, we have not fully investigated the nature of human limitations and loss; we have not stretched our hearts and minds to encompass all that we inevitably must think about and feel in order to live fully.

Helen remained embittered toward life until her death. An intelligent and artistic woman, she had always prided herself on being "discriminating" and "having a good critical eye." Her judgments tended to be quick and global, and as her Parkinson's disease progressed, she became increasingly less tolerant. She honed in on what was lacking, in her circumstances and in other people, and she viewed these shortcomings as "impossible to forgive or forget."

Forgiving is different from forgetting. Forgetting about the people or things dear to us that we have lost is neither possible nor healthy. We also remember the hurtful acts and the people who caused them; to forget would put us at risk, deprive us of important learning in order to care for ourselves well. Forgiveness is the space we create around those memories, space for understanding that we sometimes lose what we love, and space to feel our grief. Forgiveness provides some slack. It helps us to loosen our emotional grip on the past, and to free ourselves from the experiences that have reined us in.

The word forgiveness implies a response: letting go of resentment toward a particular person for a specific wrongdoing. Many people understandably feel that they have suffered offenses that are unforgivable, that no amount of space or time could erase the sting of certain experiences or the people connected with them. Forgiveness comes within reach of all of us if we can conceive of it as an *attitude* we hold toward the world generally rather than just an *action* we take on specific occasions. I like to think of forgiveness as a generosity of spirit we bring to the present, in spite of what has happened in the past. We can decide against letting the individual angers and sorrows build into lifelong bitterness and suffering. It is less a question of undoing the hurts than of setting them down so we can move about more freely. "Forgiveness is giving up all hopes for a better past," according to a newsletter from The Center for Attitudinal Healing.[18]

People who have not resolved their grief over the losses of illness usually have little hope of a better *future*. Those who have lost all hope see no future at all.

Suicide

To a person contemplating suicide, there are things worse than death: being trapped in unbearable circumstances, whether physical or psychological, with no apparent means of escape. Hope, ironically, seems to reside in death, perceived as the only way out.

Cherry, a support group member with chronic fatigue syndrome, was awaiting a decision regarding her application for disability benefits. She had been living on the financial edge for a long time, meeting monthly obligations by supplementing general relief checks with rapidly dwindling savings. The pain and limitations of her illness were draining her emotional and spiritual resources as well.

The final decision on Cherry's case was scheduled for June, the same month her savings would run out, leaving her unable to pay for rent, utilities, and food. If her application was denied, she said, June was also the month she would take her life — the only alternative she saw to living on the street, homeless. In chilling detail, she described her plan to dispose of the few possessions she owned, with the exception of her car. Her car, she explained dispassionately, was her method of suicide; she would breathe in the toxic fumes. Her words conveyed a sense of inevitability that was alarming.

Cherry's social connections were as meager as her finances. She had a distant relationship with her family, and few friends. The people in the support group, she said, were her "lifeline." Luckily, she attended the meetings regularly and felt she could talk about her feelings openly. People who live with serious illness understand both the kind of desperation that breeds suicidal thoughts and also the kind of caring response that can help defuse them.

June was approaching, and the group members tried to help Cherry find both a reason to live and the practical means to do so. She seemed closed to suggestions of accepting financial help from others, sharing expenses with a roommate, or any of the other ideas offered. The many months of worry and fear had exhausted her: "If my disability benefits are denied, I just don't have the energy to go on."

Around this time, Cherry related to the group a long conversation she had with a friend of hers who was feeling suicidal. Cherry became animated as she spoke, in sharp contrast to her usual listless demeanor. After she finished a careful account of what her friend said and how she responded, I inquired, "Do you find it curious to find yourself in the role of suicide counselor?"

She looked almost startled by my question, then said emphatically, "Well, *she* has other choices."

After a pause, I stated what I suspected she had just figured out for herself: "Because your friend is feeling suicidal, she doesn't see for herself the choices *you* see. And because you are feeling suicidal, you don't see for yourself the choices *we* see. That's the nature of feeling suicidal."

Cherry's inadvertent role-reversal proved to be a self-generated method of suicide intervention. It extracted her from the vortex of conditions that pull people toward suicide: a sense of being hopelessly trapped, and the conviction that one's existence is totally separate from others and insignificant to anyone. Cherry repositioned herself on the side of life, reaffirming the power of choice and rediscovering her human worth through a caring connection with another.

Having recovered a degree of hope and energy to seek out solutions, Cherry was willing to follow up on the possibility that her general relief payments might be increased temporarily, in case the decision was delayed or while she appealed the decision if her application was denied. She was quickly granted the increase in monthly payments and eventually granted disability benefits.

Stories of close calls and previous attempts at suicide are not unusual in the support groups. Suicide is a frightening topic, but many group members have stared it in the face at one point or another. In the context of that common understanding and collective courage, suicidal fears can be expressed and examined rather than stifled and silenced. Taboos and judgments that cut off discussion of suicide don't put an end to the issue; they merely sever the connection with the person, already feeling isolated and misunderstood.

When I've asked people what has driven them to the point of suicide, three factors stand out as central: 1) *Trapped in pain*. Suicide is seen as a choice, the only tolerable choice, by a person who feels trapped in a life — in a body — tormented by suffering. In the context of a severely painful and disabling illness, the constricted area of freedom and choice can choke off the will to live. 2) *Stripped of hope*. Without choice, there is no hope of change for the better, only fear that things will get worse. If a suicidal person were to graph the quality of his or her life, it would either be a flat, horizontal line, representing a continuous level of misery; or the line would plunge downward, depicting the eventualities of worst fears and "what ifs." Suicide is a gamble, based on the hunch that there will be no improvement, in either our circumstances or in our ability to experience and transcend those circumstances. 3) *Isolated from others.* Suicidal individuals are willing to leave life behind because they no longer feel a part of it. The isolation and sense of worthlessness are so complete, they insulate the person from the relationships and sense of purpose that furnish life with connection and meaning. One woman recalls a suicidal period of feeling "numb" and experiencing the world as "barren": "I looked at life as a detached observer, standing outside a cardboard cutout. Nothing in my life felt substantial enough to draw me in."

I've also asked people who attempted suicide in the past whether, with hindsight, something or someone might have made a difference. There is agreement that chastisement from others was the antithesis of what they needed at the time. Ethical arguments against suicide coolly disregard the larger-than-life physical and/or emotional desperation that drives a person toward death. Labeling suicide as immoral or selfish burdens a person who is already feeling weak of character and unworthy of love with additional reasons to feel guilty and inferior, merely for the desire to end the suffering. A censuring attitude or heavy-handed approach can backfire. As Earl A. Grollman cautions in his book, *Suicide: Prevention, Intervention, Postvention*, "In the debate with the downcast person, you may lose not only the argument but also the individual."[19]

Carol came to a meeting distraught over increasingly pervasive thoughts that life with rheumatoid arthritis wasn't worth living. She said that when she tried to express those thoughts to others, the conversations were quickly aborted with the formulaic "think of what it would do to the people left behind." Like many people who are suicidal, Carol was not lacking concern for her husband and young son: she was just lacking conviction that she could be anything but a burden to them. People who are suicidal have so devalued their own worth, they have little to invest in their relationships.

In Carol's particular case, admonishments about the legacy of suicide paled against her own life experience: her older sister had ended her life with an overdose when they were teenagers. The dark memory of finding her sister, and the aftermath of confusion and grief, kept Carol "riveted to life." And yet, in the depths of her despair, her vow never to inflict that kind of pain on others was wavering.

The profound and life-threatening anguish of suicidal individuals naturally impels those close to them to "act decisively." At the same time, an impulse toward suicide has to be handled with great delicacy, lest we unintentionally exacerbate the very stresses that put a person at risk. Overpowering someone with advice or descending in a rescue mission is a way of saying, "I am concerned," but it is also a way of saying, "*I* am strong and decisive, and I will save you from yourself." A preemptive rush toward heroism may trample whatever independence and dignity the person has left, and increase the sense of entrapment and desire to escape.

In answer to my query about what *is* helpful, those who have been through the experience concur that the most direct way to reach people who are suicidal is simply to *be* with them and to *listen.* Contrary to outward appearances, offering a steady, compassionate presence to a suicidal person constitutes a bold, decisive act. It takes a great deal of courage to enter that nether world, and the willingness to do so confirms our love and affirms the other person's worth. To people who seriously doubt that their existence even matters, acceptance and attention from another person may make a critical difference.

We can't prevent people from taking their own lives; we can only promote their search for a reason not to. Those ready to end life can usually come up with the means. People choose life over suicide not because they lack a method but because they possess a desire to live. That's where others can be of help — in recovering the connection with life, not just removing the instrument of death.

Listening to someone's suicidal feelings is not a substitute for more dramatic moves that may be necessary, to lessen the person's risk or to respond when a suicide attempt seems imminent. Rather, an ongoing relationship establishes a trusting context for any other actions or decisions that might have to be made on another's behalf.

Also, a willingness to listen to someone's suicidal thoughts should in no way be construed as a sign of approval of the act itself. We listen to the reasons a person is tempted toward suicide to increase our understanding, and therefore our ability to help clarify alternatives. We accept expression of feelings, not acts of self-destruction, encouraging the former in order to prevent the latter.

At the support group, Carol found individuals who wanted to know her honest feelings, who were concerned enough to listen to her struggles and who understood enough to accept them as valid. The message she heard was that we deeply cared whether she lived, and that we knew the reemergence of her own strength and resourcefulness, not our interventions, were what would ultimately keep her alive. Hearing that other people had walked that same narrow edge added to a growing sense of trust and connection. It also sparked her interest in learning how other people steadied themselves, and kindled some hope that she could regain her own balance.

For Carol, as for anyone who slips into suicidal thoughts, the starting place was a simple question: Why haven't you taken your life so far? Carol talked about her family, sweet moments with her son at the beach, and about her spiritual connection with nature. Carol said that suicidal thoughts were "gnawing at her," that she was "fighting against them but afraid they would win." We talked about making a concentrated effort to remember why life is worth living, especially identifying those things that overshadow physical condition and capabilities in importance. Write them down, keep adding to the list, we advised, and keep it handy. Then, when the gnawing thoughts intrude, grab the list, read it, remind yourself, in your own words, of the reasons to cling to life, however tenuous they may seem at that moment.

We also talked about the importance of having a plan in mind for the times we reach the point of desperation — thinking ahead about who to call and where to put our attention. Suicidal feelings are not rational; a sense of doom fogs perceptions and also the capacity for problem-solving. We look at the sky and see only clouds. Carol said she would feel comfortable calling certain family members, people in the support group, or the crisis line if she felt on the brink of ending her life. We also encouraged Carol to let the people close to her know how they could help: by listening, by acknowledging that she sees suicide as a choice but helping her generate other choices.

Because her rheumatoid arthritis prevented Carol from doing vigorous physical work, she perceived herself as worthless. She grew up on a farm, laboring long and hard under the watchful eye of a relentlessly demanding father. Carol exacted the same standards of herself as an adult; her physical strength and the products of her labor became emblematic of her value as a person. Coupled with inactivity was the inability to contribute to the family income, which meant her husband was working two jobs. "Seeing my gardening tools just lying around unused reminds me of how useless I am," she told the group members in a quivering voice.

Others at the meeting spoke of their own similar frustrations with physical limitations but also of their efforts to shift their goals toward things they could accomplish and from which they could derive some satisfaction. People also encouraged Carol to take credit for the uniquely challenging and enormously significant responsibility of child-rearing, the major role she now assumed in her family.

I asked Carol about uncoupling the opportunity to use her landscaping skills and tools from the issue of earning an income. Although she couldn't manage the demands of a job, how would she feel volunteering her services? She lit up, said she would love to be active and, at the same time, help someone out. We talked about places in the community that could use her assistance in designing and overseeing their landscaping projects.

The doctor who was treating Carol for her rheumatoid arthritis had informed her of the diagnosis with minimal information and even less compassion. In subsequent appointments, the doctor remained detached and uncommunicative, and each office visit left her feeling more hopeless and depressed. The group members described their own patient/doctor relationships — some good, some bad, and some that changed from bad to good by switching doctors.

Within a few weeks, Carol had contacted another doctor, found several places that welcomed her gardening expertise, and developed a new sense of pride in her daily household and childcare responsibilities. "What changed?" I asked.

Carol answered the question easily: "I realized at the meeting that I can do small things and feel a sense of accomplishment. I gained some hope and some confidence about working around things rather than against them." Then she added a poetic afterthought: "You know, I'm finding the change of seasons beautiful. The leaves on the sycamore trees and the oak trees are just beginning to show some color."

Through careful listening and gentle inquiry, the group members found out what was important to Carol, which of those things were present in her life and which things were missing. The suggestions offered grew out of that framework and, equally important, conveyed the belief that Carol had the strength to act on those suggestions if she chose to. The hope that others offered was not false reassurance that things would be easy. Rather, it was the perspective, based on firsthand experience, that illness, as a part of life, as bad as it is, is not *all* that there is. As one member put it, "Pain is inevitable, suffering is optional."

One of the stories Carol heard at the meeting was Judy's account of her "sandbagging operation," an unsuccessful suicide attempt that she and the group members recall with humor — but, of course, only in hindsight.

In a desperate moment, Judy had tied a ten-pound bag of sand around her waist, hid it beneath her coat, and hitchhiked to the ocean headlands in search of an isolated spot to drown herself. She was determined, and the sandbag, she thought, was a foolproof method. At the time, Judy was feeling so remote and inaccessible, she could barely manage the brief note she had scribbled to her lifelong partner: "This will sting, but you'll get over it."

When she got to the headlands, it was swarming with people. Although it was a Monday, it was Memorial Day, a detail that Judy hadn't taken into account.

> I trudged around for four hours and couldn't find a single private corner. In my distraught state, it didn't occur to me to put down the sandbag while I walked around. Feeling utterly ex-

hausted and defeated, I decided that this just wasn't the time and hitchhiked home.

Although Bob hadn't found the note yet, he knew how upset I had been and suspected what I might be up to. When I arrived home and saw the look on his face, I knew, in a way I had never appreciated before, how devastating it would be for him and for my family if I ever took my life. And the memory of that moment has kept me from ever sinking again so dangerously close to the bottom.

Those who say they would never consider suicide, as well as those who say they would never attempt it again, give a variety of reasons, but in one way or another, they have decided that life is precious. People who express themselves in religious or spiritual terms hold life sacred, a gift, and to end it would be a violation, a renunciation of the divine. Others who conceive of life in practical rather than metaphysical terms think of potentials and opportunities. Small things can improve the quality of life, they happen day by day. Pain and suffering may dominate the present, but suicide is forever.

Unfortunately, certain illnesses, and terminal stages of illness, can create such intractable suffering that death, rather than life, would constitute a gift, a blessed pain-killer. Under those circumstances, would not a high regard for life be consistent with leaving it as gracefully as possible? Would a prolonged torturous existence be more "natural," more "life-affirming" than an early release guided by compassion for both the patient and loved ones? The heated controversies over physician-assisted death, and the general concern over end-of-life decisions and the right to die, reflect our basic human dilemma: to live and die as individuals the best we can, within our limited understanding of life and death.

I recently read a moving account of a man with AIDS who chose his time to die. It appeared in a Buddhist publication called *Inquiring Mind* and was written by Maria Monroe, a longtime friend of the man. She not only detailed the physical and emotional changes that marked his last days, but also reflected on their shared history as individuals deeply committed to Buddhist principles — which traditionally prohibit the taking of any life, including one's own.

> Four years after he was diagnosed with AIDS, my dear friend Ric told me that he'd looked into ways to end his own life if, as the disease progressed, he wanted to take that option. I was accustomed to knowing he would die, but I didn't want him to commit suicide. It rubbed against Dharma teachings I'd taken very much to heart.[20]

When Maria received the call telling her Ric had died, she asked if he had ended his own life.

> Yes, he had, and as the story of Ric's last days and hours and moments were filled in, to my surprise I felt my heart filling up with gladness.... The story of his death was one of mastery of the moment...."[21]

Suspicious of her "unexpected comfort with his manner of dying," Maria began questioning various fellow Buddhists practitioners and trusted teachers about the "unwholesome action of suicide."

> Everyone I spoke with thought we needed a different name for what Ric had done; "suicide" didn't fit. A friend of Ric's, who is only eleven, said, "Ric didn't commit suicide because suicide is angry and is done to hurt people. When I heard Ric died, I thought he died of AIDS, and when I heard a few days later how he died, it didn't change anything. He still died of AIDS. If he didn't have AIDS, he wouldn't have died.[22]

Ric's own words were recorded by his friends hours before he died with the help of a doctor:

> Today is the last day of my life. I never thought I'd be saying that because people don't know when the last day of their life is. So I'm feeling very grateful for yet another gift I can be appreciative of, that God has allowed me, very graciously, to take his role over for a few minutes here. Yet I'm not taking over anything.... He might have wanted to wait a little longer to take me but I wasn't willing to suffer like that.... He didn't want me to suffer so he sent me a friend who could help me out.[23]

Whatever the reasons leading up to suicide, there is only one result. And the enormity of the decision to end life by one's own hand, whatever the circumstances of that life, inevitably raises the most troubling kinds of questions we may ever ask ourselves. The suicidal person wonders, "How can I continue to live in such pain?" "What do I have to look forward to?" "Would anyone really care if I died?" Family and friends ask, "What alternatives could I offer?" "Can I provide some hope?" "How do I communicate my love?" And in the aftermath of a suicide, there are yet more questions, persistent and haunting: "Was there more I could have done?" "Couldn't *someone* have done *something*?"

There are no easy answers; they come about painfully and slowly, and sometimes too late or not at all. Patience, enormous patience, is what is being asked from both sides of a suicidal encounter. Suffering that becomes greater than the patience to endure it drives people to take their lives. And impatience with the suicidal person who appears unwilling to take our suggestions may drive us away at the time our love and compassion are needed most.

Patience is tested most severely in the wake of a suicide. Forbearance toward the person who did the deed and toward oneself for the inability to prevent it may seem an impossible task. Yet what else can we do but forgive ourselves for being human? Our humanness resides, after all, in our capacity to feel deeply and also in our freedom to choose. I wish more than anything that no one would ever be faced with overwhelming pain, and that the choices we each make would never cause hardships for others, but we do not live in an ideal world; can we be patient with the world, as it is, as we are?

Although, like most people, I have had fleeting moments of "wanting out" of a situation, I personally have never felt suicidal and would hope that I continue to find enough quality in my life to prevent me from ever reaching that point. But I appreciate there is a large element of grace in that and am humbled by those whose experiences have been otherwise. Although I consider life sacred, I can't (can anyone?) honestly say, "I am certain I could never get to the place myself where either physical or emotional pain would make life unbearable." If I should find myself in that place, I would want to have a choice. And I hope that, by confronting death, I would choose life.

Part Three

In Good Company:
Illness and Relationships

And remember, we all stumble, every one of us.
That's why it's a comfort to go hand in hand.
— Emily Kimbrough[1]

Illness is a universal human experience. The failings of a mortal body will inevitably impact each of our lives and the lives of those close to us. Yet ironically, illness often separates us from one another — from loved ones, from friends, from health care providers, from the very people who figure most significantly in our comfort and well-being. It is as if there is the world of the sick and the world of the healthy, each viewing the other through a haze of misunderstanding and each confused about where to find some common ground.

The common ground is simply our humanness, the willingness to meet one another openheartedly and share the concerns that touch us all. Experiencing an illness and witnessing it each bring their own kind of pain and fear, and each of us will come to know both. Recognizing this fundamental truth establishes the basis for the closeness, understanding, empathy, and trust that is essential to any healthy relationship. When each person in the relationship humbly acknowledges the enormity of both tasks — living with illness as well as trying to help alleviate it — they stand on the same side, on the side of compassion. I don't know anyone who has said this as simply as Elisabeth Kübler-Ross: "I'm not OK, you're not OK, but that's OK."[2]

Healthy relationships require the same kind of care and attention that we bring to our bodies. Just as we monitor symptoms, we must listen to and honor the signals we receive from one another in order to take care of problems in the relationship before they become more serious. Healing from illness involves inner resources — self-reflection, intuition, creativity — as well as medical care;

similarly, healthy relationships require that people be as committed to understanding themselves and each other as to understanding disease.

A serious illness demands attention and action, but if the focus shifts from the welfare of the individuals involved to merely the illness itself, the relationship suffers. When illness-directed interventions replace human-based interactions, the vital healing effects of a warm presence and close connection are sacrificed. Agendas or judgments about what could or should be happening can distract us from sharing what *is* happening. Evaluating the results of our efforts becomes more important than accepting each other as we are. The result is two lonely people.

Illness profoundly strains relationships. It tests commitment, stretches patience, and challenges our communication skills. It places burdensome responsibilities and high expectations on both the ill person and those trying to help. All we can truly ask of one another is the willingness to participate in a process, fully, honestly, and flexibly. If we can appreciate each other's good intentions and also be generous toward each other's limitations, relationships can grow and flourish, regardless of the medical outcome. Rather than a wall of separation, illness can be a doorway between those who are ill and those who care about them. Since none of us remains only one or the other, it serves us well to make that passage.

Chapter Seven

Health Care Providers

We are not truly human until we see
another person's suffering as our own.

Albert Schweitzer, M.D.[1]

Trading Places

Several years ago, my husband Larry injured his knee. It required arthroscopic surgery, and being a physician himself, he had the resources to prepare himself fully for what was about to take place. He reviewed his X rays, consulted with colleagues, and discussed the details of the operation with both the surgeon and anesthesiologist. On the morning of the operation, Larry was matter-of-fact as we arrived at the hospital and completed the necessary paper work. It was comforting to him to have surgery at the hospital where he was a staff physician. He had a warm and personal relationship with the nurses and other employees, and he was familiar and confident with the level of care they provided.

We chatted lightheartedly with the admitting clerk as we walked down the hallway. When we reached his room, I turned to Larry and saw that all the color had suddenly drained from his face. His gaze was fixed on the empty bed, as if realizing for the first time that he would be the person *in* the bed rather than the one standing beside it.

There is no substitute for "in the bed" experience. The view from the bed grants health care providers an important credential not acquired through education or training: the ability to identify with the *people* they are treating, not just identify the *problems*. Ideally, each of us could choose our health care providers by learning not only where they were trained and what degrees and licenses they hold; we could also ask, "Have you, or has anyone close to you, had significant pain and loss?" "What is your experience with it?" "Do you reflect on it when you are taking care of your patients or clients?" I would love to see on the walls of medical offices, hanging alongside the diplomas, the following quotation by Rumi:

> Each has to enter the nest
> of the other imperfect bird.[2]

My "*next* to the bed" experience was also transformational. I was now at the giving rather than the receiving end of care and assistance. From my own experience of living with an illness, I was acutely aware of the importance of offering help rather than imposing it, of asking what is needed rather than taking charge, of being a quiet presence rather than a controlling force. And yet, I saw how tempting it is to jump in and "fix"; to say, "Let *me* do that"; to do everything that is humanly possible, and hopefully a little more. I could understand how a health care provider, possessing a great deal of knowledge and expertise, could get lost in the doing and forget about being.

Not long ago, the director of the nursing education program at the local hospital asked me to help with one of the training sessions. Because of my own illness and my work with the support groups, she requested that I talk with the nurses' aides to "sensitize" them to the needs of people living with chronic illness. In preparation for the discussion, I asked the group members to tell me what thoughts they would like me to pass on to the nursing staff, what things had been difficult for them as patients in the hospital and what things had been helpful.

Few people focused on the details of medical treatment. Most of the comments concerned the need to be understood and respected as fellow human beings. When chronically ill people are admitted to the hospital, it is usually for acute episodes within ongoing conditions. They want to be relieved — hopefully cured — of the immediate problems, but they also want support for their continual efforts at healing, at remaining whole and intact despite their physical limitations. The following list is representative of the suggestions gathered from the group members, based on their experiences as hospital patients:

"See me as something more than a diagnostic label or abnormal lab test. Because I am a patient, that doesn't mean I am no longer a person."

"I want people to validate my experience, my suffering, my need to shed tears. I am not weak. These are natural, normal responses to my situation."

"Remember that people living with illness struggle with isolation and low self-esteem in an ongoing way."

"Ongoing medical care and repeated hospitalizations mean that people bring with them memories of past medical experiences that may have been negative ones. Know that people may have a history of feeling frightened, trapped, out of control, diminished, distrustful. Try to understand why the patient might feel the need to put up a barrier. Try not to take it personally."

"A chronic illness represents the limitations of modern medicine. The patient with the illness often feels like a failure in the eyes of those who are taking care of him or her. Don't blame the patient for failing to get well."

"Encourage my freedom of choice and a clarification of my priorities. Allow for my individuality and dignity; invite my input and trust my experience with my own condition."

"Meet me beyond the roles of patient and staff. Make a connection."

"Be aware of the difference between pity and compassion, between distancing yourself from people in pain and approaching them with an open heart."

"Let me be honest, and be real with me in return."

"Be gentle and patient so I don't feel like I am being zoned in on by a mechanic."

"Small, simple, nurturing things become very important — sips of water, having my hair washed."

"Remember that people are overwhelmed. They need help sorting out confusing information; give simple, detailed explanations."

"Ask more questions, like 'What would be helpful to you?'"

"Listen more — without thinking you have to come up with answers or suggestions."

I appreciated the opportunity to share these comments with the nursing staff, but I was also eager to hear their experiences and perspectives and to bring them back to the support group. I believe that anything that promotes mutual understanding between ill people and those who care for them is healing.

The nurses' aides with whom I spoke were empathic, sensitive individuals. They seemed willing to see themselves mirrored in their patients, to remember that we are all potential patients. They enjoyed the direct, hands-on care they provided people and recognized the importance of a nurturing, receptive attitude toward someone in pain. But they felt thwarted in their work, frustrated with administrative demands and rigid procedures that kept them from being as present for their patients as they wished. They felt they were in the best position to know what would comfort a patient but had the least authority to implement those measures. I was hearing from the staff of the hospital the same sense of powerlessness that is expressed by patients.

Of course, the staff of this small, rural hospital is not representative of hospital employees everywhere. But they serve as a reminder that, just as it is impossible to understand fully an ongoing illness until faced with one, we cannot appreciate the challenges of a health care worker without being in that role.

I've also had a front row seat to the standard education and training of physicians. Larry and I married just as he began medical school, and we've journeyed together through internship, residency, a private practice in internal medicine, and emergency room work. I've watched him struggle to retain his compassion, humility, and idealism in a system that seems to promote emotional distance, arrogance, and cynicism. I was mystified that people being trained to participate in the most profound and intimate of human encounters were encouraged to remain aloof and separate.

I understand the emotional toll involved in making life-and-death decisions, in witnessing horrifying levels of suffering and pain, and in knowing that, all too often, one's accumulated knowledge, skills, and expertise have little impact. The heaviness Larry carries in his heart at times is almost palpable.

What I have *never* understood is how training people to be "clinical," detached from their own feelings and those of their patients, could possibly enhance their ability to do their work effectively (not to mention the dire consequences of numbed feelings for their personal psychological health). There is a huge difference between swimming in an emotional pool, on the one hand, and operating in an emotional desert, on the other hand. To me, imagining oneself in the place of the patient, with all the attendant feelings, would provide essential information to a physician, not detract from his or her ability to make intelligent decisions.

Over the years, Larry and I have discussed these issues, as well as the rich mix of joy and pain in his own work, for he is among those caring doctors who have "let their patients in." Since I've developed an illness myself, and subsequently stepped into the role of serving others living with illness, I have also had my share of encounters with physicians and have heard endless stories from others about their own encounters.

It would be easy to indict the medical profession and to build a case with the numerous accounts of uncaring or incompetent doctors. But that creates defensiveness, counterattack, and a growing polarization between those who would like to bring about change and those who would resist it. Rather, I would like to make a case for the kind of interactions that would serve the health and well-being of both the patient and the doctor.

Patients and physicians often bring different expectations to medical appointments. They agree that the business at hand is a diagnosis, cure, or treatment, but few patients are satisfied with a doctor who is strictly business. The healing of the human body is not merely a case of mechanical repair, nor a simple exchange of information between owner and technician. We need physicians to share something of themselves, to be touched by our fears and hopes, to be moved by the sacred trust placed in their hands.

A doctor could justifiably protest, "I can't be expected to be an astute clinician, a gifted teacher, and an enlightened spiritual guide, all rolled into one." Yet a physician must be willing and able to assume elements of all these roles at various points — as well as to receive learning and healing from patients in return.

"Flexibility rather than perfection is what I look for," says a woman who healed her relationship with a doctor by writing him a letter. "I traveled 150 miles for a consultation with him, and he rushed through the appointment and had no time for my questions. I wrote him a letter, honest but not hostile, expressing my frustration, and he wrote back *thanking me*. 'Please help me remember,' he said."

Problems often develop when there are no solutions to medical problems. Doctors may become impatient with patients who "expect too much," and patients often feel their doctors have "written them off." At such an impasse, what if the physician and patient could agree that they were just two people trying to get through a difficult situation together? What if the doctor could say, "I've come to the end of my expertise. I'm frustrated that I can't give you what you came for. I'm not able to take away your illness, but I am able to add something else — connection, support, hope. Tell me how can I best provide that to you."

Would such an invitation to partnership be "unprofessional"? Would such an admission of humility, of concern, constitute substandard care? Would it interfere with either the physician's or the patient's continuing efforts to investigate treatment options? Wouldn't it clarify expectations and create a healthy bond?

Since the health care profession is counted among the "human services," the human factor should be the very ground upon which that work is based. It doesn't *replace* knowledge or skills or appropriate action, but any help extended is, after all, from one human being to another. Sometimes there is nothing tangible doctors *can* offer — then being human is enough.

The Medical Maze

"It was like going through a car wash — without a car." Those were my words as I left the large San Francisco medical center where I had been undergoing extensive outpatient procedures in the hope of arriving at a diagnosis. I shuffled from one department to the next, my hands clutching the endless papers, my feet following the colored lines. I felt only minimally in control of the rest of my body. Laboratory technicians dispensed and collected the vials of substances that entered and exited my body at designated hours. The radiology staff poked and prodded me into the required positions as they aimed their machinery at selected anatomical sites. I changed in and out of hospital gowns designed to expose one area of my body or another, never quite sure what would be done, how long it would take, or if it would hurt. Most of the people performing the procedures seemed unaware, or unconcerned, that I, and my fellow unclothed and confused waiting room companions, might need explanations or reassurance.

The low point was a gastroscopy, a procedure involving a flexible fiber-optic tube that permits visual inspection of the stomach. Inserted into the mouth, the patient "swallows" the tube, which passes through the esophagus and into the stomach. The gastroenterologist performing the procedure was casual and chatty. In my confused state I took this as a sign that what I was about to undergo would be no more than a minor discomfort. As he was about to begin, he asked, almost as if an afterthought, "Would you like some IV valium?" Not inclined to take drugs unless it is absolutely necessary, I answered, "Not if I don't need to."

At the end of what seemed an eternity of gagging and heaving and suffocating fear, he removed the tube and offhandedly remarked, "*No one* ever does this without IV valium."

I tell this story to illustrate the *unnecessary* physical and emotional distress patients often endure. It exacerbates the "necessary evils of illness," a term used by a stroke patient who describes his medical and rehabilitation treatment with equanimity. Although the medical world may feel like a foreign land, we shouldn't have to wonder if we are in enemy territory. Honest and patient explanations can go a long way toward defusing the alienation and fear. It shouldn't be necessary to know the answers beforehand in order to know which questions to ask.

The simple act of listening to patients also would eliminate much of the tension and misunderstanding that fog the atmosphere of medical facilities. During my examination by the gastroenterologist, I explained that, in addition to digestive problems and profound fatigue, I was having severe muscle and joint pain. Indeed, during those few days of outpatient procedures, I could barely walk through the hospital. Had he been listening, he couldn't possibly have come up with the explanation that he did: "When healthy people get sick, they feel like they 'hurt all over.' Once your digestive problems settle down, I'm sure all your other pains will go away."

The tests results were normal except for an inflamed pancreas (an exocrine organ sometimes affected by Sjogren's syndrome). The doctor concluded I had some unexplained inflammation of the pancreas that was of no cause for concern. Basically, it was the common, and maddening, "There is nothing wrong with you physically."

I do not fault this doctor for missing the diagnosis of Sjogren's syndrome. The symptoms are confusing, it is a difficult disease to diagnose, and gastrointestinal problems are not that common among Sjogren's syndrome patients. But he may have had a better chance if had been listening to me as carefully as he had gone over the laboratory reports. At the very least, he could have said, "I don't have an explanation for your symptoms. I think you should see a rheumatologist to evaluate your muscle and joint pain."

After several months of questioning my sanity, I did consult with a rheumatologist who, after several more months, accurately diagnosed my condition. I was grateful to him for his thoroughness and perseverance, but tucked in between his Sherlockian sleuthing and pedagogical explanations were also a few brief moments of personal connection that helped me feel recognized and understood.

Early on, before he had arrived at a diagnosis, he put his hand on my shoulder as I was leaving his office. He looked me in the eye and said, "This must be very hard for you to feel so awful and not have an answer. We'll keep going until we find one." I walked out of the office reflecting on the truth of a statement I had heard somewhere: "People don't care what you know as much as they want to know that you care."

After I was diagnosed, the rheumatologist and I were discussing lifestyle adjustments to a connective tissue disease. I told him I had a passion for gardening. He advised, "Just be sure to avoid awkward positions for long periods of time; after all, gardening is good for the soul." The soul? A doctor who was interested in the soul?? In *my* soul??? That was crucial information to me.

The search for and adjustment to a diagnosis are, for most people, among the more traumatic aspects of an illness. Having to acknowledge significant bodily changes is frightening, and having others investigate those changes is humiliating. And there is a strange unreality about the possibilities that must be considered. When I still had a sense of humor about it, I taped onto the refrigerator door a Gary Larson cartoon showing a man sitting on a chair facing his doctor. The man had little cows growing out of his elbows, knees, and shoulders. The caption read, "Mr. Jones, I'm afraid you have cows." The cartoon lasted only as long as my patience, which wasn't very long. "Cows" seemed about as close to a diagnosis as I was getting, and in a moment of utter hopelessness, I ripped the cartoon off the refrigerator and threw it in the trash.

The way physicians go about making a diagnosis is confusing to many people. The method, or seeming lack of one, appears haphazard: series of questionable tests, trials of medications that don't work, and frustrating about-faces. The support group members commonly grumble that "my doctor just seems to be guessing," "he keeps changing his mind," "we seem to be back where we started."

People are usually surprised to hear that there is actually a name for what their doctors are doing. As I learned from my husband Larry, it's called "differential diagnosis." I've explained to many that, although it may seem indirect, this procedure is one that doctors learn in their training; it's considered the "standard of care." By a process of elimination, they consider one by one the possible diagnoses, ordering tests and ruling out the most serious first. Where necessary, they prescribe treatment for the relief of debilitating or possibly life-threatening symptoms; such treatments are based on a "working diagnosis." It would only take a few minutes for a doctor to explain this — and would eliminate weeks and months of frustration and confusion for the patient.

Although there is an accepted protocol for arriving at a diagnosis, physicians are given few guidelines for delivering to the patient the news of a serious or life-threatening disease. Over the years there has been a shift away from "coddling" patients, withholding information they are not "strong" enough to handle, or placating them with statements like "Don't you worry, just leave everything to me." But judging from the accounts of many people who have left their doctors' offices feeling devastated by the news of their diagnoses, there has been an overreaction in the opposite direction. Assuming that their patients want "the truth," many doctors limit their explanations only to facts and statistics — that is, *scientific* truth.

Statistics, however, are based on groups of people. They don't say anything about a given individual. And no one can deny the "truth" of the remarkable cases of recovery that fly in the face of statistics. They may be rare but not as rare as we commonly think.* That always leaves room for hope. It would be wonderful if doctors diligently collected files of such cases for the illnesses that they treat, and shared this information with patients who are newly diagnosed. It wouldn't comfort just the patient; it would be encouraging to the doctor as well.

---

* *Spontaneous Remission: An Annotated Bibliography*, by Brendan O'Regan and Caryle Hirshberg (1993), is the outgrowth of The Remission Project of the Institute of Noetic Sciences (Sausalito, California). The eight-year program assembled the largest database of medically reported cases of spontaneous remission in the world, with more than 3,500 references from more than 800 journals in 29 different languages.

Giving people some hope isn't setting them up for disappointment. It doesn't mislead them about the possibility of improvement or recovery. It just *allows* for it.

A physician may "know" that a given illness has a poor prognosis. But none of us can predict a particular person's survival time as if we were discussing the shelf life of a grocery item. Human beings, with their unique combinations of biology and psyche, are more complicated than that. A physician may "know" that there is no standard Western treatment shown to alter the course of a certain condition. But many people (more than one-third of Americans, according to a 1993 survey published in *The New England Journal of Medicine*[3]) seek alternative treatments and constitute a growing number of "anecdotal" cases of remission or cure. "Western medicine has nothing to offer" gives a far different message to the patient than "Nothing can be done."

What I consider to be critical information is rarely mentioned when a patient is presented with a diagnosis: an acknowledgment of the limitations of proven science, a humility before the human variables that lie beyond the reach of even the most competent physician. Were such things discussed along with the harsh facts, physicians would be offering patients the incentive to gather the inner and outer resources that just might make a significant difference in their physical health or overall well-being. That is an integral part of good health care.

Also, communicating to patients a belief in the ability to heal, even when a cure is unlikely, is of enormous significance when delivering a diagnosis. It is an essential component of ongoing treatment as well. Unless circumstances demand it, few of us distinguish between physical health specifically and a robustness for life in general. The difference between the two may be one of the most important pieces of information a doctor can share with a patient who is seriously ill.

Patients often come away from medical appointments dizzy with information. Many of us have understandable difficulty remembering and digesting *what* was said, yet most of us retain a crystal clear impression of *how* things were said. It was "a good appointment" if the doctor listened patiently, responded thoughtfully, and acknowledged our individuality and unique circumstances by inviting our input and participation. We "feel better" after seeing a doctor who has recognized our struggles, validated our strengths, and bridged the "professional distance" with understanding and compassion. These personal qualities of a doctor should not be written off as simply "bedside manner," which sometimes has the connotation of distracting the patient's attention from inferior medical care. Rather, it is within an open and trusting relationship that a patient derives the greatest benefit from a doctor's knowledge and skills.

Are these pleas for a more personal approach and humble attitude from medical practitioners placing extra demands and unreasonable expectations on those already burdened with overwhelming practical concerns? I don't believe so. On the contrary, I suspect that much of the pressure in the medical profession has its source in the traditional assumption that doctors can never say, "I don't know," or "This is hard for both of us." It is my sense that developing a comfort with one's own vulnerability can only make it easier to accept and respond to human frailty in others.

The World of Alternatives

Although grateful that my arduous journey through the medical world resulted in a diagnosis, I was hardly won over by the scenery or ambiance. Nor did I feel much of an affinity for either the prognosis — just learn to live with it — or the treatment — drugs. Consequently, I headed into the world of alternative medicine, with its more natural setting and expansive views.

Although I am not cured of my illness, some of the alternative methods I've tried (most notably acupressure) have improved my overall health and sense of well-being. One treatment in particular (evening primrose oil) has markedly improved my symptoms. The world of alternative treatments extends across a vast territory, and the adventure through it can be overwhelming as well as vitalizing.

But it is an environment where I feel comfortably at home, where I feel a kinship with many others who "speak the same language." It is this aspect of alternative health care that I wish to explore more fully here, leaving the discussion of specific treatments to the many other available publications that cover them in depth.

If I had to isolate a single factor that draws me to alternative approaches to treating illness, it would be this: the assumption that each of us has inherent self-healing abilities that can be mobilized toward a fuller and more balanced life. This powerful premise establishes the basis for a special kind of relationship that evokes the innate wisdom and strength of the client, each of us the budding author of our own healing scripts. The health care practitioner may supply the props or provide some cues, but it is always the client who has the ultimate say in how the story unfolds.

Such a relationship is the ideal one, but it is not universal among all alternative care providers and those they treat. Overzealous "healers" frequently push themselves into the limelight, seeking top billing in the recovery dramas of their clients. Enamored with their own techniques rather than the healing capacities of their clients, such practitioners begin to bear a striking resemblance to the more rigid of their counterparts within mainstream medicine. They could be counted among those psychologist Abraham Maslow had in mind when he cautioned, "If the only tool you have is a hammer, you tend to treat everything as if it were a nail."[4]

A woman in the support group described to the members a Christmas dinner where she received a spontaneous healing: "spontaneous" not because her health improved immediately (or later, for that matter) but because the two people sitting on either side of her at the table decided, on the spot, that they would heal her with a laying-on-of-hands, right after dinner.

Beside providing a good laugh for the group, this story served as a catalyst for a thoughtful discussion about the nature of a healing relationship. Several of us in the group had experienced positive results in working with alternative practitioners. We wondered wherein lies the healing: in the practitioner? in the client? in the method? in the interaction of all three?

Although researchers are beginning to investigate these questions scientifically, at this point no one can fully explain why some people recover and some people don't. It seems we do have an inner mechanism for healing, even from devastating illnesses. Something or perhaps several somethings can activate this mechanism — and here it gets mysterious. I believe that, in spite of how meticulously we study the process, it will, to a large extent, remain a mystery, which seems "logical" to me. I have a hunch that healing comes about for each individual through a special kind of relationship that enhances the interaction of good medicine (whether conventional or alternative) and personal inner resources. My intuition suggests that the right mix of these factors is unique to each individual, as are the particular relationships that provide the right environment. I am content to trust that process without having to understand it.

It is much more difficult to explain the mechanism of a healing relationship than it is to recognize it. A wonderful "picture" of such a relationship appeared in the *Inquiring Mind* a few years ago. A radiant-looking Buddha is walking hand in hand with an wide-eyed chicken, and below the drawing is a riddle. *Question:* Why did the Buddha cross the road? *Answer:* To escort the chicken safely to the other side.[5]

I like the word escort because it connotes companionship, two people doing something in tandem. One person may be guiding the other, providing safe passage, but they are taking the path together.

I am wary, however, of the term healer when applied to health care practitioners. Ideally, it would mean someone who, regardless of the specific modality, facilitates self-healing in others: someone who reflects back to the clients their own strengths, and encourages and witnesses whatever transformations take place. Unfortunately, the word healer is often used to focus attention on the celebrated powers of a practitioner who, perhaps without the participation of the client, sets about dispensing his or her healing gift. Healing here implies one person doing something to another person, rather than two people involved in a relationship that promotes healing — in both.

Mutual healing is an inevitable by-product of a truly authentic helping relationship. When someone entrusts us with his or her pain, we recognize it as something familiar. It enters the place in us where we store our own pain, and a kind of alchemical reaction takes place. The warmth that comes from sharing pain transmutes it from something base into something precious, the human capacity to care for another.

Similarly, when we create the environment for others to stretch to their full physical, intellectual, emotional, and spiritual stature, we stand in that space with them. It gives *us* the room to move and grow as well.

Support groups are often included in the listings of alternative approaches to health care. They certainly qualify in terms of the nature of the relationships that characterize support groups in general, and in terms of the mutual healing aspect in particular. Because the only credential most of us bring to the meetings is life experience, there is no agenda other than to share that with one another. We see how we fit together. And we find if we stand close enough, none of us falls through the cracks.

I like to ask people if they see themselves as strong. Often the question takes them by surprise. Although many of us can recite a long list of ways we feel diminished by illness, few of us ever consider whether that tells the whole story. In thinking about it, many people are as surprised by their own answers as they were by the question: "Well, I guess I must be, if I'm still here," or "I never really added together all the things I've overcome. I guess I am stronger than I thought."

Sometimes the answer to the question, "Do you see yourself as strong?" starts out with a flat "no" but, after some discussion of what constitutes the "self" and what "strong" means, there is a shift. At first labeling herself as "broken," a woman came to appreciate that a broken body, all by itself, can't break the spirit. She also allowed that a shorter list of accomplishments didn't mean she was shrinking as a person.

Often I am asked what I *do* in the support groups. Perhaps hoping to hear about an exotic form of healing, some seem disappointed with my answer: "I mainly encourage the members (and they, me) to remember that we are whole. As long as we are alive, we are using our life experience, whatever that is, to reach the fullest expression of ourselves. We encourage each other to embrace life with that in mind."

I have found that if you let people talk long enough, they often come up with their own insights and solutions. Some thoughtful questions along the way may facilitate the process, but there is something about unqualified respect and undivided attention that instills confidence and invites self-exploration.

Lawrence LeShan, a psychotherapist who has worked with cancer patients for over thirty-five years, offers a remarkable account of the power of "respect for the patient's uniqueness; our encouraging him/her to grow in his/her way, not in the path of our own preferences."

> Pedro was a slim Hispanic youth of twenty. He had grown up in a devastated area of New York and joined one of the toughest gangs in New York at eleven. He loved gang life and rose in it to the highest position — "Warlord." When he was nineteen, the gang dissolved due to attrition, deaths, army draftings, prison sentences, and so forth. He could find no satisfactory substitute and within the year developed a rapidly advancing Hodgkin's disease. At that time this was a fatal syndrome, with no treatment available that did more than briefly delay the end. When I first got to know Pedro, he was in a hospital bed, going downhill and not responding at all to an experimental chemotherapy program that was later abandoned as ineffective.

> During our discussions it became clear that gang life had two special qualities that particularly appealed to him. The first was the group of men who always knew that they could depend on each other and whose relationship had been forged in periods of danger and tension. The second was the rhythm of life with its lazy periods of talk and easy pace, alternating with periods of excitement and danger. When Pedro realized that this was the life of a fire fighter, he became interested, for the first time, in the possibility of a regular job. In the hospital he began to study for the necessary high school equivalency diploma. At about the same time he began to respond positively to the chemotherapy program. He ob-

tained the diploma and, now on outpatient status, began working, with my help, on a job history, partially made up of whole cloth that would sound reasonable to an examining board. Presently, he showed no signs of Hodgkin's on x-ray examination, took the physical, passed it, and a year later went through a fire fighter's training successfully and obtained the appointment.

That was over twenty-five years ago, and there has been no sign of disease recurrence. He loves his life, is married with two children, and has upgraded his life on all levels.[6]

Pedro's medical recovery is extraordinary, but even had he fared less well physically, the story stands as an example of an exceptional "healing": a therapist who found out what made sense to his client, and together they improvised from there.

One of the main criticisms of Western medicine is its authoritative attitude. Many of us bristle at the expectation that patients should trust their doctors to make all the decisions, often without clear explanations or adequate discussion. To go blindly into an alternative treatment with a practitioner who doesn't acknowledge a client's individuality or right to information is equally undermining. And expectations about outcome always need to be open-ended; no matter how efficacious the intervention or enlightened the practitioner, none of us can "save" everyone we try to help. It is not simply for lack of belief or lack of will that some clients don't respond to treatment. They should not be intimidated or burdened with a sense of personal failure. Rather they should be applauded for their efforts.

As far back as my first day-camp experience at the tender age of five, I realized that when I hear the words, "How about if everyone," I tend not to hear the end of the sentence. We each have a different propensity for falling into step with the rest, but when we are ill — when we feel shaken to the core — most of us have a strong need to stand our individual ground. The person who is willing to remain there beside us, and to move with us when we are ready, is a true partner in healing.

Chapter 8

Family and Loved Ones

People change and forget to tell each other.
— Lillian Hellman[1]

Go Away Closer: Intimacy and Boundaries

Less than a year after my diagnosis, my husband Larry and I separated. We had been married for seventeen years, quite happily by our own account, "the perfect couple" according to others. (That label had always made us squirm.) We lived apart for almost two years, "dated" each other about half that time, and have been back together again for nine years.

During the confusing period of our separation, I remember saying to friends, "My relationship with Larry is like the coastal summer weather report: partial afternoon clearing with night and morning fog." At one moment, I would feel confident with a decision. Then a phone call or letter could bring about a total change of heart. I not only was stymied by our seeming inability to resolve the issues that had come between us; I also considered them totally unique.

The layers of history embedded in our almost thirty-year relationship are, of course, our own unique construction. They reflect, as in any relationship, the individual contributions and combined participation that become the "we" of any long-term partnership. But hindsight, conversations with others about their own relationships, and good psychotherapy have clarified some of the more common stumbling blocks that can trip up any of us as we go about building a "we." The added element of illness has the potential to dismantle a relationship entirely. It also can invite a closer collaboration, a greater commitment to do the necessary work.

Relationships are the backdrop against which we sort out our dual, seemingly conflicting, human needs for both autonomy and intimacy. (Intimacy is used here in a broad sense, referring to an emotional closeness of which sexuality is only one component). We want our personal boundaries recognized and our individuality respected. We also want to merge with others, to melt away our separateness and sense of isolation through deep and enduring connection. Although these needs are universal, we each have unique ways of balancing them and styles of achieving them. Because an illness tests commitment in a relationship so profoundly, it can fuel any already-existing fears of abandonment. Similarly, because an illness represents such an intrusion into physical and psychological boundaries, it can fuel any already-existing issues around intimacy as well.

It was clear at the outset of our relationship, at nineteen, that Larry and I had different styles. I had a greater need for solitude than he, which during our difficult times he experienced as "withdrawal." His need for togetherness exceeded mine, which during our difficult times I found "overbearing." A key factor in our reconciliation was realizing we had always wanted the same thing. Like many couples who struggle over similar issues, we both wanted intimacy but had different ideas of what that meant. For Larry it was tied to actively doing certain things together; for me, it also included just being with each other, sharing time "around the nest." Few other problems came up between us that couldn't in some way be traced back to this underlying dynamic. If someone were to ask, before I developed an illness, how we handled that difference, we would probably say with confidence, "We've learned to work around it." Looking back now on that period of time, I would have to answer, "We learned to sweep it under the rug."

The onset of my illness intensified my need for solitude. I was committed to continuing my usual activities — teaching preschool, studying piano, gardening. These things had become emblematic of my hard-won autonomy, and I was determined that nothing would have to change. Naturally, everything took longer to do because of my health limitations. And I also needed time for internal work, the inevitable soul-searching, the initiation rite of illness.

During this time, Larry's own need for togetherness also intensified. (It was a therapist who later suggested we try to see these needs as complementary rather than conflicting.) Larry didn't want things to change either. If my health limitations demanded that something would have to go, he wanted to be sure that it wouldn't be any of our time together.

My long period of denial before my diagnosis was a stressful time for both of us. Now the adjustment to the diagnosis brought a new round of problems — or, more accurately, another version of the ongoing one. The relationship wasn't working for either of us; we were both disappointed in each other and in ourselves. Whether I was reading Larry correctly or projecting onto him my own insecurities, I felt I was failing him. He, in turn, was frustrated that there seemed to be little that he could do, medically or otherwise, to "make it like it used to be."

At the time, 1986, both of us had been actively involved in the anti-nuclear movement. Publicity began appearing about the upcoming "Great Peace March," a nine-month walk across the United States to spread the message of peace and nuclear disarmament. The project immediately grabbed Larry's attention. He was deeply committed to the cause, and it also appealed to his love of adventure. He had already been thinking about a several-month sabbatical from his work and had been looking for another physician to take over his medical practice.

When Larry first told me of his interest in the Peace March, he simultaneously suggested that I could ride along in one of the support vehicles. I appreciated his desire to include me but pointed out what we both knew to be true. Even at the peak of my physical health, when I could have made the trip on foot, I still would have fared poorly. Given my particular psychological makeup, if I spent twenty-four hours a day with several thousand people, no doubt personal rather than global peace would become the pressing issue.

I also would find it hard to remain grounded in Buddha Land while bedding down each night in a different town.

I understood that Larry, however, found the challenges of the Peace March exhilarating. I encouraged him to go. Although we acknowledged it would be a strain on our relationship, we mainly skirted that issue. We comforted ourselves and each other with re-assurances that our love and commitment would override any potential problems. That did turn out to be true in the long run but certainly not in the short run.

Basically, our relationship was in trouble at the time, and we both wanted a break from it. Neither of us had the courage to face the problems squarely or suggest that we get professional help. We called it politics instead. We found a kosher way to have a separation and called it by its true name only after the fact.

Although we made some attempts to bridge the physical distance, we couldn't overcome the psychological one. Long-distance phone calls and occasional weekend rendezvous only made it more apparent — painfully apparent — how far apart we had grown. Yet something still held us to each other. We spent six months trying to determine, across the miles, whether it was love or history. Eventually, Larry left the Peace March three months early. He moved to San Francisco, a four-hour drive from Mendocino, and began to see a therapist.

Living apart was revealing. Without Larry there to assume his usual role, I had to provide my own distractions. "I bet there's a beautiful sunset," I would think. Without a moment's hesitation, I would drop what I was doing, hop in the car, and drive four miles to the ocean just to catch the last bit of color.

Larry, on his end, was still watching sunsets but dashing about much less than usual. Without me there, he was developing his own set of brakes. "I just finished repotting some houseplants," he would tell me over the telephone. At first, it took some imagination on my part to picture it.

We had an unusual opportunity to experience the deeper meaning that lies beneath the clichéd expression, "opposites attract." We came to understand that together our differences provide balance: Larry — the "motor," I — the "anchor."

When the other person in a couple expresses the underdeveloped part of our own psyche, we find it both satisfying and uncomfortable. It is satisfying because it provides a missing piece. It is uncomfortable because it's a piece of ourselves we are inclined to avoid. Individual growth and maturity is the lifelong process of befriending all the parts of ourselves. A relationship facilitates that integration process to the extent we learn to recognize and accept aspects of ourselves in the other. In the words of Jungian analyst Jane Hollister Wheelwright, "The drama of the opposites and their reconciliation is both the theme and the ideal of a true marriage."[2]

At one of the low points during our separation, the drama seemed like it could go on forever, while the reconciliation prospects appeared increasingly remote. Larry and I agreed it was time to get a divorce and went to see a lawyer. As we talked in her office, the lawyer looked deeply puzzled. About midway through the meeting she finally said, "Excuse me for interrupting all this, but WHAT ARE YOU DOING HERE?" She explained that the typical couple who comes to her for a divorce can barely stand to be in the same room together. They want to get the most they can from each other and then bolt out the door. She accurately pointed out that Larry and I, in contrast, were obviously extremely concerned about each other's well-being. In addition to being financially generous with one another, we were caring, even tender, in our interactions.

We assured this perceptive woman that ours was a firm decision and asked her to draw up the papers. Skeptical though she was, she agreed. We walked out of her office in a daze and stood for several moments in stunned silence. Taking leave of one another this time had enormous significance; neither one of us could say good-bye.

Larry had originally planned to drive back to his apartment in San Francisco. Instead we decided to go back to our house "to talk." We talked all afternoon and then decided to have dinner together. After dinner we talked some more. Larry wound up staying the night.

In the morning, we joked about whether we were having a honeymoon or getting a divorce. We opted for a honeymoon. More importantly, we made a commitment to work through our problems rather than ever allow them to split us apart. The harsh reality of divorce was our "rock bottom."

A short time later Larry moved back home. We decided to mark the event — reconsecrate our marriage — with a brief ceremony on the day of our reunion. As the date approached, we talked about how much we wanted harmony between us; we wondered if there would be a bit of "walking on eggshells" for a while.

I began saving eggshells. On the day of our ceremony, I wrapped them in a linen napkin. At our original wedding, Larry stepped on a wine glass wrapped in such a napkin. Eighteen years later, with much fanfare, we stepped on the eggshells. It signified that we were on solid ground.

We vowed to enter fully into the relationship as two vulnerable people, with some hard moments (i.e., life) ahead. My illness had exposed not only my own fragility but the fragility of our relationship at the time. We had both faltered when put to the test of "in sickness and health," "for better or for worse."

Within families and in close relationships, people often make an unspoken and unconscious agreement with each other to conceal their vulnerability. An illness insists that our common vulnerability be recognized. The integrity of the relationship demands that the original agreement be replaced by a new one that promises mutual acceptance of each other's susceptibilities as well as appreciation of each other's strengths.

As Larry and I grew more comfortable with the issue of vulnerability, we found it easier to resolve our conflict over boundaries and intimacy. When we moved back together, we invited in our "shadows." We made space for our darker sides, became intimate with them as well. The closeness and deepened trust that has grown from a more complete understanding of ourselves and one another paved the way toward greater forgiveness, flexibility, and unconditional support.

Larry and I agree that we've reversed our old push-pull cycle to work in our favor, but we disagree about the reason. It is a chicken-or-the-egg kind of debate. He says that because I am now more emotionally available generally, it gives him joy to support my periodic needs for solitude. I, on the other hand, say that because

Larry shows more sensitivity to my personal boundaries, I relish as much as he does the time we spend together. But we agree that we don't have to agree about cause and effect. We wholeheartedly concur that the relationship is working well for both of us.

Many other stories begin, "After I became ill, our relationship fell apart." Far fewer resolve as happily. Larry and I recognize that we had the luxury of time to work on our relationship. Without the added pressures of children and tight financial circumstances that many people face, we could focus on each other. I sense that many couples share the same love, history, and commitment, but run out of patience under the stresses of daily life.

It is also my sense that many of the relationships that don't survive an illness perish in battles over boundary issues. Often fuzzy to begin with, boundaries are easily confused when someone in a relationship becomes ill. Offers of help to the ill person, or requests for help from the healthy partner, may be perceived as "intrusive " or "overstepping the limits." Intimacy becomes difficult when boundaries are drawn as battle lines. "Chronic illness tends to smash people together, and then it drives them apart," writes Sefra Kobrin Pitzele in *We Are Not Alone: Learning to Live with Chronic Illness*.[3]

One way or another, illness intensifies the connection between people in a relationship. Couples often say they are "stuck with it." The "it" refers to the illness, but people may also become increasingly entrenched in unhealthy patterns of relating that predated the illness. The relationship itself is wounded; subject to continual re-injury, it can never quite heal.

Fortunately, illness sometimes has the opposite effect on relationships, as it ultimately did in my own marriage. Psychiatrist Irvin D. Yalom has observed that "cancer cures neurosis."[4] Illness can precipitate emotional healing between people as well as within them.

There is an expansive quality to the relationships that successfully adapt. They leave room for illness. Each person provides for the other a safe and accepting space to grow strong and whole. "Love...consists in this," according to poet Rainer Maria Rilke, "that two solitudes protect and border and salute each other."[5]

...once the realization is accepted that even between the *closest* human beings infinite distances continue to exist, a wonderful living side by side can grow up, if they succeed in loving the distance between them which makes it possible for each to see the other whole and against a wide sky![6]

Continuity and Change

In close families and loving relationships, much is taken for granted. We move, often unquestioningly, within established priorities, comfortable roles, and predictable patterns. Illness disrupts this familiar choreography. In the scramble to reposition ourselves in the new arrangement, few of us adjust without some loss of balance, some lack of grace. Accustomed and attached to the usual routines, we tend to resist the changes. And in relationships that were only precariously balanced in the first place, those changes expose issues we may have been dancing around for a long time.

Others naturally hope their loved ones can cure themselves quickly so things can get "back to normal." But the ill person may be moving beyond, toward horizons broader than physical health. The changed circumstances are usually less disturbing to a relationship than the changed person. Although overwhelming and exhausting to implement, the practical adaptations demanded by illness are straightforward. Responding to another's internal shifts in direction, style, and pace is a far more complicated matter.

As discussed in the second part of this book, an ill individual's personal steps toward reintegration constitute a grieving process. Ultimately, everyone close to a person with a serious illness undergoes grief, as it becomes apparent that change and loss may become a way of life. One man in the support group says, "My wife's illness shattered my idyllic vision that she and I would always be able to count on our health, and it forced on me an awareness of my own vulnerability." Yet each of us grieves in our own fashion; we cannot synchronize the rhythm and sequence of our emotions with those of another. Because of the varying patterns of grief crisscrossing a relationship, people trying to trace a path through illness together may find themselves bumping up against each other instead.

Often those in relationships affected by illness do not even identify the grieving process as the framework for the emotional upheavals that each person is experiencing. Because grief is most commonly associated with death, many assume that only a terminal diagnosis is an occasion for grief. When we become ill, those close to us rally — with much-needed assistance, advice, and reassurance as expressions of their love. It is less common that a family member or intimate friend will say, "Let's grieve together." If, together, we can acknowledge the disappointments and losses, and understand our emotions as a natural response, the connection with one another need not be added to the other losses. If we can accept that the grieving process is part of healing, of moving beyond the losses, we can join together to resurrect hope and build meaning on what remains.

Three years after an automobile accident that left Don with permanent brain damage, he and his wife Kathy decided to reaffirm their wedding vows in a ceremony at their church. "It was difficult to be married to a man who was so different from the one I had married fourteen years earlier," said Kathy. "I was confused about how to grieve because my husband had 'died' and yet he was still here. The ceremony was a public statement that I was accepting this new person as my spouse forever, that I wanted other people to join me in acknowledging and honoring the changes." Their vows were adapted from *Ecclesiastes*, "To everything there is a season": "Today our season has come. Today we remember what was, and with the breath of wisdom blow it gently in the past. Today with truth and honesty we acknowledge and accept our new growth...."

Kathy does not minimize the devastating changes that followed the accident but neither does she consider her adjustments particularly remarkable. "All along, I felt in my being what needed to be done."

Finding the Way Home

On November 13, 1984, on the eve of our fourteenth wedding anniversary, a turn of events took place, shattering all that we were or ever would be again. Returning from his routine trip to San Francisco to pick up supplies for our floorcovering store, Don's truck ran off the road and hit a tree. The load shifted and crushed him, breaking nearly every bone in his body and causing serious head and internal injuries....

...After several surgeries, he was in a coma, could not breathe without a support system, and was at risk of losing his left arm. He had lost his spleen, a third of his liver, and looked like an erector set with all the metal holding his bones together. I was numb, and with robot-like movements, moved through what felt like a twilight zone....

And then the news, the bones would mend but he would be left with permanent brain damage. He would never be the same again. To what extent they did not know, but be sure, he'd never be the same again. Devastation, pure devastation. I sunk to my knees and wept. Don was my husband, my partner, my pal, and my playmate. All that we did, we did together. It had been two months now. I was so afraid to proceed without him and quickly I realized I was without him....

For five months Don received daily therapy, and we both continued to experience the torture of such a tragic accident. Yes, Don did have brain damage, and I was overwhelmed with the change in him. After so many months, he had made no significant progress. His behavior was aggressive, and he was incontinent, unable to speak, walk or dress himself. We tried endlessly to help him rediscover himself with the aid of photographs, drawings, maps, and other aids and visits by family and friends. I would not be put off by the poor prognosis he continued to receive. I was convinced that no one knew Don like I did and that faith and time alone would bring us to our ultimate destination.

Now seven months later...we set a date and began to make ready for Don's homecoming. It was not an easy one. Numerous adjustments were needed and Don continued to tug at my heart with his changes. I missed my old Don terribly. There was a portrait of him on my dresser, and I would study it and grieve the loss of him. My new Don could not but for a minute remember what had just happened. This man who used to be able to lift a three hundred pound carpet was not yet able to walk. He was timid and clingy. I was growing weary, physically and emotionally, trying to run the business without his support and caring for his every need. He was not the man I married, and I began to fear it might not work....

Don's recuperation was painstakingly slow and my patience and fortitude were tested daily. He continued to overwhelm me with his inability to problem-solve, the loss of his short-term memory, and his physical and speech changes. I drifted mentally from the old Don to the new Don, though not intentionally. I tried to stay focused but it wasn't easy when the appearance of the man was both the old and the new. If I was having this problem, imagine how everyone else was feeling. Most everyone was rejoicing because they were witnessing the physical recovery and hadn't a clue about the extent of his brain damage. And I wore a badge of courage, implying that we were doing fine.

But Kathy also describes some changes, both in Don and in their relationship, that have been for the better. There is a kind of tender honesty that wasn't there before, and the desire to nurture it ultimately led to the decision to make a renewed commitment to their marriage.

I have a tremendous admiration for Don. He gives a far higher percentage of what he's able to give than most people do. Before the accident he was extremely shy, introverted, not terribly communicative. Now he has a gracious way of reaching out to others, even to strangers. He is more trusting and patient, and this openness has improved our relationship. We have more arguments than before, but it's healthier. We both live on the edge; there's no room to carry any false feelings.

The turning point came for Kathy when she recognized the simple yet profound care and love that had grown from their struggles together. It was a toothbrush that finally convinced her to bid farewell to the past and wholeheartedly embrace the present.

One morning I entered the bathroom and instantly spotted on the vanity my toothbrush deliberately positioned alongside of the toothpaste, ready for my use. Don had placed it there. It was a gesture of love and thoughtfulness that I had not seen since his accident. It came after so many months of providing total care to Don, still in a wheelchair, incontinent, and unable to feed himself. It was his way of telling me that I was loved and special. And now I had the faith that I could be special to this man, not as a caregiver, but as a wife and a companion. I took one last look at the portrait on my dresser before tucking it away with our mementos of the past. I resolved to build a new relationship together, as we are now.

Kathy says that she was forced to grow and learn, see and make choices, and "travel by faith more than by sight." She found the strength to do that from "the enormous presence of a divine power being transmitted through the actions of others. Clearly we were not alone; I was humbled by the outpouring of unconditional love from the church community and from friends."

Unfortunately, the grief of illness is not always so clearly acknowledged and resolved in relationships. People often grieve silently and alone, confused by their emotions and angry about their losses, overwhelmed by the present and frightened of the future. Although there may be close collaboration on practical matters, people may drift apart emotionally on separate waves of grief. Many describe an illness as something that has "moved in" on the household, forcing its way into the relationship, to some extent replacing it.

Two women in the support group, both ill themselves and with young children who are ill, say of their relationships with their husbands, "All we talk about is *stuff*." Linda has AIDS, and her children, seven and nine, are HIV-positive. Elizabeth has lupus and her three-year-old daughter has diabetes. Each of their husbands has assumed a majority of the household responsibilities. Linda's husband admits to being "tired" but verbalizes little else about how he is feeling. Elizabeth's husband is "perfect" in terms of the way he supports his family, an image of invulnerability that is his trademark. Both of these women are introspective and express their feelings openly; their husbands listen but rarely respond.

At a support group meeting Linda and Elizabeth shared their reluctance to "complain," to expect anything additional from their husbands who are already giving so much. Elizabeth described an outburst that she surprised herself with as well as her husband: "I'm tired of feeling grateful that you haven't left me!" He reassured her that she shouldn't feel "grateful"; he stayed because he wanted to. Linda, in turn, described tearfully how at Easter her husband didn't pull it off quite right and now her children know there is no Easter bunny.

The shifting of the usual roles in a household inevitably strains the relationship. Without the opportunity to discuss the feelings about such changes as well as the strategy, the relationship suffers additional stress. Each person, in his or her own way, fears a loss of identity, has lost the familiar moorings. The ill person feels helpless, removed from the normal flow of life; the helpmate feels overwhelmed, thrust into a foreign sea of responsibilities.

"When one is sick...two need help" is the motto of the Well Spouse Foundation, an organization that offers emotional support to its members, raises public awareness about the role of caregiver, and advocates for programs to address the practical and social needs of families dealing with chronic illness. The foundation's president says, "We're the people others usually look past, the people pushing the wheelchair." A support group member with breast cancer describes her own husband's sense of being "invisible":

> His "quiet resentment" accumulated as he saw an outpouring of attention and care in my direction, while my illness put everything on hold and he took over the responsibilities of our three-year-old and six-year-old sons. He was expected to be strong, really stronger than he was, and felt alone and unsupported. His men friends never spoke to him about my illness. After a group of people gathered in a healing circle for me, my husband blurted out, "Does that mean that I have to be dying to get people to pray for me?"
>
> I protested, "I'm not dying!"
>
> He said, "I just want someone to care for me."

From my own experience, and from talking with people who come to the support group with family members and loved ones, it is clear that illness makes us afraid. We fear its impact on us and on those close to us, whether we have the illness or are witness to it. Fear puts us in a survival mode, and I believe that much of the stress on relationships is the result of fear-based interactions. Wants and needs get confused, and old wounds become tender again. Control becomes an issue, and we are poised for fight or flight. Because *each* person in the relationship needs extra care, seemingly minor things can take on major importance. The differences between people tend to become exaggerated when self-preservation is at stake.

A couple attending the support group talked about their diametrically opposed perceptions of their home environment. He, characteristically quiet and slow-paced, now fatigued and in pain from an undiagnosed musculoskeletal condition, experienced their household as "chaotic." She, an extremely ambitious and energetic person, found the atmosphere "like a hospital." They each felt they were giving as much as they could and receiving little of what they needed in return.

"He who is all wound up in himself makes a very small bundle," according to an old Chinese proverb.[7] But an illness encases each person in a relationship with some degree of fear and instincts toward self-protection. It takes conscious and consistent effort on everyone's part to resist the natural pull toward self-absorption exerted by illness. I've often heard people say, "Well, it's family," or "He (or she) is like a member of the family," as if that constitutes a license granting unrestricted privileges. Certainly, the love, trust, and understanding that bond close relationships allow for acceptance and slack under difficult circumstances; we expect to be comfortable and "real" with one another rather than polite. But even when we feel overwhelmed with our own needs and emotions, either as the ill person or as a loved one, we cannot forget or ignore the needs and emotions of those close to us. Making a practice of respecting each other as distinct individuals and of nurturing our relationships with care and attention helps to establish a kind of bottom line beneath which we are less likely to slip during hard times. Even when the ill person seems to be bearing up stoically, or a loved one appears willing to give unconditionally, we all have our limits.

An illness disrupts relationships not only between spouses or partners but between parents and children as well. If a daughter or son becomes ill before the parents do, it violates our sense of the natural order of things. And it seems no matter what the chronological age, the failing health of a parent violates our cherished notion that mothers and fathers remain invulnerable. The unique bond between parent and child undergoes constant change during the years a family shares together. That bond is tested and redefined as both child and parent try to balance their coexisting needs for independence and intimacy within the relationship. We somehow assume we have infinite time to work out the details of these relationships and find it almost inconceivable when serious illness threatens the person with whom we share our closest biological connection.

The people who attend the support groups vary in age; there is also a mix of ill people and family or loved ones. Therefore, the group members have an opportunity to hear how other people's parents and children respond to illness, minus the history and emotional charge that surround our own filial relationships. I don't want my parents, at seventy-eight and eighty-five, to worry about my health. But I've become more realistic as I've listened to a woman of my parents' generation, whose fifty-year-old daughter has lupus, talk about her "mama lion" instinct. She reminds me what a tall order it is for parents to relax in the face of any risk to their offspring.

Sjogren's syndrome is an illness that has a genetic component. Present at birth, it predisposes an individual to develop the disease later in life. Not everyone with the gene marker develops Sjogren's syndrome, which seems to involve an as yet undiscovered environmental trigger, possibly a virus. This fact was explained to me at the time I was diagnosed, but I saw no reason to include it in the explanation I gave to my parents about Sjogren's syndrome. Several years later my mother had a routine history and physical from her doctor. When he asked her about diseases in the family, she told him about me and my illness. Although my mother does not have Sjogren's syndrome, a blood test came back positive for the gene marker.

Fighting back the tears, my mother told me what she had learned from her doctor. On top of being concerned about my health problems, she now felt responsible. I could, with total honesty, tell her that I had never looked at it that way. In fact, I was grateful for the genetic material I had inherited: I enjoyed wonderful physical health until the age of thirty-seven, and given the range of other diseases one could be prone to, Sjogren's syndrome was relatively mild. Furthermore, since she didn't have the disease herself, there was clearly some non-familial factor that accounted for my illness. And since my mother obviously didn't originate the gene marker but, like me, had inherited it, I asked her if she held my grandmother, or her grandmother, responsible. "Of course not," she said.

It was a tender time for both of us, and we shared some feelings about my illness in a more intimate way than we had before. She talked about how difficult it is for a mother to see her child vulnerable, and I talked about how illness had taught me how to look beyond physical vulnerability. She said it was frustrating that there was nothing she could do that would really help. I said that there was something that always helps: to focus on my wholeness, my larger self, not my physical self only, which is just a part of who I am.

When a parent becomes ill, it shifts the very ground upon which we've established our give-and-take relationship over the years. Parents take care of children as they are growing up; they do for them what they cannot do for themselves. In healthy families, there is no shame involved, no talk of being a burden. But because our culture glorifies independence and self-sufficiency, we are conditioned to see the need for help as a personal shortcoming once we are adults. For many of us, our worst fear is that we will become dependent or a burden to someone else. In that context, "being cared for like a child" is a distressful, unnatural condition. As parents, we are loathe to find ourselves in that position; as children, we find it almost unthinkable that our parents would be the ones in

214

need. Even in the closest of families, the adjustments are awkward. When the family history is a troubled one, the health problems of a parent often bring additional episodes of disappointment and misunderstanding.

Some parents are deeply hurt that their children seem too busy or self-involved to respond, "to offer even a fraction of the care and attention that was lavished on them when they were growing up." Other parents object to being "infantilized," having children they raised from birth now telling them what is best. Yet others describe children who seem to deny or ignore obvious changes, depending on their parents to function as they have in the past. "My children continue to see me as a dispenser," says one woman.

There are as many reasons for the behavior of children toward their parents as there are families. And certainly, there are selfish, demanding people in this world, and they each have parents. But beneath a seeming lack of understanding or compassion among adult children of ill parents, there is often a great deal of sadness and confusion. Many people whose parents are gravely ill describe to me a feeling of abandonment that surprises them. "I can't believe that, at the age of forty-five, I feel like an 'orphan'." When my husband Larry received the news that his father had died, he was standing next to his older brother, Robin. He fell into Robin's arms and sobbed, "Oh, Daddy." He had not called his father "daddy" since he was a small child. I sensed I was watching a little boy who had lost his young father, not a grown man whose frail father had come to the end of his life.

In addition to this underlying resistance to seeing our parents as vulnerable, there are the strategic problems of responding to an ill parent. Three generations living under one roof as an extended family has become the exception rather than the norm in our society. People are torn, or stretched, between two households, often separated by many miles. They feel "sandwiched" between the responsibilities of partner and/or parent and that of daughter or son. For this reason, many people face the difficult decision of having a parent move in with them, and the reluctance is often on both sides. It is an arrangement that requires solid commitment, continual flexibility, and "an ever-present sense of humor," according to

215

two women I know — one taking care of her elderly father in her home, the other living with her children.

A friend whose mother recently died describes her years of care-taking her mother as "an opportunity to learn more about each other." No matter what our relationships are like with our parents or with our children, no matter what decisions are made about how much caregiving responsibility can be realistically assumed, we can always learn more about each other, and about ourselves. And there is usually some healing in the process.

For Linda, the challenge of accepting illness into the family is triple-fold. Three years after she learned that she and both of her children are HIV-positive, Linda began a newsletter. She calls it *Diary from a Mother in the Time of the Plague*; in it she shares how she and her family are learning to live with their "pet monster, 'HIVI'."

> I refuse to let the trauma of HIV in my family be without some ecstasy. I know dark clouds have silver linings. Now I embrace it as a mantra which inspires me to live with curiosity and passion.
>
> Our gift from HIV is that it forces us to live today. Whether we have enough "rehearsal" time, preparation time, or time enough to live at all, is inconsequential. Our point of power is always in the moment. There comes a moment once. God help us if we're too chicken to live it!

Because Linda's family believes that "it's fear that creates a life-threatening situation more than just the presence of HIV," they are all involved in AIDS/HIV education programs. She writes in her newsletter, "Treat our kids like the normal kids they are." The need for education became painfully apparent when parents began withdrawing their children from the preschool attended by her son (whom she describes as "fearless, like a baby samurai"). Of her nine-year-old daughter, she writes, "Alora feels that part of her mission on earth is to educate you so you needn't live in fear.... Alora can assist your children by telling her version of the 'HIVI' story."

Linda contracted the virus before her marriage to her husband, who is HIV-negative. Both he and Linda speak in the public schools and at community forums on AIDS awareness. After hearing Linda on a panel of HIV-positive adults who participated in a high school symposium, a student named Kyala Shea wrote the following for a local newspaper:

> One of the panel members in particular spoke with such warmth and honesty, and was so convincing of her conviction in herself, her sexuality and her husband, I could not escape the feeling that presumptions were being dispelled even as she spoke. Her endearing personality broke my heart; she could have been my mother, could have been me in thirty years if I turned out so well.[8]

As Linda's symptoms increase and she's able to do less, she describes her connection with her family with an air of bittersweetness.

> Alora and I are working on a science project together. The whole family put in the veggie garden yesterday. My time with them is precious. I don't want to waste a drop. I see how different my time is than other people's. I want to feel I've gotten as much time and fun with my kids as possible. We're working on our memories — all of us.

If, as Linda suggests, we work on creating memories with the people closest to us, it keeps our attention on each other and what is still possible, rather than on the illness and expectations from the past. *What* we do is not what connects us; what counts is that we are together.

We can truly be together only if we are communicating. Understandably, attention is often focused on the external details concerned with illness at the expense of the internal realities of the individuals involved. But unless we allow ourselves the "luxury" of talking with one another from the heart, we cannot hope to resolve the inevitable strains and problems inherent in life with illness. We may begin to nurture the illness instead of one another, become angry with each other instead of at the circumstances. The growing separation may ultimately be more unhealthy to the relationship than the illness itself.

Few of us are expert communicators, even under the most favorable conditions. When something like an illness creates extra demands on relationships, the ability to express ourselves becomes, at once, especially difficult and especially important. An essential component of communication skills is the willingness to shift perspective, to put oneself in the other's place. Through the give-and-take of open and honest conversation, each person gains a deeper appreciation of the fact that present roles could easily be reversed. That awareness helps us to forgive each other — for having an illness, for being human in our responses.

Communication

Martin Luther King, Jr., didn't create the racial problem in the South by talking about it. He called attention to it in order to draw people together to address the suffering. Similarly, talking about illness doesn't give it more life; words help clarify the experience, make it easier to share.

The goal of communication is understanding and connection: to understand and connect with our own feelings and the feelings of those close to us. By talking and listening, we come to know the two things that ultimately will carry a relationship through an illness: that we are understood and that we matter.

As Henry David Thoreau said, "It takes two to speak the truth — one to speak and another to hear."[9] The "truths" of illness are difficult to speak about and difficult to hear. People vary widely in terms of how quickly and how deeply they can plunge into discussions about such intimate and life-altering issues. These differences are to be respected. Sometimes the ill person is eager to talk, and loved ones respond with discomfort or silence. Other times these roles are reversed.*

---

* Although the patterns are thankfully beginning to change, men and women in our culture typically have different styles of communicating. Women talk to share feelings and be close; men talk to trade information and problem-solve. This vast subject,

I remember well the moratorium I declared on any discussion of my health problems at the onset. I still have periods of time when I grow too weary of dealing with my illness to talk about it. Yet during my most insecure moments, I also engage my husband Larry in overly long inquiries into how he is *really* feeling about my illness, the changes in me, the limitations on our life together.

Many seek out support groups because of thwarted attempts to share the inner experience of illness with those closest to them. Cindy says, "It is where I can go in and say, 'I just don't feel like life is worth living.'"

> ...people will talk about how they have felt suicidal from time to time. And it's okay to talk about it there. At the time I felt that way, I had a partner, but I was not able to talk to him about my feelings — it would have upset him too much, and he would have been too concerned about me.[10]

Another man attending the meetings became increasingly frustrated with his "upbeat" family toward the end of his father's life: "My father is close to death, and both he and my mother act as if it's not happening. We're losing a precious opportunity to be close as they carry out this charade." Under such circumstances, one individual's need to approach painful realities with caution is as valid as another's need to face them head on. These divergent approaches each reflect an attempt to integrate the experiences and emotions in a way that feels tolerable, manageable. We can't expect others to match our personal styles of exploring, sharing, or expressing emotion. But we can offer an invitation: "I have many thoughts and feelings about what is happening that I would like to share with you. I understand and respect your wishes not to do so right now, but any time you are ready — to listen or to talk —

---

beyond the scope of this book, is explored in Deborah Tannen's *You Just Don't Understand: Women and Men in Conversation,* and in many other books as well. This gender difference often, but not always, is a significant factor in the communication problems and misunderstandings that develop around illness.

please let me know." Such a gentle invitation is both honest about one's own needs and also respectful toward another's. There is often a great deal of fear behind the reluctance to talk about painful issues, and a non-threatening approach is more likely to encourage a dialogue.

It is natural to want to protect those we care about. Out of a concern that the full implications of a diagnosis or prognosis would be "too much to handle" for a loved one, ill people may downplay the facts, or mask the pain or fear they are feeling: "I share very little about my illness with my father. He has a weak heart." Sometimes family members conspire to shield the "whole truth" from the person with an illness, to spare him or her from additional worry: "My husband has never liked delving into things or dwelling on things that are unpleasant. I figure the less he knows about what might be in store for him with diabetes, the better. Although I'm scared myself, I don't let on." But an atmosphere of secrecy in an intimate relationship leaves everyone on their own, just at the time we need each other the most. The closeness and trust created by an open exchange of thoughts and feelings are, in fact, what help us cope with things that are hard. Genuine connections with others fortify our inherent strength to absorb difficulties and participate in the decisions that directly affect our lives.

Being honest, however, doesn't mean violating the rights of each person to process information and emotions at their own pace. It means taking cues from one another and finding a comfort zone, an area of trust and safety, in which to have a sensitive yet forthright exchange. This comfort zone is often the entry way toward the deeper, more intimate soul-searching that draws people together on an odyssey through illness. Finding that comfort zone is largely a matter of paying attention, close attention, to what we hear and what we say.

A friend and I had a conversation about the power of words. We agreed that it is easy to become casual about the way we listen and the way we speak. We both know people who show minimal regard for the art and skill involved in good communication. "It's just words," they say. My friend is a gifted artist and craftsman and is adept as well as careful in the use of the wide range of tools he employs in his work. I reflected on the fact that words are tools. "Power tools," he added. Like any other tool, words have the potential both to create a beautiful effect and to do a great deal of damage.

Don't our relationships deserve as much attention as any material creation or work of art? Shouldn't we handle the tools of communication with as much respect and care as tools designed to achieve material ends? "Just words" is one of the main ways we have to share our humanity. The commitment to listen with concern and respond with sensitivity is the ultimate way we can honor one another.

Listening is not a passive process, not if our intention is truly to hear the other person, to understand deeply the thoughts and feelings carried by the words. There are critical actions we need to take in order to be present to receive another person. The act of listening is much like meditating; it is serious business that requires full attention, one-pointed concentration, and an unwavering concern for the task at hand.

Creating the space to listen is the most essential aspect, and in some ways the hardest. To experience the world of another, we must temporarily empty ourselves. By quieting the inner chatter, we hear the other person's voice rather than our own. By clearing the mind of interpretations, judgments, and agendas, we listen to the whole symphony of thoughts and feelings being played, not just the selected parts that harmonize with ours. A woman returned from an extended stay with her elderly parents and credited the support group experience with her increased ability to listen: "I realized how different it was this time. I could really hear what they were saying because I was listening with my heart wide open, not filled with what I expected or wanted to hear."

Our brains work more rapidly than our tongues. As we listen to someone speak, our minds have the time, and usually the inclination, to fill in the blank spaces. Ideally, we are reflecting on what we just heard, but often this is not the case. Personal concerns, unrelated to those under discussion, may intrude. Pulled along these sidetracks, we find we are no longer together with the other person on the same train of thought: "When I try to talk to my daughter about fears that my upcoming checkup will show a recurrence of my cancer, she seems more concerned about how driving me to the appointment will affect her busy schedule." We all know people who say, "I have such a terrible memory; it's amazing how quickly I forget what someone has just told me." I don't find it that amazing. In my experience, these are often the same people whose eyes glaze over frequently during a conversation, their attention obviously elsewhere. They can't remember what they haven't heard in the first place.

The point of listening is to hear another. The time to formulate our responses is after the other person is finished speaking. But many people listen for opportunities to insert their own ideas. Although it may not be a literal interruption, a string of questions can push the conversation in a different direction; a running commentary on the speaker's thoughts and feelings may block their full expression. Giving feedback is important and helpful, it is part of being a good listener. But if it is premature, it can be disruptive as well as inappropriate. Hearing a person out to the end of what he or she has to say gives us additional information; it may change the nature of our feedback — or our sense that feedback is even necessary: "I'm reluctant to tell my partner that I'm having a bad day. I barely get the words out, and she begins her 'you'd feel better if' tape. She doesn't listen long enough to find out I've already tried most of the things she's suggesting." In an article about the needs of people in grief, the author quotes a clergyman: "...we have two ears and only one tongue. Therefore, we should listen twice as much as we speak."[11]

When we empathize, we reflect on how we might feel in another's place. This naturally awakens in us any similar emotions or parallel circumstances we may have personally experienced. As we listen to someone's story, it is tempting to tell our own. It creates a bond, lets the other person know we understand. As with other responses, it is important not to steer the conversation away from the person's current concerns. It is one thing to say, "Parts of what you are describing are familiar to me. I'd like to tell you about my experience later." It's another to say, "Boy, the same thing happened to me," and immediately launch into the full account. The first response indicates a sincere desire to identify with the other person and, at the same time, a deep respect for the individual's uniqueness. The second response reveals a short-lived interest in the other person and a superficial understanding of his or her circumstances.

A peaceful, receptive listener communicates care, understanding, and acceptance. Such a person is like a sturdy vessel, trustworthy and spacious enough to hold our individual truths in safekeeping. In that presence, even silences are honored, as needed time to reflect, not awkward interludes to be filled. "An angel passed" is what Chilean people say of such quiet moments, according to author Isabel Allende.[12]

"Finding the right words" is a matter of looking in the right places. The place to start is the heart. Sharing the questions — the questions within the questions — rather than providing answers often nourishes the deepest connection between people whose lives are disrupted by illness. The search for wise interpretations or helpful advice is an understandable but frequently misguided quest. A linear approach to illness-related problems bypasses the curves of conversation that bring people to their own — therefore authentic — insights and solutions. The questions we ask are often more significant than the statements we make.

Some questions gently lead people deeper into territory they have already begun to explore. This kind of inquiry encourages clarification, elaboration, reflection: What is the hardest part of this for you? Are your struggles concerned more with fear of the future or your present circumstances? What changes can you think of that would help you feel more confident and in charge of your life? Such questions communicate a respect for the individual priorities and inner resources of the other person. Questions of a pushing or probing nature, however, violate personal boundaries: When are you going to ask for help? How do you expect to feel well if you don't take better care of yourself? Why haven't you joined a support group? This aggressive form of concern can leave one feeling intimidated, cross-examined, judged.

Knowing how to respond in a discussion about sensitive issues becomes a complicated task only when the mind enters with theories and agendas that separate us from each other, and ourselves from our intuition. We don't need to *know* anything to show that we care. We merely need to ask ourselves, "What would I want to hear if the roles were reversed?" I personally would rather hear "I don't know what to say," rather than a hollow phrase or empty reassurance. It is an honest response that communicates, along with *real* feelings, an appropriately humble respect for the uniqueness of another's experience and the enormity of his or her challenges.

Initiating discussions about sensitive issues requires as much thought and attention as listening or responding. Illness is a large and difficult subject; a careful choice of words, good sense of timing, and some skill at editing are helpful if we want our words to have a full and sympathetic hearing. A detailed and exhaustive account of everything we are thinking and feeling can easily wear out even the most devoted family member or intimate friend. So can reruns of discussions about tired issues. Bringing up *any* issue at a time when the other person is feeling unusually weary, vulnerable, or preoccupied is unlikely to result in a satisfying dialogue. In healthy relationships, some compromise can usually be reached: "My husband is fine about having one of our 'marathon talks,' as long as I give him twenty-four hours notice," says a support group member. Support group meetings, individual counseling, journal-keeping, and letter-writing all offer healthy outlets, beyond our usual circle of confidants, for a pressing need to talk.

Effective communication requires the ability to be assertive. For many, myself included, illness has been a catalyst to learn more straightforward ways of expressing needs and priorities. A failing body instills a sense of urgency about taking care of oneself; ignoring or minimizing personal concerns becomes a habit too dangerous to perpetuate.

Since she developed Lyme disease a few years ago, Nedra has been trying to be more forthright with others about what she can and cannot do. Having spent her whole life in the same small town, Nedra had always made herself available to a large network of family and friends. She has explained to them the nature of Lyme disease and her limitations, but the message has not gotten across. Her "911" reputation has been hard to live down. Ideally, Nedra's telephone would be ringing off the hook with offers of help rather than requests. However, this hasn't been the case. She is finding that she can't change other people's patterns; she can only clarify her own position.

Assertive behavior claims our legitimate right to have our needs and priorities, along with those of other people, acknowledged and respected. Aggressive behavior, however, violates the rights of others, and it usually provokes a counterattack or defensive stance in return. Language that is aggressive sabotages communication. The specific issues are likely to get lost in an avalanche of global condemnations — "you always," "you never." When we lose our tempers, we usually lose the possibility of hearing or understanding each other as well.

The simplest and wisest advice I've ever heard for restoring connection and understanding between two angry people comes from Thich Nhat Hanh. I personally have tried it and it works. He suggests that each person ask the other, "Do you think I understand you?"[13] The answer, of course, in the heat of an argument, will be a resounding "no!" But this mutual invitation puts a halt to the cycle of accusations and shifts attention to the real issue. The identified goal is to understand and be understood, not to be right.

Communication under difficult circumstances such as illness often requires listening "between the lines," decoding the spoken word for hidden meanings. A woman describes her family as extremely verbal and articulate — except when it comes to discussing her cancer. "Then we struggle to understand each other as if English were a second language." Sometimes comments that land like a painful blow are merely a reflection of the pain and grief of the person uttering them. The message sent is not always the message received. Many ill people are deeply hurt when a loved one says, "I can't believe this is happening to me." They feel disregarded, that their own suffering is being discounted. "I'm the one with the illness," is a common retort.

An illness does happen to everyone in a relationship. If that comment were rephrased, "happening to us," it might land more softly. And there would be more understanding and compassion if the underlying feelings were also verbalized: "I'm scared, I'm confused, I'm worried I'm not strong enough to handle this."

"You *look* good" is a comment that many ill people take as a mixed message. At one of the support group meetings, several people described their irritation with this "double-edged compliment." The wife of a man gravely ill listened intently but looked confused. I asked what was puzzling her. "Well, some days my husband looks better than others. I like to let him know that, and that I notice. Is that wrong?" she asked.

Why are ill people almost allergic to the words "You *look* good"? It is an ambiguous statement that can have several interpretations. Most of them leave a person feeling dismissed. It may mean "You must be cured if you look that good" or "You can't be as sick as you say you are." The implication here is that the other person is a better judge of good health, and that the ill person's credibility is subject to question. Another interpretation of "You *look* good" is "I don't want to take the time to hear how you really feel; I'll just short-cut the conversation by saying you look fine." Or "You represent human vulnerability to me; I'm too uncomfortable with pain and suffering to get close or learn the truth."

As the puzzled woman in the support group pointed out, sometimes, maybe much of the time, "You *look* good" means simply that. It is an attempt to connect, not to create distance. "So what should I say to him?" asked the concerned wife.

"You look good; how do you *feel*?" is what the group came up with. The compliment is communicated, but the ill person's reality is also validated. That makes all the difference in the world.

As I was writing this section on communication, I wondered why I had ventured so far into the territory of basic communication skills. But when I reflect on my own experience and the experiences others have shared with me, I keep coming back to the same conclusion: Some of the most painful moments of living with illness are the ones spent lost in the thicket of miscommunication, in search of understanding, of a way out of the isolation.

Sometimes things that seem so obvious are difficult to implement. This is certainly true of communication skills. It is also true of friendship and helping relationships. We undervalue the small, simple interactions that are the very substance of life.

Chapter Nine

Friendship and Helping Relationships

> If I am not for myself, who will be?
> If I am only for myself, what am I?
> If not now, when?
>
> —Rabbi Hillel[1]

Counting on Each Other

A loyal friend is someone we can count on. For what? In the shadow of illness, the outlines of friendship can become fuzzy. Commitment, companionship, assistance take on a different cast. Friendships often pale under a cloud of uncertainty about expectations. Sometimes they disappear altogether, unable to transcend the darkness and fear.

The fear is "too much responsibility"; the darkness is "too much pain." Someone who is frightened off by the illness of a friend somehow assumes that a relationship with the illness must now replace the relationship with the person. The concern is that everything will be different. Interactions will be based exclusively on need and assistance rather than love and companionship, tragedy and grief rather than hope and healing. Alice, who has liver disease, watched one of her closest friends withdraw right after her diagnosis. They had a conversation at that time in which Alice shared some of her feelings. "I find that illness is isolating," she told her friend, who then immediately stopped calling.

Her friend later explained, "I thought you were saying you wanted to be left alone." But it turned out to be more than a misunderstanding. Alice's friend ultimately told her that if she became seriously ill, she couldn't continue in the friendship. Having grown up with a brother who had hemophilia, she needed to keep her distance from disease and hospitals.

Without stopping to consider "What is being asked?", friends of an ill person may become wary they will be drawn in too deeply, called upon too often, expected to be too strong. "I've got a life of my own," they reason. In healthy friendships, the ill person is not asking a friend to sacrifice his or her life, only to continue sharing it. I look to my friends for unconditional love and acceptance, not unconditional help. And I can, even with an illness, offer that in return. The mutual give-and-take woven into any genuine relationship may take a different pattern when one member becomes ill. But it is unlikely to unravel as long as each person expects what is reasonable and gives what is comfortable.

Isolation is one of the most toxic aspects of illness. In keeping the relationship alive and healthy, a friend is helping restore the ill person's own sense of vitality and well-being. Being ill excludes us, in ways both obvious and subtle, from normal intercourse with the larger community. Meaningful personal friendships help lift that psychological quarantine, lead us back from the hinterland.

I recently drove a friend named Lindsay home from the hospital. She was recovering from major surgery. Generally in excellent health, she had undergone a hysterectomy to alleviate symptoms of endometriosis. Lindsay was exhausted from the operation, nauseous from the drugs, in pain from the incision, and uncomfortable with the catheter. On the way home we stopped at a pharmacy. She waited in the car while I picked up her prescriptions. When I returned she said, "I've been sitting here watching all these people move around effortlessly, with plenty of energy and bodies that work. The kind of things I'm thinking about now are probably the last thing on their minds. I feel like I'm worlds apart."

I knew what she meant, and *she* knew that I knew what she meant. A sensitive and devoted friend, Lindsay had "sat in the parking lot" with me on many occasions. I always felt her empathy and appreciated her willingness to accompany me through difficult times. Now I had the opportunity to enter her own private place of pain that was "worlds apart." It deepened our relationship, brought a new level of intimacy.

The climate of illness is characterized by a wide range of conditions and unpredictable shifts. In describing the reaction to her diagnosis of HIV, Linda says, "I feel I'm watching a tornado moving through my friends." For a friendship to adapt successfully, both people need to be flexible and mature. Some friendships weather illness but to a limited degree. They tend toward one extreme or the other, either letting the issue of illness dominate the relationship entirely or allowing it hardly any space at all.

There are several reasons for this lopsided response to an ongoing illness. One explanation is that physically healthy people are more familiar with acute medical conditions than chronic ones. They are inclined to respond as one would to an infection or injury that resolves with treatment. When an illness fluctuates or progresses instead, it creates discomfort and confusion.

A friend who sincerely wishes that we "get well soon" may direct conversations and interactions exclusively toward symptoms and treatment. "Although I greatly appreciate my neighbor's concern and generosity, after a point I feel like we are discussing whether my eyes are still blue," says a woman who has had arthritis for thirty years. Friends who have been ill for only short periods of time often try to squeeze an ongoing, systemic illness into that limited frame of reference. They eagerly share information about the remedy that worked wonders for a bad cold or a pulled muscle. During the flu season, the "how I cured myself" conversations become epidemic. I distinguish those superficial comparisons, however, from the heartfelt and humble concern of friends who say, "I thought about you when I was sick with the flu. I realize you feel like that much of the time."

Disease is a medical condition; illness is the human experience of it. Another reason that friendships become overly-focused on the unwell part of the person with the illness is the assumption that disease and illness are one and the same. A disease causes symptoms and discomfort. We try various treatments or turn to health care providers to relieve the *pain*. Our friends and loved ones, however, can relieve the *suffering*, the loss of connection, of meaning, of hope. "When people get stuck on your symptoms, they patronize you, write you off as less than whole," says Judy. "But I'm still up for living."

While some friends seem to relate only to physical limitations, other friends appear to forget them entirely. They avoid any discussion of illness or else make light of its impact. They have unreasonable agendas and register surprise when the ill friend cannot meet those expectations. The support group members are frequently frustrated with the seeming inability of a friend to remember, after repeated explanations, why certain things are difficult or impossible for them to do: "My well friends don't distinguish between 'won't' and 'can't,'" is the way one person sums it up. Linda finds it a continual challenge to respond to the stream of out-of-town friends who want to visit her, most of whom never consider that houseguests might be a problem to someone who has AIDS and two children who are HIV positive. "Although everyone offers to help out, and *sometimes* they actually do, few of my friends offer to stay elsewhere. I'm learning to be very direct. It's strange. People want to spend time with me because they think I'm dying, yet they have a hard time understanding that I feel *sick*. They have no idea how much time and energy illness takes."

Why do friends so often overshoot the mark, either denying the realities of illness, on the one hand, or focusing on them exclusively, on the other hand? I believe the reason underlying both of those responses is the same: It is more difficult to accept pain and vulnerability into our immediate circle of experience than to try to eliminate it. We want either to fix it or push it away. The friendships that continue to thrive "over the long haul" are the ones where both people are willing to acknowledge and share the uncertain nature of human existence, to face the inevitability of personal pain, loss, grief, and mortality. "Illness separates out those who care from those who don't," say some who feel abandoned by certain of their friends. Although that is sometimes the case, I believe there is also another explanation: It separates out those who can handle pain from those who can't.

Author Reynolds Price, paralyzed by a spinal cord tumor in 1984, describes a cocktail party where he was sharing perspectives with another man in a wheelchair. The other man leaned over to tell him, "I consider all these people who are walking around to be 'temporarily abled.'"[2] That is an uncomfortable truth brought home by the illness of someone close to us.

"How are you?" becomes rather like a trick question to a person living with an illness. We must quickly assess if the person is referring specifically to our physical health and whether we are interested in discussing it, at that moment or with that individual. Most people who live with illness develop a unique way of negotiating around that question, usually some compromise between total honesty and personal comfort. I privately reword "How are you?" to "I've been thinking about you; do you feel like filling me in on what's been happening?" I find it easier to respond to the second question. I can acknowledge the person's concern and still have the freedom to determine how much and which part of my circumstances to share.

In our awkwardness around the question "How are you?", we too can overshoot the mark. We may assume that the individual inquiring wants an extensive report on our physical and emotional adjustments to illness. Too much detail or bad timing can stretch the patience of even the most devoted friend, let alone a caring acquaintance or concerned co-worker. "No one wants to hear an 'organ recital,'" cautions one of the support group members.

Too much caution, however, causes a credibility problem. Many of us who live with illness respond to "How are you?" with an automatic "fine." We create a pleasing social surface that belies the symptoms and limitations that underlay our daily existence. When I announced that I was closing my preschool because of health problems, the parents of the children were surprised, confused and, in some cases, incredulous. I had done my best to hide my symptoms for the first few years of my illness and had obviously succeeded.

I was, in turn, surprised, confused and, in some cases, incredulous at their responses. Some suggested I could continue to operate the school if I only adjusted the hours, got more help, scaled down the curriculum. Although I appreciated the compliment embedded in their strong desire to have me remain the teacher of their children (I had checked to make sure that other good preschools had openings), I wanted them to take me at my word. It was too difficult, too late. I had already been pushing myself to the limit for three years. With hindsight, I've come to appreciate that it is challenge enough for physically healthy people to imagine day-to-day existence with an illness, even when given complete and accurate information. Withholding information makes the moment of truth that much more difficult to comprehend.

My cover-up story is not unique. I've asked people in the support groups if they feel their friends and acquaintances understand how illness affects their lives. Many people who say "no" acknowledge that the reason is their own reluctance to discuss it: "I don't want people to see me differently or treat me differently." Others say they don't bother trying to explain because "no one else can really understand." Almost all of us have encountered those who *think* they understand, based on limited experience with something only vaguely similar to a chronic, systemic illness. Few of us are inclined to share much information with someone who quickly assures us, "I know *just* how you feel."

Intended to establish a connection, that statement usually has the opposite effect. It makes most people cringe. Drawing parallels between the inconveniences of a sprained ankle and the adjustments to living with multiple sclerosis does not indicate a depth of understanding. Recovering from a strenuous backpacking trip does not feel "exactly" like living with a connective tissue disease. A systemic, possibly progressive disease that potentially can affect every organ in the body whispers doubts and fears not appreciated by those suffering from "low energy." Comparisons that trivialize or invalidate the life-altering changes of illness feel abrasive. They wear away at the self-esteem we work so hard to preserve. They smooth over the personal mark we make on our circumstances, rub against us like sandpaper.

Someone who *has* undergone an experience similar to ours is probably the least likely to say, "I know just how you feel." That person recognizes that beneath familiar circumstances lies a private, individual world of illness. Others may visit that place, but they can never truly inhabit it. The friend who understands and re-

232

spects those boundaries is more likely just to listen and *then* say something like "I am thinking about my own experience to try to imagine what it must be like for you." That communicates a humility and respect that is missing from the response of the person who immediately evaluates our situation and "knows" all about it.

The issue of boundaries between friends comes up literally as well as figuratively. We each characteristically seek differing amounts of solitude and company, depending on where we fall along the continuum of introvert/extrovert. Illness, like any other intense emotional experience, tends to intensify our typical inclinations. Extroverts are comforted by the steady presence of others; introverts may find the same degree of social interactions overwhelming.

I have always cherished my friendships, even more so since I became ill. I consider my friends an integral and essential part of my life as well as of my healing. Yet, ironically, when I am feeling my lowest, I am least desirous of company. This is no reflection on my friends. If the healing goddess herself turned up at my door on those occasions, I would probably say, "Not now. Please come back another time."

Many would respond quite the opposite: "Do come in. And please bring all your friends." These people find visits a welcome distraction from their health problems. I welcome visits too, but only up to a point. At the times my health problems are most severe, *they* distract me from the person who is visiting. My friends warmly reassure me that they are just offering their company and expecting nothing in return. But I find it unsatisfying not to be present for people I deeply care about, and exhausting to try.

Those who feel differently are more at ease integrating their friends into the ebb and flow of illness. Their "off" times are not also "off limits." I've questioned my own degree of privateness and talked with many who have feelings similar to mine. We seem to have a different way of shifting gears. We operate "manually"; it takes more time, more energy, more thought to make the transitions that others make "automatically." We can't internally process what is happening and simultaneously share it with others. We need a bit more space. I was reassured by a therapist that an introvert is a legitimate way of being, not a pathological state. "And the sign of a true introvert," he explained, "is the need to be alone at times of stress."

Even the most outgoing people I've spoken with say that since developing an illness, they spend more time alone — by choice. Solitude functions as a cocoon, a place to undergo the necessary inner changes that can only happen in private. Some solitude is necessary for self-reflection and creative work; it is an opportunity to increase our connection with ourselves. Linda yearns to spend time in her studio, to draw, to paint, to write, just to think, as a way of making peace with AIDS. In a fair imitation of Greta Garbo, she likes announcing in a low, dramatic voice, "I vant to be alone."

Solitude is different, however, from isolation. Isolation leads to self-absorption rather than self-expansion. It narrows our perspective and widens our distance from others. The difference between solitude and isolation is not just the amount of time we spend alone; it is also a matter of the quality of that time. Solitude is time used productively. We emerge from a period of solitude feeling nourished and better able to go back into the world. Isolation is an escape. We are emotionally unavailable not only to others but to ourselves. A period of isolation leaves us depleted rather than replenished.

How is a caring friend to distinguish the times an ill friend needs solitude from the times he or she has slipped into isolation? How does one offer one's presence without being intrusive? Asking "How are you feeling about company these days?" elicits not only a "yes" or "no" but also the thoughts and feelings behind it. The question "Do you like having people drop by?" is never intrusive as long as any answer is acceptable. An open-ended offer to visit "when it is a good time" is like a gift placed under the Christmas tree. It is a reminder of someone's love, a present carefully selected, waiting to be opened.

As one woman put it, "A friend is willing to hold your hand, even when your hand is in your pocket." This is not to suggest that the terms of a friendship be dictated only by the needs of the ill person. We have to make room in our "pocket" for that generous hand, to satisfy our appetite for solitude and still feed our friendships. I try to thank my friends for the slack they allow me in the same way I would thank them for stopping by to visit. And when I am feeling energetic and sociable enough to get together, I am happy to adapt to their needs and schedules, rather than expect that they continue to adjust to mine.

Friends who sensitively accommodate to one another, rather than have agendas for one another, can usually make whatever shifts are necessary and still remain close. It requires a kind of peripheral vision, careful attention to the context of the situation, the history of the relationship, and the contours of the personalities. There are no simple, straightforward solutions that can be stretched to fit all people, in every circumstance, across time.

Honoring that truth paves the way toward a common ground between ill people and those who care about them. Mutual respect, honest dialogue, heartfelt compassion, and sound intuition all help establish the parameters of that meeting place. But because we are human, we inevitably go awry on occasion. We need to allow each other some latitude, a comfortable margin of error.

I occasionally meet up with a woman in the post office who always makes a point of coming over to me to "discuss" my health. She invariably says, "I can tell just by looking at you if you are having a good day or a bad day, and I can see that this is a good day." (Some days the verdict is "bad.") She takes my hand and smiles warmly at the end of this "conversation," and seems pleased to be reaching out and so "in tune" with me and my circumstances.

This woman isn't asking for a response, so I just smile back and collect my mail. I could ask her how she determines the state of my health in a split second, or I could tell her how often she has guessed wrong. But why? Would it be helpful either to her or to me? Because I anticipate her comment when I see her coming, I now find it amusing rather than irritating, which I did at first. I try to appreciate it as her way of showing concern. Some individuals reveal a wealth of insight and sensitivity in their responses to people who are ill, but they are relatively rare. Toward those with fewer resources, I have adopted an attitude borrowed from a support group member. She translates from Yiddish a favorite saying of her grandmother: "Don't look for fifty cents where there is only a quarter."

Not all awkward encounters around illness strike people as humorous, well-intentioned, or innocuous. People are often deeply hurt by comments that seem inexcusably thoughtless or heartlessly cruel. That such people are "doing their best" seems questionable. A woman with asthma tells of a friend who likes asking her, "Why do you need your asthma?"

"I feel like saying, 'Actually I don't. Would *you* like it?!'"

Many of the comments are like braids of accusations / presumptions / judgments, twisted into various patterns: "I know someone who has exactly what you do, and he's doing great. He gets out and goes, instead of giving in." Less visible, but also deeply woven into these pointed remarks, are strands of ignorance and fear. As a culture, we respond to vulnerability, illness, aging, and death with aversion. We find them threatening and keep our distance; the less we know the better. It is from that dark void of fear and ignorance that hurtful ideas and words are shaped and directed toward those who are ill.

I consider the people I find most difficult my Dark Angels. They carry a message and deliver it with a hard blow to my most vulnerable spots. I have no choice but to heed the call, to pay attention to where I am hurting and why. My friend Kate wrote a poem about these unsparing teachers, without whom "we are doomed to fail / knowing who we are...your Dark Angel will tell you / the thing you love most / by naming the thing you fear." The thing I fear is losing my integrity. I fear my illness will make me less than whole. When my Dark Angels suggest that this is true, their words press along every fault line in my being. And my patience begins to crack.

Anger, however, only scatters my energy, leaves me feeling fractured. When, instead, I can gather my indignation into a clear and direct response that beams some ray of understanding into the ignorance and fear, I feel restored.

A hostile confrontation, intended "to take care of unfinished business," may only create more unfinished business. The point isn't "to put people in their place," which reinforces the separation, but to enlighten them about ours. It is to remind them we are all ultimately in the same place — human, vulnerable, and mortal.

Buddhist teachings encourage us to see each other, and ourselves, as Buddhas-to-be. The assumption is that wisdom and compassion are part of our essential nature as living beings, whether or not it reaches full expression at any given moment. When we "lose it," as we inevitably do during episodes of anger or fear, the "it" is the ability to recognize in another, or recover in ourselves, the patience and understanding of which we all are capable.

Shortly before his death, Aldous Huxley made this observation: "It's a bit embarrassing to have been concerned with the human problem all one's life and to find at the end that one has no more to offer by way of advice than 'try to be a little kinder.' "[3]

The Give-and-Take of Helping

Last night my husband and I attended a performance of Schumann's piano quartet. Before we left for the concert, I had been reviewing my notes for this section of the book. "There is truly an art to helping," I thought, thumbing through the jumble of papers overflowing the manila folder.

As I sat at the concert, I marveled at the pianist, watching her nimble fingers skim across the keyboard, alighting on each note with precision timing and beautiful tone quality. I was reminded of advice given me by a piano teacher years ago. At the time, I was playing a piece of music that required a rapid succession of leaps across several octaves. Her technique: Fly like an airplane, but land like a bird.

"That's it," I thought, as the music carried me back home to the folder on my desk. "That's the essence of helping: doing what needs to be done, directly, efficiently — but always delicately." Help that descends like a jumbo jet in the middle of the front lawn is overpowering. Often people living with illness are already frightened of losing control. Gestures that seem to erode further their sense of competence can inadvertently send those being "helped" into a tailspin.

Eleanor was my first hospice client. A few weeks after I completed the volunteer training, a nurse named Ann called to ask if I was available to be a bereavement counselor to an eighty-five-year-old woman whose husband had died that morning. That morning, shortly before he died, was also the first time Eleanor called the hospice office for help. For the previous four years, she single-handedly cared for her bedridden ninety-five-year-old husband in the weathered cabin in the woods they had shared for sixty-five years. Except for weekly grocery deliveries, she ran the household without any assistance; she even chopped kindling and hauled firewood for the woodstove, their primary source of heat.

When I arrived at Eleanor's house, Ann was trying to generate with her a list of things with which she could use some help. "The light bulb in the bathroom needs changing," was all Eleanor could come up with. With some coaxing, she thought of a few other things I could pick up at the store along with the light bulb. When I returned, Ann took the bulb from the bag, a small ladder from the kitchen, and headed toward the bathroom. Eleanor and I were talking together at the time. As soon as she realized what Ann was doing, she scooted after her calling out, "Now you get down from there. Let me do that."

"Why not me?" asked Ann, from midway up the ladder.

"Because you're tired. You work so hard. It's too much for you," said Eleanor, motioning Ann to come down.

"How about letting me change the bulb?" I asked as Ann stepped to the ground.

"It's a rickety ladder. You'll hurt yourself," answered Eleanor as she pushed her way past both of us and put a determined foot on the first rung.

Ann and I exchanged a long look, shrugged our shoulders, then quickly positioned ourselves on either side of Eleanor, firmly gripping the ladder to steady it. A woman with a mission, she accomplished it without mishap. We laughed good-naturedly about the incident later, turning it into a "light bulb joke":

How many hospice people does it take to change a light bulb?

Three: one client to change it and two workers to hold the ladder.

The best help supports people, makes it easier for them to do what they can, rather than doing it for them. To be of value to others is to give them a sense of *their* worth. When it comes to helping, more isn't necessarily better. Too much help, or unwanted help, may leave people feeling *more* helpless, undermining their independence and sense of dignity. Obviously, Eleanor's age and circumstances made her appear much more fragile than she was. Although one might understandably assume such demanding caregiving responsibilities would wear a person down, in her particular case, they seemed to make her stronger. Even though her patient was gone, she continued to derive her strength and sense of purpose from giving care rather than receiving it.

Our natural response to the struggles of another reflects our most precious quality as human beings — the awareness of our connection with, and therefore responsibility for, one another. Our eyes fill with tears, our hearts ache with the imagined grief, our breaths become punctuated with sighs, as personal boundaries dissolve in the heat of the pain. We literally want to offer a part of ourselves — a sympathetic ear, a helping hand, a strong shoulder on which to lean.

Then the confusion starts: "What should I say?" "What should I do?" Our heartfelt desires to "fix it," even situations that are not fixable or perhaps don't need fixing, often result in a flurry of words and actions that leave us feeling like we fumbled the handshake. In the effort to do everything possible to relieve another's suffering, the need to be a helper can interfere with the ability to understand what is being asked. The greater the identification with the helper role, the less the identification with the one who is being helped. This creates distance and inequality in the relationship. The person being helped is diminished, and his or her true needs get lost in the role playing.

What one person finds helpful, another might find intrusive. And the same person's needs change over time. Some of us welcome suggestions and fresh perspectives; others of us need to speak rather than be spoken to. Still others find comfort in sitting silently with a trusted friend. People often appreciate help with the details of daily life, but many individuals prefer to remain in charge of those details themselves. And physical contact, a hug or a hand to hold, might reassure one person but create discomfort in another.

Personal perceptions and priorities are not necessarily an accurate gauge of another's needs. Asking directly is the best way to assess where and with whom we can be of service. "Would you like help?" is a yes or no question. If the answer is "yes," the appropriate response is simply "Tell me what I can do." A concerned but respectful answer to "no thank you" might be "Is it okay if I continue to ask now and then, in case you change your mind?"

Sometimes pride or awkwardness keeps those desirous of help from requesting or accepting it. "I've always been the one that others come to for help," explains a woman caretaking her husband, critically ill with myeloma and congestive heart failure. Although "let me know if I can do anything" may be a sincere offer intended to be non-intrusive, this woman, and many others, find it indirect and vague, an "empty gesture." "Can't they see the dishes piling up in the sink and the weeds taking over the garden? Although they say they want to help, they leave it up to me to initiate it. I guess I want people to read my mind."

What is a sensitive way to respond to those whom we suspect want help but have trouble asking, or those who seem too overwhelmed even to know what they need? "Would you like help making a list of things that I and other people could help you with? Then when people offer, you can be specific and they can choose." A woman in the support group, also caring for a husband with cancer, expresses deep gratitude for a friend who volunteered to organize the help of six other friends. "Just tell me the kinds of things you eat and what time you have dinner. You'll have a meal delivered at your door seven nights a week, no obligation to socialize, no strings attached."

For some people, personal comfort rather than pride or awkwardness about being helped accounts for "no thank you" to offers of assistance. We each have different privacy needs, membranes that are more or less permeable. I am among those whose personal boundaries extend to living space; it is like my skin. Having someone else intimately involved in my home surroundings would feel rather like someone else giving me a bath. The time may come, for both of those things, and when it does I will be grateful for the help. But for now, I am not ready.

Some of us also find the coming and going of helpers may require more energy than taking a little longer to do things for ourselves. Life with illness is already unpredictable; it can become increasingly so when the details of daily life are also subject to other people's schedules. Those of us who need some degree of quiet and order to rest easy may prefer to manage as many things as we can on our own, or to streamline life sufficiently that it minimizes the things that require help.

On the surface it might seem curious that everyone with an illness wouldn't welcome help, any laborsaving offer that would make life easier. During an acute illness or a short-term crisis, having friends to do the laundry or watch the children is a blessing. But the disconnection from regular routines is only temporary.

"Having other people 'do your life' gets old quickly," says a woman with Crohn's disease, an inflammatory bowel condition. "It is not a brief respite or welcome vacation from responsibility. My illness is chronic. For me, peace of mind comes from assuming personal responsibility for as much as possible, as long as possible."

Because long-term assistance is a reminder of losses, caregivers often become the targets of anger. Those they care for may resent both the inability to do things for themselves and those upon whom they must rely to do them. Under the glaring light of indignation, nothing a caregiver does may appear "right."

For me, the "drudgery" of household tasks has become strangely appealing since precarious health makes it uncertain how long I can continue to do them. I don't have the energy for major mop-up operations, so I give things care and attention in small, regular ways. It sustains a connection and continuity with daily life that I find grounding, somehow intrinsic to my sense of well-being. A woman with whom I correspond by mail, and who also has Sjogren's syndrome, shares the same sentiment.

...I come closer to the time when I must have more help if we are to stay in this house.... In trying to work out what I would have the person help me *with*, I have been surprised at how many of the little household chores I would hate to turn over to someone else...not because I don't trust people, but because I love those chores! The time I spend making a bed or doing dishes is precious thinking time. When would I arrange and rearrange my thoughts? As for ironing, everybody's bugaboo, I *love* to iron! Something about a freshly ironed shirt stirs in me feelings of love and domesticity — and pride that I can do it so well. I used to feel the same way about a row of jars of homemade jam on a shelf, back when I did that sort of thing. There is a war going on in me all the time between the domestic me and the me with a brain, but the fight is over the allocation of available time. There seems to be room in this old body for both halves to coexist.

During a hospice volunteer training I attended, a nurse described a situation that illustrates well the importance of treading lightly on someone else's living space. A volunteer came to a home that, by her standards, looked messy and chaotic. She assumed it would be a great relief to the patient and family to have the house clean and orderly and set about that task while the patient was asleep and the family was out. They were not pleased. Things had not gotten out of hand because of the disruptions of illness; the state of affairs in the house was the way it always had been. It was comfortable, that was the way they liked it. Now it seemed antiseptic, lifeless.

If the dynamic of a relationship or an offer of help has a patronizing or controlling quality, it feeds any reluctance to seek or accept assistance. We tend to back away from those armed with their own agendas. "Cold water in the face" is chilling. It can make us go numb, stop listening, respond defensively, run in the other direction. We are more likely to trust and accept help that bathes us in the warmth of understanding and respect. Human beings do change but usually because of inner motivation, not external pressure from someone else. A man with a spinal tumor describes a neighbor intent on "saving" him. "For a while he insisted that I let him pick up my groceries. He would return with food *he* had chosen, 'for my own good.' I finally ended that arrangement."

Not only do continual attempts to fix others imply that they are broken and invalidate their own choices; they also lead to burn-out — a never-ending sense of responsibility that drives an enormous but misguided expenditure of energy toward effecting changes in other people. We look for ways to help another, in part, so that we don't feel helpless ourselves. But when we focus on concrete results or a measurable outcome of our efforts, we confuse the helping relationship and exhaust ourselves in the process. The need to play a recognizable role and have a dramatic impact on the life of an ill friend blinds us to the ordinary kindnesses that are extraordinarily helpful, the simple acts that have profound effects. Doing the natural, human thing in the presence of someone in need, when we don't "know" how to help, is often the most helpful. Just touching and being touched by the experience makes a difference.

A few weeks before she died of breast cancer, a woman looking back over her life identified the following incident as among the most significant.

> About thirty years ago I had some strange, very disturbing symptoms that indicated some kind of endocrine imbalance. None of the doctors I saw could figure out what was going on. I remember spending a grueling day in a large medical center and leaving there sobbing. The doctors were not only of no help; they showed no concern, no respect, no understanding of what I was going through.
>
> I waved down a cab and rode home slumped over in despair, my head in my hands, still quietly crying. As I got out, the cabdriver looked me straight in the eye and said, "Young lady, I have no idea what your illness is, but I really do hope you recover."
>
> By the time I walked up to my apartment, I decided I *was* going to recover. I resolved to change my diet, start meditating, and doing yoga. I did those things and my symptoms did go away, as mysteriously as they came. I credit that cabdriver. To know that a total stranger could really care what happened to me restored my confidence and faith.

A man recovering from major abdominal surgery describes a friend who came to visit him in the hospital: "The man stood in the

243

doorway, radiating fear. He called out, 'Let me know if there is anything you need,' then quickly left. At the time I was too sick to have any idea what I needed. I later told him, 'What would have helped enormously was for you to come in my room, pull up a chair and sit down, and take my hand and pray with me.'"

Since Elizabeth has lupus and also a three-year-old daughter with diabetes, she needs all kinds of practical help and appreciates whatever assistance comes her way. But something that stands out in her mind as uniquely helpful is a small gift given to her daughter Becca by a friend, shortly after Becca was diagnosed. The package contained a toy tiger and a set of play syringes; the tiger was "diabetic" and it was Becca's job to care for him. The child enthusiastically began injecting her charge, substantially diminishing her own fear of needles in the process.

Although it might seem that sending cards is the thing to do when there is nothing else to do, most people are deeply touched by any messages sent from the heart that say, "I am thinking about you." When feeling too ill for a phone call or visit, letters or notes are reassurance that friends understand and have not abandoned us. And someone willing to field phone calls during those times is of significant help. It allows for needed rest and also the peace of mind of knowing that friends are not being ignored.

For those who don't have a family member to accompany them through hospitalizations, medical appointments or procedures, or meetings with social service agencies, a friend to serve as an advocate can be enormously comforting. Someone to interpret overwhelming information, ask questions to facilitate communication, or run interference during misunderstandings can soften the sense of isolation and fear often connected with those encounters.

Offers of food are usually plentiful. In contrast to situations where help is faulted for being "too little too late," food seems to arrive "too much too soon." Following hospitalization, or a flare-up or complication in symptoms, people often bring food, to help those who are ill regain their strength and to save them the trouble of shopping and cooking. But the appetite of the person recovering may be no match for the amount or elaborate nature of the meals that sometimes arrive. Appetite tends to recover more rapidly than strength, but offers of food that would be appreciated at a later point tend to slacken off.

This pattern applies not only to offers of food but to other offers as well — of practical help, visits, the general ways of keeping in touch that feed relationships and provide emotional sustenance for those coping with illness. A woman whose husband died of lymphoma describes how "the continuous flow of people at first was followed by an awful lot of time alone."

Along with food, ill people are often inundated with food for thought. Also too much too soon, abundant advice starts arriving before a diagnosis and its implications have a chance to be digested. Although well-meaning, people who want to play a role in the cure may, in fact, be an obstacle to the healing. It can create an added strain to find a loving way to respond to seemingly endless suggestions from people who often understand little about what it means to live with serious illness or about the particular disease process occurring. And few stop to think that theirs might be just one of the many recommendations offered that day (no different from any other day), all of them loving, well-intentioned, and often convinced that theirs is the one right method.

Some of the cures suggested to me have been for physical problems that are, at best, similar to mine in only the most superficial way or, all too often, totally unrelated or even the opposite. Immune systems can be deficient, as is the case with AIDS or chronic fatigue syndrome. Or they can be overactive, as is the case in autoimmune conditions such as rheumatoid arthritis, lupus, and Sjogren's syndrome. Those eager to share information about boosting the immune system don't pause long enough to hear or understand that my immune system indiscriminately attacks my own tissue. Also, the muscle and joint inflammation from a systemic illness such as Sjogren's syndrome reflects a different process than osteoarthritis, a wearing away of cartilage due to aging. And a flare-up of a connective tissue disease causes constitutional flu-like systems. It is more complicated than the localized musculoskeletal pain and discomfort associated with overuse or injury. After twelve years of misplaced enthusiasm from those long on advice but short on information, I now say, "If you could get me the phone numbers of people with *Sjogren's syndrome* who have been helped by that treatment, I would be very interested in calling them."

An avalanche of advice about curing the body can crush the spirit. A man who took his ulcer attack as a "wake-up call" says, "Advice makes me feel that I'm trapped — in my old life — that I am only acceptable if I return to my previous level of health and way of living. People don't want me to move forward with this illness, or beyond it."

Many advise the way back to physical as well as emotional well-being is by reading a book. I have always loved to read and have found material about my own illness and certain books or articles about coping with illness to be comforting and helpful. But that is not true for everyone. Nor, avid reader that I am, do I want to be handed a book that I "must read," the book that will make me well. Just as "Would you like help?" is a yes or no question, so is "Do you like to read?" or "Do you want more written information?" Unsolicited books can stack up like unasked for suggestions, creating a pile of work if we attend to them, or a mountain of guilt or awkward excuses if we don't.

It is, of course, simplistic to suggest that reading a book will cure all our ills. I've learned that even *writing* a book about personally gained wisdom is no guarantee. I had been facilitating the support groups for several years when a new member told me, "I decided to come to your group after reading your booklet. It was really helpful to me. I realized I need to take better care of myself, to get more rest; it's okay to take a nap."

"Really? I guess I need to reread the booklet!" I laughed, as I was just recovering from several days of pushing myself, sorely in need of a good night's sleep, let alone a nap.

In a manual for support group leaders, I came across some valuable advice about giving advice. The acronym, WISE advice, stands for Willing, Informed, Success, and Empathy.[4]

WILLING. People must first be willing to hear advice. Not everyone who has an illness wants or needs suggestions. They may be overloaded with recommendations from others and appreciate the chance to talk with someone who validates the choices they have already made.

INFORMED. People often find advice irritating because of the lack of information on the part of the person offering it. Suggestions made without first asking what has already been tried are sometimes so obvious they border on insult. Frequently people don't bother to find out from the person who is ill the personal priorities and unique circumstances that factor into his or her decisions.

SUCCESS. Changes are difficult to make. Improvement in the quality of life makes it worth the effort. Yet advice is often given quite casually, with little concrete information or first-hand experience to back up claims of success. Suggesting that an ill person devote time, energy, and often expense to something rumored to be more health-promoting than what they are already doing is confusing and can be counterproductive. The best exercise program is the one we actually do; the best diet is the one we actually follow.

EMPATHY. Advice is meaningful only in the context of a caring interaction. When people first feel heard and understood, they are more inclined to heed the advice they receive in return. Suggestions should always be put forth as an offering, not a demand.

Although the issue at hand is not illness, a story that psychologist Lawrence LeShan tells about advice-giving goes to the heart of the matter.

> And one of the great teachers of the mystic way, Rabbi Zusya, was once asked by his congregation to undertake a particular action. He refused, saying he did not do that. The elders said that if Moses were their rabbi, he would have done it. Zusya replied, "When I die and rise and stand before the Throne, God will not ask me, 'Zusya, why were you not Moses?' He will ask, 'Zusya, why were you not Zusya?'"[5]

There is confusion on the receiving end of help as well as on the giving end. How much and what kind of assistance is appropriate to accept or request from friends or loved ones? Just as someone offering help should be sensitive to cues from those they are helping, those in need of help should be respectful toward personal characteristics and styles of giving. Many people like concrete tasks that provide a sense of accomplishment; they like to see they've made a difference. Others prefer to offer emotional support; they feel nourished by the sharing of feelings rather than the sharing of chores. Asking people how much time they have to help and what things they would like to help with allows them to find a comfortable role. And it is important that people agree to let each other know should either one overstep the bounds, requesting or offering too much help. Otherwise an ill person may become unnecessarily dependent or overly demanding, jeopardizing the well-being of both individuals as well as the relationship.

What is a graceful way of declining unwanted help or discouraging inappropriate advice? A response that acknowledges the other person's good intentions might be a version of the following: I appreciate your offer and concern, but I am managing fine and have made some choices that seem to be working well for me.

Much of the awkwardness around helping relationships has its source in the erroneous assumption that love and concern flow in only one direction. We fail to recognize the undiminished capacity in each of us to give, to nourish and enrich our relationships, even when our bodies are compromised. This awkwardness disappears if we meet each other as wounded healers — with ever-changing strengths and weaknesses. Then we give what we can and accept what we need. There is no accounting of favors.

I find it easiest to accept help from those who quietly accommodate to my physical limitations and then acknowledge the rest of me, encouraging me to contribute something meaningful to the interaction. I feel well cared for when my husband Larry registers concern about any physical problem I might be experiencing but doesn't discount me because of it. After we've talked about my health and he's done all that he can to make me comfortable, he often says something like "There was a confusing situation at work today. I'd really appreciate your perspective and input." Asking for *my* help, even when physically I can do no more than lie on the couch, helps both of us.

In *A Death of One's Own*, historian and author Gerda Lerner accounts her time with her husband as he was dying of a brain tumor. Lerner beautifully expresses the opportunity for mutuality in a helping relationship: "Dependence on others can be an act of grace, an acceptance of our common human weakness. Acceptance of help without false pride is the last gift the dying can make the living. It is a handshake, a handhold, celebrating our mortality and our transcendence of it through kindness."[6]

Another mutual gift in any caring relationship is humor. Human suffering is never funny, but our attempts at coping can be amusing. Our imperfections and lack of control frustrate us in serious and profound ways. Yet some of the warmest moments occur when someone helps us notice the misplaced detail or the plan that wandered off in a different direction. It encourages us to step back and consider, "Is there anything funny here?" — even when the issue is our own vulnerability. Bringing some humor into the life of a person who is ill isn't the ability to tell jokes or be funny; it is the ability to "see" funny, to offer a different perspective. It is developing together honest but sympathetic observations about the paradoxes and incongruities, the unexpected angles and overlaps, that comprise the human predicament.

Watching children play reveals the close connection between humor and fear. "Playing sick" is one of their favorite dramas, the bigger the "owie" and the bandage, the better. They casually switch back and forth between the roles of patient and doctor, and it's all in good fun.

Because children are in the habit of playing with their fears concerning illness or injury, they tend to communicate about those issues directly. They often approach people in wheelchairs more easily and talk to them more openly than the adults around them. A woman tells of a young boy who inquired about her amputated foot. "Why are you in that chair?" he asked matter-of-factly.

"Because I only have one foot," she explained.

"Where *is* your other foot?" he asked, looking directly at her amputated limb.

"I left it in my other pair of pants," she answered playfully.

"I bet you fell off a cliff!" he stated with a mix of expectation and certainty.

"I had an infection that was so bad that they had to remove my foot in surgery," she told her disappointed listener.

The boy nodded and turned to go. As he walked away, she heard him say quietly to himself, "She *must* have fallen off a cliff...."

Humor has a leavening effect. If only temporarily, it lightens the weighty realities of illness. Joking releases tension, creates the space for a smile in the midst of pressing concerns. As I was leaving Linda's house one day, she picked up a book lying on the kitchen counter. It was about strengthening the immune system, and she had just finished reading it in the hope it would help her cope with AIDS. Because we had laughed together in the past about combining her immune system with mine, an overactive one, she suggested, "Maybe you should read this book backwards." In the support groups, we have joked about planning a field trip to Lourdes. And one of the members, overloaded with advice from enlightened friends, has posed the question, "If 96% of us are from dysfunctional families, how is it that we feel qualified to create the New Age?"

Whether it's laughing together or crying together, helping always begins with a sharing of experience. The simple desire to help raises complicated issues that stir the heart and soul, but that is exactly where to find some guidance. We can take our cues from the wisdom of the soul and the generosity of the heart. Our innate genius for helping emanates from our soulful connection with others and our heartfelt desire to be of service, from the understanding that comes because we care enough to pay attention. "It is only with the heart that one can see rightly; what is essential is invisible to the eye." — Antoine de Saint-Exupéry in *The Little Prince.*[7]

In the Buddhist tradition, a Bodhisattva represents service. It is an incarnation of self as an instrument to relieve the suffering of others. In many temples, the image of the Bodhisattva is depicted as a being with one thousand arms, an eye in the palm of each open hand, and a heart in the center of each eye. The hands symbolize action, the eye, understanding, and the heart, compassion. Compassion moves us to act, understanding leads us in the right direction.

This section on helping would be incomplete without some mention of those who, in addition to being ill, are alone in the world. They have no one with whom to work out the subtleties and complexities of a helping relationship. Fear of becoming a burden assumes there is someone willing to care for us; concerns about privacy imply we do not live in continual isolation. Too much advice or the wrong kind of help might be most welcome to those who fare with none at all.

Telling Our Stories

During a recent visit to a video store with my young nephew, I realized we have entered a whole new era. My nephew's updated version of "I didn't read the book, but I saw the movie" is "I didn't see the movie, but I read the box."

As a culture, we have little patience for "the whole story," a low threshold for taking in all the details that are part of the complete telling. Yet telling our stories, in our own words, is the way we each make sense of our life and discover its meaning. Gathering the pieces into a satisfying fit gives an overall shape and orientation to scattered events and experiences. And the texture of the past changes when revisited in the present. We see that although a hardship like illness may be a major theme, it alone cannot turn a story into a tragedy. A tragedy is not to live fully the life we are given.

A theme in Joe's story is structural change. Over a period of years, he has kept a journal/record/sketchbook of the evolution of a fanciful "tower house" he constructed for himself and his family. The stages of ankylosing spondylitis, which led to the fusion of his spine, are chronicled on the same pages. The book and the story it tells, which he eagerly shares, reflect Joe's ironic wit and unconventional creativity.

The direction of Joe's life is skyward. An avid tree climber from early on, he limbed trees for a living in his youth. Even with a fused spine, he has mastered the ability to make a slow, careful ascent up almost any tree that needs trimming around his property. He is at home in the trees, and his tower house graphically reflects that. It is a multilayered collection of rooms, alcoves, lofts, and decks, angled and stacked according to whimsy as well as principles of sound construction. The "design" has always been to be as close to the trees as possible.

Joe approached the structural challenges of his body in a similar way. He was determined to maintain his expansive view and likes telling the story of how he accomplished that.

> What saved my life were prism glasses. They are a set of glasses that allow you to lie completely flat on the bed and either read a book that sits on your stomach, watch television, or look out the window. The prism glasses were a technological gift that allowed me to lie flat and fuse straight, vertically. A lot of people with this disease fuse in a bent position, so they can't look up.[8]

Every story needs someone to listen, someone who does not put us in a box without knowing the contents, who is not distracted by the "packaging." A factual accounting of "what" and "when" does not satisfy our inborn need to confide. The real story unfolds only in the presence of another person who is willing to explore with us "why" and "how," and to know the emotional territory we cover in meeting those questions.

When we share our stories with one another, we also recognize that our personal patterns and themes are part of a larger narrative. Each individual life contributes a singular volume to the collective human experience. When she first became ill, Judy felt Meniere's disease separated her from the rest of the world. "Now," she says, "I'm trying to relate to the world in a broader way, to be part of the circle of energy that I used to feel when I was singing on stage. Even in the post office, something passes between people."

People move through difficult circumstances like illness more easily when they are able to place it in some meaningful context. Friends can play a significant role in helping to facilitate that process. Inviting people to tell their stories is inviting them to heal. And offering to participate in the process with them is offering much more than a sympathetic ear. When we accompany someone on a soul-searching journey such as this, we act as a refuge, a witness, a mirror, a midwife.

Only when we feel safe do we talk openly. To establish that environment, a companion must become a human refuge — quiet, spacious, secure, and free. It is undivided attention, unhurried patience, unwavering trust, and unconditional acceptance that encourage people to roam the far corners of soul and psyche. Although we may not be able to rescue someone from the areas of pain, we can provide a sanctuary of love and concern to contain them.

What creates that feeling of safety? Why do I openly share my experience with certain people and reveal as little as possible to others? What tells me that someone is less trustworthy than I thought, and leaves me regretting that I said as much as I did? It's the difference between pity and compassion — between a handout and an invitation to sit at the table.

Pity is not a healthy environment. The atmosphere is thick with condescension and judgment. It hovers from a distance, like the unwholesome haze that hangs over a crowded city. When I am in the company of people who patronize me because I have an illness, I feel stifled: unseen, unheard, and unacceptable the way I am. Their vantage point is fear, and from that position all they see is my physical condition, not the person inside. When they reach out, with platitudes or advice, they touch me only on the surface. And it is largely for their comfort.

Compassion feels like home. It warms me with a sense of belonging and connection. I can express myself openly and breathe freely. Exposing the fragile, wounded parts of myself to a compassionate friend doesn't make me strange or unfamiliar. It is within "our" experience. And if compassionate friends do offer advice, I hear it more easily because they talk *with* me, not *down* to me. They are not trying to save me, or save themselves from feeling pain.

Illness has a way of erasing us. Our struggles seem invisible to those around us; unable to keep pace, we sometimes disappear from view. A witness is someone who knows and understands what is happening to us. It is another pair of eyes, an additional set of ears, to validate the life-altering changes. A witness remains alongside us so we don't have to bear our experience alone.

"I have one good friend with whom I feel I don't have to prove anything," says a man recovering from a stroke. "He sees my wheelchair, but he still sees me. He sees my losses but also the gains I've made through rehabilitation. He sees it all because he sticks by me, and listens."

A trusted friend is also a mirror, someone with whom we are comfortable not only arm-in-arm but face-to-face. This is a sensitive position to assume. Merely shoving a psychological looking glass in front of someone who "needs to see" tends to foster resistance rather than self-reflection. In a true helping relationship, there is a mutuality, a collaboration. We are mirrors for one another, three-dimensional ones, that penetrate the surface. We reflect back not only the wounds of the other person but evidence of healing, which often goes unnoticed by the one living the story.

A few years ago, a close friend listened with care and concern, as she had on many occasions, while I wandered through a maze of insecurity and self-doubt. In her gentle reflection, I could see that although the particular circumstances were new, the pattern of insecurity and self-doubt were not. A few days later, I came home from a medical appointment and saw an oddly shaped package lying on my doorstep. It was about three feet long and tubular. I opened it to find a giant pencil, boldly striped in red and gold, with a small note from my friend tied around it. It said, "To Gayle, a woman who has always known how to write her own script."

Sooner or later, each of us will look in the mirror and see the image of illness or death. Although some of us reach that point earlier in our stories than others, it is an inevitable turn of events. If we want to be a steady source of reflection to those who are ill, we cannot turn away from the human frailty, our own vulnerability, that they mirror back. If we behold ill people in all their aspects, the inherent wholeness of the human spirit also will be mirrored back. Linda tells of tearful and awkward good-byes from friends who have been visiting since her diagnosis of AIDS. "They look at me and see death — *my* death. But we all will die sometime. I would like to think I reflect other things, just as they do, and just as they will when they are dying."

As midwife to friends who are ill, we attend the vital, natural force within them that is moving toward healing. We nurture that potential for growth and transformation and also confirm that there is some element of mystery in the process. Ill people often have all the inner resources they need; what they lack is confidence and faith. A good friend can bring to life what people already know by drawing out their stories and helping breathe hope and meaning into them.

Within a few years of becoming ill, the idea of somehow connecting with other people around the issue of illness started to germinate inside me. A friend named Susan helped bring that idea to fruition. I shared with her, in conversation and in writing, some thoughts and feelings about having an illness that were taking form but lacking direction. Susan invited me to talk with her clients at the senior center, as if that was the obvious next step. She reassured me that my own words, in my own voice, were all that was necessary. She conveyed a trust that the fundamental shifts and changes emerging out of my illness were life-affirming.

Although reluctant at first, I took Susan up on her offer — after which she made another offer: to include me in a grant as a facilitator of a weekly support group. That sequence of events began a whole new chapter of my life. Susan never pushed me; it was more that she received me. She stood like a lighthouse, radiating possibilities, illuminating the way.

We each have a different style of giving. Not every friend will be able to assume the role of refuge, witness, mirror, or midwife. That's why there are support groups. People who have gone through the fire know what hot means. They understand the searing effects of illness; they share the same burning questions. They like hearing tales of the phoenix rising from the ashes.

Linda calls the support group "The Club." Her name captures the special fellowship that comes from feeling like an "insider." Since the inside of illness is a dark and lonely place, it is natural to seek out others who have been there and are also still learning their way around. When I read that Albert Einstein said, "How do I work? I grope," I appreciated the company. Knowing that others grope — having others to grope *with* creates a kinship. "There is a camaraderie in being with other people trying their very best to live each moment of the day with some kind of equanimity," says a longtime member. This kinship often transforms total strangers into intimate confidants within a few sessions. "Now what are we supposed to say when we run into each other at the market?" joked a new member as she left her first meeting. "After the 'big talk' at the group, the 'small talk' seems microscopic."

People unfamiliar with support groups often find this immediate intimacy difficult to imagine. They also wonder how pooling stories of the struggles of illness could make it any easier to wade through them. "I wouldn't be strong enough to handle such pain and suffering" is a response I commonly hear when I describe my work.

The group members *are* strong. They bring a remarkable level of commitment, compassion, and courage to the meetings. But they also bring a kind of strength that may not look like strength at all; ironically, our own vulnerability, our own wounds in the process of healing, gives us the strength to meet other people's pain. We know how to touch the tender places in another because we know how those places feel inside of us. We believe others can heal emotionally because we observe that healing in ourselves. This wisdom and trust arise from our own experience with the human story, with the wounding and healing that comes with being alive. It is not a question of being strong enough to "take on" the pain of others or, conversely, to keep it at a distance. The challenge is not to endure increasing amounts of pain but to see each experience as another form of the pain that we all share.

Kindness extended to others is mutually soothing. One of the members describes the meeting as a "group massage." Another says, "I *share* the pain of other people but what I *absorb* is their strength." And another: "If there are six other people at a meeting, I don't feel like I leave with six additional problems. Rather, I feel like each of us had six minds and hearts to help with the load we carry single-handedly the rest of the time."

There are no experts in the group. We meet as peers, credentialed only in personal life-experience. Authoring our own stories of healing doesn't make us authorities on anyone else. All we can do is encourage each other by example and support, offering ourselves rather than solutions. In fact, people often come to the group for help in delineating their own paths through the crisscrossing advice of family and friends. They seek respite from those trying to deny, change, or fix their experiences. We each want to have our reality validated, not rewritten.

People who have largely made peace with their illnesses often continue to attend support groups. Why? The desire to help others is only a partial explanation. "Talking with those newly diagnosed keeps the 'cancer message' fresh," explains Laoma, who is several years beyond breast cancer, surgery, and chemotherapy, both in terms of chronology and psychological adjustment. An experience with a serious illness propels our stories forward, in unexpected directions. It is important to remember how we arrived where we did and take stock of what we gained along the way.

The genesis of the support group I began facilitating almost a decade ago was the need to understand my own illness and also be of service to others. It turned out to be an exodus, a radical departure from my previous life and its untested assumptions. The privilege of exchanging stories with my traveling companions, people I would never have otherwise known, has been one the most rewarding parts of the journey.

But illness is ultimately a part of everyone's story. Support groups work because they foster a strong identification with others who are ill, but they shouldn't alienate us from those who are not. "I don't want to become 'cancer-centric,'" says one member. If we consider our stories exclusive, we continue to exclude ourselves. Rather, support groups should give us the spirit and confidence to rejoin the rest of the world and to celebrate our stories.

There is an invisible thread that weaves together the lives of all of us, regardless of physical condition, age, or lifestyle. We share a common desire to touch that nameless source that gives our lives meaning, and each of us is perplexed at times that the search is so difficult.

The choices we make throughout our lives are just our unique and manifold ways of "paying attention," of experiencing what it means to be human. That expression of our humanity is healthy and enduring in each of us, protected deep inside the soul.

An illness tests our courage and will to engage creatively with the unknown. We are asked to greet the challenges of life with the same intensity as we greet our passions. In the process, we discover the strength of our convictions — our integrity — and hopefully emerge declaring, "In spite of everything, I wouldn't trade my life for a half-lived one, no matter how long, or how perfect the body living it."

Epilogue

Life can only be understood backwards,
but it must be lived forwards.

—Kierkegaard[1]

About halfway through the writing of this book, I began to question the whole endeavor. Originally I made a verbal agreement with the publishers to complete the manuscript within a year. It was in a moment of wishful thinking. I declared 1993 "The Year of the Book" and entered "writing" in every available space on my calendar. Six months later, I was on schedule, but my life bore little resemblance to my words.

I had to face the painful irony that working on this book about wholeness and balance was leaving me fragmented and uncentered. Driven by an unrealistic goal, I had drifted far from my stated position about being rather than doing. The constant strain hardly exemplified a graceful adaptation to limitations. My words said that an illness forces us to pay attention, to remember what is real, to honor life in the present. In order to author those words, however, I feared I was fitting life around a book instead of the other way around. I couldn't call the book honest — and it was never intended to be fiction.

Writing a book, in and of itself, wasn't the problem. Writing has always nurtured me, helped me to clarify my thoughts, understand my emotions, enlarge my perspective. I had imagined the book as an evolving synthesis of ideas about illness, a vehicle to convey the collective wisdom of people who have shared their experiences with me. I assumed that working on the book would enhance my own adaptation to living with illness, not undermine it. I anticipated the project would increase my connections with others, not interfere with them. I wanted to write a book that would reflect my life, not alter it beyond recognition.

When the book became linked to a publisher and a deadline, it became a case in point: How do we balance the healthy drive toward creativity with the limitations of illness? Can meaningful goals be generated that are not product-oriented and outwardly-directed? Does the expression of our uniqueness necessitate the assertion of our ego? And is not living with illness, indeed life itself, an ongoing creative endeavor? I talked with Renée about these issues. She says that because her lupus so often saps her creative energy, her multitude of unfinished musical undertakings wind up feeling like "chronic projects."

I reached a point where I wondered why I thought I had to put words to lived experiences and auspicious interactions. They had happened. *That* was significant, not my book, which was threatening to take on a life of its own.

In the midst of all this soul-searching, I recalled the first time my husband Larry and I went camping. We were living in Chicago at the time. Having been born and raised there, we had spent little time away from a big city. The summer after we married, we went to northern Wisconsin for a weekend to try camping. The first night out, I looked up at the clear, star-studded sky. It truly seemed like a different sky than any I had ever seen. It was magical, I was awed, I said, "Oh, Larry, it's just like the planetarium!" I had reversed what was real and what was representational, and I wondered if the same thing was happening with my book.

Around that time I wrote a letter to a friend describing my shifting perspective. I said, "As long as I can have quality time with those close to me, continue to meet with the support groups, take care of daily things, and spend time in nature, I am content. If I manage to finish this book, or bring to fruition some other creative yearning, that would be a bonus. Not too ambitious, but illness can kill ambition. Right now, haiku seems appealing: three lines at a time, unless you want to write another one."

With hindsight and from talking with others, I suspect that some of my angst was standard for any substantial creative project, especially a first book. In addition, I was physically exhausted. Since I was about half finished, the thought that I had the same amount ahead of me during the next six months dampened my resolve to carry it through. I explained all this to the publishers, an extraordinarily perceptive and compassionate couple. They supported my need to reestablish the balance in my life that I had lost while so diligently writing about it.

We left the deadline open-ended, which lessened my anxiety considerably. (The first definition listed in the dictionary for the word deadline is "a line drawn within or around a prison that a prisoner passes only at the risk of being instantly shot.") Yet the enormity of the project I had undertaken still weighed heavily on me. With each and every sentence I wrote, I asked myself, "Does this reflect the truth?" — not truth with a capital "T," but true to my experience, true to the accounts of those who live with illness daily. The unique versions of the universal experience of illness, converging here, diverging there, took me deep, sent me far, spun me around.

I found that writing about illness has a great deal in common with having one. It's another place to get lost, another opportunity to meet fears and then find a way beyond them. As writer Alice Walker put it, "When your balloon string has been cut, you may not know where you're going to drift — but what a view."[2] Stretches of creative energy seem capricious, as unpredictable as stretches of good health. At times, I am as suspicious of my creativity as I am of my body, and I periodically feel abandoned by both.

Yet, like my illness, creative moments bring me clarity. I've come to appreciate that living within limitations, physical or otherwise, is a honing process, a refining and redefining of what is essential. Along with messages from my body, the content of the book was a continual reminder not to lose my way in the writing of it. I didn't always heed those messages; the book became a crucible. But it has enriched the journey immeasurably, as I continue to find my way home.

Notes

Part One
Living the Questions: Illness and Uncertainty

1. Rainer Maria Rilke, *Letters to a Young Poet*, translated by M.D. Herter Norton, rev. ed. (New York: W.W. Norton & Company, 1954), p.35.

2. John Muir, *The Yosemite*, illus. Galen Rowell (San Francisco: Sierra Club Books, 1989), p. 19.

3. Rachel Naomi Remen, audiotape *Living Next to Cancer* (Bolinas, CA: Commonweal — The Institute for the Study of Health and Illness).

Chapter 1: To Know We Are Vulnerable

1. *Face to Face Quarterly Bulletin*, Sonoma County AIDS Network.

2. Nancy Mairs, *Plaintext: Deciphering a Woman's Life* (New York: Harper & Row, 1986), p. 6.

3. Issa, *Snow Falling from a Bamboo Leaf: The Art of Haiku*, trans. Hiag Akmakjian (Santa Barbara: Capra Press, 1979), p. 85.

4. Sam Keen, "Dying Gods and Borning Spirits," *Noetic Sciences Review*, no. 24 (Winter 1992), p. 28.

5. H.L. Mencken, *Passages Journal*.

6. Idries Shah, "The Man Who Was Aware of Death," *Tales of the Dervishes: Teaching Stories of the Sufi Masters Over the Past Thousand Years* (New York: E.P. Dutton & Co., Inc., 1970), p. 77.

7. Karren Silver, "Behind the Buzzing Needle," *Mendocino County Outlook* (February 19 - March 4, 1993), p. 15.

8. Karren Silver, "The Symbology of Death in Tattoos," *Mendocino County Outlook* (August 21, 1992), p. 15.

9. Linda Weltner, "Good Luck, Bad Luck," *New Age Journal* (November-December 1990), p. 128.

10. Lucinda Pitcairn, "On Trying to Find a Possible Life," *The Common Thread* 5, no. 2 (July 1992), p. 3.

11. Ram Dass and Paul Gorman, *How Can I Help? Stories and Reflections on Service* (New York: Alfred A. Knopf, 1985), pp. 27-28.

12. Anne A. Simpkinson, "In Memoriam: Treya Killam Wilber, 1946-1989," *Common Boundary* (May-June 1989), pp. 5-6.

13. Nancy Mairs, *Plaintext: Deciphering a Womans's Life* (New York: Harper & Row, 1986), p. 20.

14. Rachel Naomi Remen, from a talk given at a meeting of the Sjogren's Syndrome Foundation, Marin chapter.

15. Andrée O'Connor, "One-Breasted Woman," *Ms. Magazine* (September-October 1992), p. 33 and "Metamorphosis: A Rose Replaces a Breast," *Mendocino Commentary* no. 417 (May 8, 1992), p. 8. (A more complete account appears in "One-Breasted Women: Andrée O'Connor," *The New Settler Interview* no. 72 [Winter 1992-1993], pp. 28-42.)

16. Sara O'Donnell, "The Unbroken Circle," *The Common Thread* 5, no. 2 (July 1992), p. 3.

17. *Ibid.*

18. *Ibid.*

19. Rumi, "The Friend," *Night and Sleep*, trans. Coleman Barks and Robert Bly (Cambridge, MA: Yellow Moon Press, 1981), pages are unnumbered.

20. Gilda Radner, *It's Always Something* (New York: Simon and Schuster, 1989), pp. 140-41.

21. Cheri Register, *Living with Chronic Illness: Days of Patience and Passion* (New York: Bantam Books, 1987), p. 239.

Chapter 2: Freedom and Choice

1. Isaac Bashevis Singer, acceptance speech for the Nobel Prize for Literature, 1978.

2. Cheri Register, *Living with Chronic Illness: Days of Patience and Passion* (New York: Bantam Books, 1987), pp. 24-25.

3. Joe Murray, "Arthritis: Patient Perspective," *Update* 4, no. 3 (Third Quarter 1989-90), pp. 1-2.

4. Laoma Bryant, KZYX Radio Interview with Beth Bosk, July 1993.

5. *Ibid.*

6. *Ibid.*

7. Thich Nhat Hanh, *Being Peace*, ed. Arnold Kotler, illus. Mayumi Oda (Berkeley, CA: Parallax Press, 1987), p. 65.

8. Viktor E. Frankl, *Man's Search for Meaning: An Introduction to Logotherapy*, part one trans. Ilse Lasch (New York: Pocket Books, 1963), p. 104.

9. Ken Wilber and Treya Wilber, "Do We Make Ourselves Sick?" *New Age Journal* (September-October 1988), p. 90.

10. Larry Dossey, "Healing and Prayer: The Power of Paradox and Mystery," *Noetic Sciences Review* no. 28 (Winter 1993), pp. 24-25.

11. Harris Dienstfrey, "What Makes the Heart Healthy? A Talk with Dean Ornish," *Advances: The Journal of Mind-Body Health* 8, no. 2 (Spring 1992), p. 31.

12. David Spiegel, "An Exchange of Letters Between Bernie Siegel and David Spiegel on Psychosocial Interventions and Cancer," *Advances: The Journal of Mind-Body Health* 8, no. 1 (Winter 1992), p. 3.

13. Jon Kabat-Zinn, *Full Catastrophe Living: Using the Wisdom of*

Your Body and Mind to Face Stress, Pain, and Illness (New York, Delacorte Press, 1990), p. 217.

14. Paula Underwood, "A Native American Worldview," *Noetic Sciences Review* no. 15 (Summer 1990), p. 20. (The Rule of Six is part of *The Past is Prologue* [PIP], an educational program based on Learning Stories handed down in Paula Underwood's family. PIP has been designated as an "Exemplary Educational Program" by the U.S. Department of Education. The PIP approach to learning and wholeness is used in schools, corporations, and in health and healing programs. Information is available from The Past is Prologue Program, PO Box 913, Georgetown, TX 78627, [512] 930-5576.)

15. Barry Stevens, *Burst Out Laughing* (Berkeley, CA: Celestial Arts, 1984), p. 140.

16. Rumi, "The Ground," *Night and Sleep*, trans. Coleman Barks and Robert Bly (Cambridge, MA: Yellow Moon Press, 1981), pages unnumbered.

17. Harold S. Kushner, *When Bad Things Happen to Good People* (New York: Avon Books, 1981).

18. Phyllis B. O'Connell, "When Life Isn't Fair," *Quest* (February 1993), p. 4.

19. Thomas Wolfe, *You Can't Go Home Again* (New York: HarperPerennial, 1968), p. 40.

20. Wes "Scoop" Nisker, *Crazy Wisdom* (Berkeley, CA: Ten Speed Press, 1990), pp. 34-35.

21. Stephan Bodian, "Love is the Healer: Interview with Joan Borysenko," *Yoga Journal* (May-June 1990), p. 94.

22. Rachel Naomi Remen, audiotape *Beyond Cure: The Psychology of Wholeness* (Bolinas, CA: Commonweal — The Institute for the Study of Health and Illness).

Chapter 3: An Evolving Perspective

1. Jack Kornfield, "Respect for Parenting, Respect for Children," *Inquiring Mind* 8, no. 2 (Spring 1992), p. 10.

2. Fyodor Dostoyevsky, *Passages Journal*

3. Lucinda Pitcairn, "On Trying to Find a Possible Life," *The Common Thread* 5, no. 2 (July 1992), p. 3.

4. Leo Lionni, *Frederick* (New York: Random House, 1967), p. 23.

5. JoAnne LeMaistre, *Beyond Rage: The Emotional Impact of Chronic Physical Illness* (Oak Park, IL: Alpine Guild, 1985), pp. 24, 126.

6. Rick Fields, Peggy Taylor, Rex Weyler, and Rick Ingtasci, eds., *Chop Wood, Carry Water: A Guide to Finding Spiritual Fulfillment in Everyday Life* (Los Angeles: Jeremy P. Tarcher, 1984), p. 35.

7. Jack Kornfield, "Respect for Parenting, Respect for Children," *Inquiring Mind* 8, no. 2 (Spring 1992), p. 10.

8. Thich Nhat Hanh, *Being Peace*, ed. Arnold Kotler, illus. Mayumi Oda (Berkeley, CA: Parallax Press, 1987), pp. 42-43.

9. Jan Trueheart, "Since I Didn't Die After All," *The Common Thread* 5, no. 2 (July 1992), p. 2.

10. Mark Twain, *Passages Journal*.

11. Yael Bethiem, "The Unhealed Life," *The Sun* no. 158 (January 1989), p. 38.

12. *Ibid.*, p. 37.

13. Richard Yaski, "In the Desert of My Soul," *The Common Thread* 7, no. 2 (October 1994), p. 5.

14. Thich Nhat Hanh, "Peace as a Path: Five Exercises," *Inquiring Mind* 8, no. 1 (Fall 1991), p. 15.

15. Jan Trueheart, "Since I Didn't Die After All," *The Common Thread* 5, no. 2 (July 1992), p. 2.

16. Joe Murray, "Arthritis: Patient Perspective," *Update* 4, no. 3 (Third Quarter 1989-90), pp. 1-2.

17. Nancy Mairs, *Plaintext: Deciphering a Woman's Life* (New York: Harper & Row, 1986), pp. 6-7.

18. Isaiah Berlin, *The Hedgehog and the Fox: An Essay on Tolstoy's View of History* (New York: Simon & Schuster, 1953), p. 1.

19. Sefra Kobrin Pitzele, *We Are Not Alone: Learning to Live With Chronic Illness* (New York: Workman Publishing, 1986), p. 210.

20. Sue Bender, *Plain and Simple: A Woman's Journey to the Amish* (San Francisco: Harper, 1989), pp. 4-5.

21. *Ibid.*, pp. 48-50, 146.

22. *Ibid.*, pp. 146-47.

Part Two
On Individual Terms: Responses to Illness

1. Diane Ackerman, *A Natural History of the Senses* (New York: Random House, 1990), p. 193.

2. Alan Watts, *Passages Journal*

Chapter 4: Crisis and Loss

1. Mary Oliver, "In Blackwater Woods," *American Primitive* (Boston: Little, Brown and Company, 1983), pp. 82-83.

2. Lucinda Pitcairn, "Neither Friend Nor Foe," *Inside MS* 11, no. 3 (Fall 1993), p. 21.

3. Pablo Casals, *Joys and Sorrows: His Own Story as Told to Albert E. Kahn* (New York: Simon and Schuster, 1970), p. 105.

4. Ibid., p. 106.

Chapter 5: The Need to Grieve

1. Elisabeth Kübler-Ross, brochure from The Elisabeth Kübler-Ross Center.

2. Thomas Merton, "Flight from the Shadow," *The Way of Chuang Tzu* (New York: New Directions, 1965), p. 155.

3. Viktor E. Frankl, *Man's Search for Meaning: An Introduction to Logotherapy*, part one trans. Ilse Lasch (New York: Pocket Books, 1963), p. 30.

4. Marjorie Lyon, "How Are You?" *Bereavement: A Magazine of Hope and Healing* 6, no. 7 (September 1992), p. 6.

5. Thich Nhat Hanh, "Precepts as a Way of Life," *The Mindfulness Bell* no. 6 (Spring 1992), p. 3. (Later published in book form by Thich Nhat Hanh, *For a Future To Be Possible: Commentaries on the Five Wonderful Precepts* [Berkeley, CA: Parallax Press, 1993], p. 25.)

6. Stephen Levine, *A Gradual Awakening* (New York: Doubleday, 1989), p. 60.

7. Colin Berg, "The Art of Return," *Parabola: The Magazine of Myth and Tradition* 12, no. 3 (August 1987), p. 64-65.

8. Catherine Ingram, *In the Footsteps of Ghandi: Conversations with Spiritual Social Activists* (Berkeley, CA: Parallax Press, 1990), p. 189.

9. Thich Nhat Hanh, "For Warmth," *Zen Poems*, trans. Teo Savory (Greensboro, NC: Unicorn Press, 1976), pages are unnumbered.

10. Jan Trueheart, "Since I Didn't Die After All," *The Common Thread* 5, no. 2 (July 1992), p. 2.

11. Joel Goodman, "Love, Laughter & Miracles: A Prescription from Bernie Siegel," *Laughing Matters* 6, no. 4 (1990), pp. 138-39.

12. Stephen Levine, *Who Dies? An Investigation of Conscious Living and Conscious Dying* (New York: Anchor Books, 1982), p. 68.

13. Harold S. Kushner, *When Bad Things Happen to Good People* (New York: Avon Books, 1981), p. 91.

14. Ralph Waldo Emerson, *Passages Journal*.

Chapter 6: Exploring the Edges

1. Yamabe no Akahito, Manse, Motori Norinaga, Izumi Shikibu, and Fujiwara no Toshiyuki, *Springs of Japanese Wisdom* (Oakland, CA: Marcel Schurman Company)

2. Flannery O'Connor, *The Habit of Being*, letters ed. Sally Fitzgerald (New York: The Noonday Press, 1979), p. 90.

3. Derek Walcott, "Love after Love," *Collected Poems 1948-1984* (New York: The Noonday Press, 1986), p. 328.

4. Arnold R. Beisser, *Flying Without Wings: Personal Reflections on Being Disabled* (New York: Doubleday, 1989), pp. 7-8.

5. Anatole Broyard, *Intoxicated by My Illness: And Other Writings on Life and Death*, ed. Alexandra Broyard (New York: Clarkson Potter, 1992), pp. 61-62.

6. *Ibid.*, pp. 19-21.

7. Thich Nhat Hanh, "Peace as a Path: Five Exercises," *Inquiring Mind* 8, no. 1 (Fall 1991), p. 15.

8. Flannery O'Connor, *The Habit of Being*, letters ed. Sally Fitzgerald (New York: The Noonday Press, 1979), p. 57.

9. Ken Wilber, *Grace and Grit: Spirituality and Healing in the Life and Death of Treya Killam Wilber* (Boston: Shambhala, 1991), pp. 338-39.

10. Sogyal Rinpoche, *The Tibetan Book of Living and Dying*, ed. Patrick Gaffney and Andrew Harvey (San Francisco: Harper, 1992), pp. 223, 238.

11. *Ibid.*, p. 177.

12. Danny Ross, "You Know I Love to Travel," *The Common Thread* 8, no. 1 (May 1995), p. 6.

13. Deborah Duda, *Coming Home: A Guide to Dying at Home With Dignity* (New York: Aurora Press, 1987), p. 291.

14. Viktor E. Frankl, *The Doctor and the Soul: From Psychotherapy to Logotherapy*, trans. Richard and Clara Winston, 3rd ed. exp.

(New York: Vintage Books, 1986), p. 66.

15. Kahlil Gibran, *The Prophet* (New York: Alfred A. Knopf, 1964), p. 80.

16. Stephen Levine, *Meetings at the Edge: Dialogues with the Grieving and the Dying, the Healing and the Healed* (Garden City, NY: Anchor Press, 1984), pp. 239-40.

17. Viktor E. Frankl, *Man's Search for Meaning: An Introduction to Logotherapy*, part one trans. Ilse Lasch (New York: Pocket Books, 1963), p. 130.

18. Excerpt from an interview with Jerry Jampolsky and Diane Cirincione, *New Dimensions* (January-February 1991).

19. Earl A. Grollman, *Suicide: Prevention, Intervention, Postvention*, 2nd. ed., upd. and exp. (Boston: Beacon Press, 1988), p. 80.

20. Maria Monroe, "A Very Human Death," *Inquiring Mind* 9, no. 2 (Spring 1993), p. 1.

21. *Ibid.*, p. 9.

22. *Ibid.*

23. *Ibid.*, p. 11.

Part Three
In Good Company: Illness and Relationships

1. Emily Kimbrough, *Passages Journal*.

2. Elisabeth Kübler-Ross, *The Elisabeth Kübler-Ross Center Newsletter* no.58 (Summer 1994), p. 10.

Chapter 7: Health Care Providers

1. Leo Buscaglia, *The Disabled and Their Parents* (New York: Holt, Rinehart and Winston, 1983), p. 186.

2. Rumi, quotation on greeting card

3. David M. Eisenberg et al., "Unconventional Medicine in the

United States: Prevalence, Costs, and Patterns of Use," *The New England Journal of Medicine* 328, no.4 (January 28, 1993), pp. 246-52.

4. Abraham Maslow, *The Psychology of Science: A Reconnaissance* (New York: Harper & Row, 1966), pp. 15-16.

5. Susie Rashkis, *Inquiring Mind* 8 no. 1 (Fall 1991), p. 30.

6. Lawrence LeShan, "Creating a Climate for Self-Healing: The Principles of Modern Psychosomatic Medicine," *Advances: The Journal of Mind-Body Health* 8, no.4 (Fall 1992), p. 27.

Chapter 8: Family and Loved Ones

1. Lillian Helman, *Passages Journal.*

2. Jane Hollister Wheelwright (in collaboration with Eleanor Haas, Barbara McClintock, and Audrey Blodgett), *The Death of a Woman* (New York: St. Martin's Press, 1981), p. 270.

3. Sefra Kobrin Pizele, *We Are Not Alone: Learning to Live With Chronic Illness* (New York: Workman Publishing, 1986), p. 61.

4. David Spiegel, "A Psychosocial Intervention and Survival Time of Patients with Metastatic Breast Cancer," *Advances: The Journal of Mind-Body Health* 7, no. 3 (Summer 1991), p. 13.

5. Rainer Maria Rilke, *Letters to a Young Poet*, translated by M.D. Herter Norton, rev. ed. (New York: W.W. Norton & Company, 1954), p. 59.

6. John J.L. Mood, *Rilke on Love and Other Difficulties: Translations and Considerations of Rainer Maria Rilke* (New York: W. W. Norton & Company, 1975), p. 28.

7. Chinese Proverb, *Passages Journal.*

8. Kyala Shea, "AIDS Symposium Dispels Prejudice, Shows Personal Woes of the Disease," *The Mendocino Beacon*, February 3, 1994.

9. John Bartlett, *Familiar Quotations: A Collection of Passages, Phrases and Proverbs Traced to Their Sources in Ancient and Modern Literature*, rev. ed. (Boston: Little, Brown and Company, 1955), p. 588.

10. Lucinda Pitcairn, "Community Outreach," *Update* 8, no. 2 (Spring 1994), p. 7.

11. Harry E. Mann, "How to Help A Grieving Friend," *Bereavement: A Magazine of Hope and Healing* 6, no. 3 (March-April 1992), p. 42.

12. Isabel Allende, audiotape (with Alice Walker and Jean Shinoda Bolen), *Giving Birth, Finding Form: Where Do Our Books Come From?* (Boulder, CO: The Sounds True Catalog).

13. Thich Nhat Hanh, audiotape, *Buddhism and Psychotherapy* (Berkeley, CA: Parallax Press, 1989). (Later published in book form by Thich Nhat Hanh, *Touching Peace: Practicing the Art of Mindful Living*, ed. Arnold Kotler, illus. Mayumi Oda [Berkeley, CA: Parallax Press, 1992], p. 53.)

Chapter 9: Friendship and Helping Relationships

1. Philip Novak, *The World's Wisdom: Sacred Texts of the World's Religions* (New York: HarperCollins Publishers, 1994), p. 216.

2. Reynolds Price, KZYX radio interview, *Fresh Air*, with Terry Gross, May 22, 1994.

3. Arnold R. Beisser, *Flying Without Wings: Personal Reflections on Being Disabled* (New York: Doubleday, 1989), p. 42.

4. *Training for Group Starters* (Los Angeles: California Self-Help Center), p. 5.

5. Lawrence LeShan, "Creating a Climate for Self-Healing: The Principles of Modern Psychosomatic Medicine," *Advances: The Journal of Mind-Body Health* 8, no. 4 (Fall 1992), p. 23.

6. Gerda Lerner, *A Death of One's Own* (Madison: University of Wisconsin Press, 1985), p. 116.

7. Antoine de Saint-Exupéry, *The Little Prince*, trans. Katherine Woods (New York: Harcourt Brace Jovanovich, 1971), p. 87.

8. Joe Murray, "Arthritis: Patient Perspective," *Update* 4, no. 3 (Third Quarter 1989-90), p. 1.

Epilogue

1. Soren Aabye Kierkegaard, *Passages Journal.*

2. Alice Walker, audiotape (with Isabel Allende and Jean Shinoda Bolen) *Giving Birth, Finding Form: Where Do Our Books Come From?* (Boulder, CO: The Sounds True Catalog).

Appendix

Coping with the Stress of Illness

The following list of suggestions for coping with the stress of illness is distilled from the collective wisdom of the support group members.

Stress is a combination of problematic life experiences and our responses to those experiences. We can reduce the level of stress by either the actions we take or the attitudes we adopt.

Actions

1. Whenever possible, initiate necessary changes to eliminate or minimize external pressures, including any concrete, day-to-day aspects of life (job, relationships, physical circumstances) that are sources of strain or tension.

2. Clarify priorities and conserve energy and time by planning and pacing.

3. Choose realistic standards and expectations, not inappropriate ones based on the past or comparisons with others.

4. Set goals focused on the present that can be accomplished in small, manageable steps.

5. Become flexible about long-term goals and open to redefining them because of unexpected changes.

6. Be willing to request information and help when necessary.

7. Schedule a daily period of relaxation to ease the struggles of both mind and body.

8. Pursue, in an ongoing way, an activity that is nurturing and absorbing, an outlet that is enjoyable and taps interests, creativity, talents, or skills.

9. Incorporate some pure fun into each day.

10. Acknowledge the inevitable strains that an illness imposes on relationships, and look for ways to improve communication, to be assertive in a loving way.

Attitudes (Beliefs, Thoughts, Feelings)

1. Develop equanimity — the ability to accept rather than battle against things as they are. This is not resignation or defeat, but an active process, aimed at peace of mind and a sense of wholeness.

2. Cultivate an openness to change, and avoid the dualistic notion of the good news and the bad news. Remember that the Chinese symbol for the word "crisis" has two characters: one means danger, the other means opportunity.

3. Appreciate all the choices that do exist, especially ways to keep from making problems worse.

4. Limit concerns to present issues, not fears about the future ("what ifs") or regrets about the past ("if onlys").

5. Retain a sense of humor.

6. Maintain a perspective larger than the immediate situation to keep current problems in proportion. See them in the context of the rest of one's life and in connection with the rest of the world. Distinguish between a crisis and an event.

7. Focus on the preciousness of each moment, and have faith that the future will bring more of these moments.

8. Remember that physical vulnerability is not a sign of inferior-

ity but part of the human condition, something everyone will confront within a lifetime. The imperfections of the human body should be approached with love and compassion, not judgments or feelings of guilt.

9. Be patient with the normal and necessary manifestations of grief that surface with the loss of good health: denial, anger, depression, bargaining for a cure, and acceptance.

10. Take credit for the increased sensitivity, creativity, courage, and inner strength that one demonstrates daily in meeting the challenges of living with illness.

11. Nurture self-esteem through a constant awareness of each person's unique capacity to enrich his or her own life as well as the lives of others, in spite of physical limitations.

Selected Bibliography

There are hundreds of books written *about* people who live with illness, but there are far fewer written *by* those people. Although many of the popular books authored by health care providers are excellent, I've limited this list to less well-known firsthand accounts. Each of these books offers both a unique perspective on illness and a pleasurable reading experience because of the quality of the writing.

Barasch, Marc Ian. *The Healing Path: A Soul Approach to Illness.* New York: A Jeremy P. Tarcher/Putnam Book, 1993.

An investigation into the nature of healing by the former editor of *New Age Journal,* based on his own experience with thyroid cancer as well as on the experiences of others he interviewed.

Beisser, Arnold R. *Flying Without Wings: Personal Reflections on Being Disabled.* New York: Doubleday, 1989.

Insights into the world of loss and disability by a psychiatrist paralyzed by polio since the age of twenty-five.

Broyard, Anatole. *Intoxicated by My Illness: And Other Writings on Life and Death.* Edited by Alexandra Broyard. New York: Clarkson Potter, 1992.

Personal essays and journal notes by literary critic for *The New York Times,* chronicling his final months of life following a diagnosis of metastatic prostate cancer.

Lerner, Gerda. *A Death of One's Own.* Madison: University of Wisconsin Press, 1985.

A narrative, from the point of view of wife and caregiver, on the journey through cancer and on the attempt to provide at-home health care before hospice services were available.

Mairs, Nancy. *Plaintext: Deciphering a Woman's Life.* New York: Harper & Row, 1986.

A book of essays by a prize-winning poet who has multiple sclerosis. The first two essays most directly address the issue of illness.

Price, Reynolds. *A Whole New Life: An Illness and a Healing.* New York: Atheneum, Macmillan Publishing Company, 1994.

Intimate account by the 1986 winner of the National Book Critics Circle Award of his attempts to reclaim his life after a spinal tumor left him paraplegic.

Register, Cheri. *Living with Chronic Illness: Days of Patience and Passion.* New York: Bantam Books, 1987.

A comprehensive coverage of day-to-day life with illness, drawn from the author's own experience with a congenital liver disease and from extensive interviews with others.

Wilber, Ken. *Grace and Grit: Spirituality and Healing in the Life and Death of Treya Killam Wilber.* Boston: Shambhala, 1991.

An interweaving of journal entries from a woman dying of breast cancer and her husband's commentaries, including his perspective on life and death as a leading theorist and prolific author in the field of transpersonal psychology.

Publisher's Acknowledgments

For permission to quote material in this book, the publisher wishes to acknowledge the following sources:

From *Letters to a Young Poet*, by Rainer Maria Rilke, translated by M.D. Herter Norton, copyright © 1954; and from *Rilke on Love and Other Difficulties: Translations and Considerations of Rainer Maria Rilke*, by John J.L. Mood, copyright © 1975: both reprinted with permission of the publisher, W.W. Norton & Co., Inc.

From *The Yosemite* by John Muir, copyright © 1989 and reprinted with permission of Sierra Club Books.

From the audiotape *Living Next To Cancer*, by Rachel Naomi Remen, M.D. of Commonweal: The Institute for the Study of Health and Illness; from a talk given by Rachel Naomi Remen, M.D. at a Sjogren's Syndrome Foundation meeting in Marin; and from *Beyond Cure: The Psychology of Wholeness*, an audiotape by Rachel Naomi Remen, M.D. Produced by Commonweal: The Institute for the Study of Health and Illness. All used with the permission of Rachel Naomi Remen, M.D.

From *Face To Face Quarterly Bulletin*, Sonoma County AIDS Network.

From *Plaintext: Deciphering a Woman's Life*, by Nancy Mairs, copyright © 1986 and reprinted with permission of University of Arizona Press.

From *Snow Falling from a Bamboo Leaf*, by Hiag Akmakjian, copyright © 1979. Reprinted with permission of Capra Press.

From *"Dying Gods and Borning Spirits,"* by Sam Keen. Published in *Noetic Sciences Review* (no. 24, 1992). Used with permission.

From *Tales Of The Dervishes* by Idries Shah, copyright © 1967 by Idries Shah: "The Man Who Was Aware of Death." Used with permission of Dutton Signet, a division of Penguin Books USA Inc.

From "Behind the Buzzing Needle," by Karren Silver (2/19/93-3/4/93); and from "The Symbology of Death in Tattoos," by Karren Silver (8/21/92). Reprinted with permission of *Mendocino County Outlook*.

281

From "Good Luck, Bad Luck," by Linda Weltner, published in *New Age Journal* (1990); and from "Do We Make Ourselves Sick?" by Ken Wilber and Treya Wilber, published in *New Age Journal* (Sept/Oct 1988). Reprinted with permission of *New Age Journal*, 42 Pleasant St. Watertown, MA 02172.

From "On Trying to Find a Possible Life," by Lucinda Pitcairn; from "The Unbroken Circle," by Sara O'Donnell; from "Since I Didn't Die After All," by Jan Trueheart (vol. 5, no. 2., July 1992); from "In the Desert of My Soul," by Richard Yaski (vol. 7, no. 2, October 1994); from "You Know I Love to Travel," by Danny Ross (vol. 8, no. 1, May 1995): reprinted by permission of *The Common Thread*.

From *How Can I Help? Stories and Reflections on Service* by Ram Dass & Paul Gorman, copyright © 1985 by Ram Dass and Paul Gorman. Reprinted with permission of Alfred A Knopf, Inc.

From "In Memoriam: Treya Killam Wilber, 1946-1989," by Anne A. Simpkinson, as published in *Common Boundary*. Previously published in *Grace and Grit* by Ken Wilber. Reprinted with permission of Ken Wilber.

From "One-Breasted Woman," as published in *MS Magazine* (Sept/Oct 1992) and "One-Breasted Woman: Andrée O'Connor," as published in *The New Settler Interview* (no. 72), by Andrée O'Connor. Used with permission.

From "The Friend," by Rumi; and from "The Ground" by Rumi; both translated by Robert Bly and Coleman Barks. Reprinted with permission of Robert Bly and Coleman Barks from *Night and Sleep*, copyright © 1981, Yellow Moon Press, P O Box 381316, Cambridge, MA 02238; (800) 497-4385.

From *It's Always Something*, by Gilda Radner, copyright © 1990, by the Estate of Gilda Radner. Reprinted with the permission of Simon & Schuster

From *Living with Chronic Illness: Days of Patience and Passion*, by Cheri Register. Originally published in 1987 by The Free Press of Macmillan, Inc. Currently out of print, it is available from the author: (Please send $12.00 to 4226 Washburn Ave S, Minneapolis, MN 55410-1521).

From Issac Bashevis Singer's Nobel Prize for Literature acceptance speech, 1978.

From "Arthritis: Patient Perspective," by Joe Murray (vol. 4, no. 3, 1989-90); and from "Community Outreach," by Lucinda Pitcairn (vol. 8, no. 2, Spring 1994): as published in the Mendocino Coast District Hospital's *Update*. Reprinted with permission.

From Radio Interview of Laoma Bryant by Beth Bosk; KZYX Radio (July 1993). Used with permission.

Reprinted from *Being Peace*, by Thich Nhat Hanh (1987); from *Buddhism and Psychotherapy* (1989 audiotape), by Thich Nhat Hanh: later published in *Touching Peace: Practicing the Art of Mindful Living* by Thich Nhat Hanh, copyright © 1992; from "Precepts as a Way of Life," in *The Mindfulness Bell* (no. 6, Spring 1992), by Thich Nhat Hanh: published in *For a Future*

Publisher's Acknowledgments

To Be Possible: Commentaries on the Five Wonderful Precepts, by Thich Nhat Hanh, copyright © 1993; and from *In The Footsteps Of Ghandi: Conversations with Spiritual Social Activists* by Catherine Ingram, copyright © 1990: all with permission of Parallax Press.

From "Healing and Prayer: The Power of Paradox and Mystery," by Larry Dossey, MD, as published in *Noetic Sciences Review* (no. 28, Winter 1993). Reprinted with permission of Larry Dossey, MD.

From "What Makes the Heart Healthy? A Talk with Dean Ornish," by Harris Dienstfry, as published in *Advances: The Journal of Mind-Body Health* (vol. 8, no. 2, Spring 1992). Reprinted with permission of Harris Dienstfry.

From "An Exchange of Letters Between Bernie Siegel and David Spiegel on Psychosocial Interventions and Cancer," by David Spiegel, as published in *Advances: The Journal of Mind-Body Health* (vol. 8, no. 1, Winter 1992). Reprinted with permission of David Spiegel.

From *Full Catastrophe Living*, by Jon Kabat-Zinn, copyright © 1990 by Kabat-Zinn (Dell Books); from *A Gradual Awakening*, by Stephen Levine, copyright © 1979 by Stephen Levine (Doubleday); from *Who Dies*, by Stephen Levine, copyright © 1982 by Stephen Levine (Doubleday); from *Flying Without Wings*, by Arnold Beisser, copyright © 1989 by Arnold Beisser (Doubleday); from *Meetings at the Edge* by Stephen Levine, copyright © 1984 by Stephen Levine (Doubleday). All used with permission of Bantam Doubleday Dell Publishing Group, Inc.

From "A Native American Worldview," by Paula Underwood (Spencer), as published in *Noetic Sciences Review* (no. 15, Summer 1990). Reprinted with permission of Paula Underwood (Spencer).

Excerpt from *Burst Out Laughing*, copyright © 1984 by Barry Stevens. Reprinted with permission of Celestial Arts.

From *When Bad Things Happen to Good People* by Harold S. Kushner, copyright © 1981 and reprinted with permission of Shocken Books; from *Frederick* by Leo Lionni, copyright © 1967 by Leo Lionni; and from a Chinese proverb quoted in *A Natural History Of The Senses*, by Diane Ackerman, copyright © 1990: All published by Random House and used with permission.

From "When Life Isn't Fair," quoted by Phyllis O'Connell in *Quest* (Feb. 1993)

Excerpted from *Crazy Wisdom*, copyright © 1990 by Wes Nisker, with permission of Ten Speed Press, P O Box 7123, Berkeley, CA 94707.

Quotation by Sri Rama Krishna from "Love is the Healer: Interview with Joan Borysenko," by Stephan Bodian in *Yoga Journal* (May/June 1990).

From "Respect for Parenting, Respect for Children," by Jack Kornfield (vol. 8, no. 2); from "Peace as a Path: Five Exercises," by Thich Nhat Hanh. (vol. 8, no. 1);.from "A Very Human Death," by Maria Monroe (vol. 9, no. 2, Spring 1993); and a riddle by Susie Rashkis (vol. 8, no. 1, Fall 1991): all published in *Inquiring Mind: A Journal of the Vipassana Community*. Reprinted with permission of *Inquiring Mind*.

283

right © 1988 by Earl A. Grollman: both reprinted with permission of Beacon Press.

From "How Are You?" by Marjorie Lyon (vol. 6, no. 7, Sept. 1992); and from "How To Help A Grieving Friend," by Harry E. Mann (vol. 6, no. 3, March-April 1992): as published in *Bereavement: A Magazine of Hope and Healing*. Reprinted with permission of Bereavement Publishing, Inc., 8133 Telegraph Drive, Colorado Springs, CO 80920.

From "The Art of Return," by Colin Berg published in *Parabola: The Magazine of Myth and Tradition* (vol. 12, no. 3, August 1987).

Poem, "For Warmth" from *Zen Poems*, by Thich Nhat Hanh. Translation copyright © 1976 by Teo Savory. Published by Unicorn Press, Inc. All rights reserved. Reprinted with permission of Unicorn Press, Inc.

From "Love, Laughter & Miracles: A Prescription from Bernie Siegel" by Joel Goodman as published in *Laughing Matters* (vol. 6, no. 4, 1990). Excerpted with permission from *Laughing Matters* magazine, edited by Joel Goodman and published by The Humor Project, Inc., 110 Spring St., Saratoga Springs, NY 12866 (Phone (518) 587-8770; Home Page: http://www.wizvax.net/humor/

From *Springs of Japanese Wisdom*, by Yamabe no Akahito, Manse, Motori Norinaga, Izumi Shikibu, and Fujiwara no Toshiyuki; published by Marcel Schurman Company.

Excerpt from *The Habit of Being: Letters of Flannery O'Connor*, copyright © 1979 by Regina O'Connor; and from "Love after Love" in *Collected Poems 1948-1984*, by Derek Walcott, copyright © 1986 by Derek Walcott: both reprinted with permission of Farrar, Straus & Giroux, Inc.

From *Intoxicated by My Illness*, by Anatole Broyard, copyright © 1992 by Anatole Broyard. Reprinted with permission of Clarkson N. Potter, a division of Crown Publishers, Inc.

From *Grace And Grit*, by Ken Wilber, copyright © 1991. Reprinted by arrangement with Shambhala Publications, Inc., 300 Massachusetts Avenue, Boston, MA 02115.

From *Coming Home: A Guide to Dying at Home With Dignity*, by Deborah Duda, copyright © 1987 by Deborah Duda. Reprinted with permission of Aurora Press, P O Box 573, Santa Fe, NM 87504.

From *The Doctor and the Soul: From Psychotherapy to Logotherapy*, by Viktor E. Frankl, translated by Richard and Clara Winston, copyright © 1986 Vintage Books; and from *The Prophet*, by Kahlil Gibran, copyright © 1964: both reprinted with permission of Alfred A Knopf Inc.

Excerpt from an interview with Jerry Jampolsky and Diane Cirincione, copyright © 1991 by New Dimensions Foundation. All Rights Reserved. Reprinted from the *New Dimensions Journal*, January-February, 1991. If you would like a complimentary copy of the journal, or a catalog featuring hundreds of "New Dimensions" radio interviews on audiotape, send $2 to

Index